Mozart the Performer

Mozart

THE PERFORMER

Variations on the Showman's Art

Dorian Bandy

THE UNIVERSITY OF CHICAGO PRESS
Chicago & London

The University of Chicago Press, Chicago 60637
The University of Chicago Press, Ltd., London

Published 2023
Printed in the United States of America

32 31 30 29 28 27 26 25 24   2 3 4 5

ISBN-13: 978-0-226-82855-8 (cloth)
ISBN-13: 978-0-226-82856-5 (e-book)
DOI: https://doi.org/10.7208/chicago/9780226828565.001.0001

This book has been supported by the AMS 75 PAYS Fund of the American Musicological Society, supported in part by the National Endowment for the Humanities and the Andrew W. Mellon Foundation.

This book also received funding from a Canadian SSHRC Insight Development Grant (430-2021-00764).

Library of Congress Cataloging-in-Publication Data

Names: Bandy, Dorian Komanoff, author.
Title: Mozart the performer : variations on the showman's art / Dorian Bandy.
Description: Chicago : The University of Chicago Press, 2023. | Includes bibliographical references and index.
Identifiers: LCCN 2023015313 | ISBN 9780226828558 (cloth) | ISBN 9780226828565 (ebook)
Subjects: LCSH: Mozart, Wolfgang Amadeus, 1756-1791—Criticism and interpretation. | Mozart, Wolfgang Amadeus, 1756-1791. Piano music. | Piano—Performance—History—18th century. | Improvisation (Music)—History—18th century.
Classification: LCC ML410.M9 B145 2023 | DDC 780.92—dc23/eng/20230404
LC record available at https://lccn.loc.gov/2023015313

♾ This paper meets the requirements of ANSI/NISO Z39.48-1992 (Permanence of Paper).

For Ruth Ezra

CONTENTS

NOTES ON THE TEXT

Translations from Mozart's letters are mine, following the text in *Mozart: Briefe und Aufzeichnungen, Gesamtausgabe*, collected and annotated by Wilhelm A. Bauer, Otto Erich Deutsch, and Joseph Heinz Eibl, 8 vols. (Kassel: Bärenreiter, 1962–2005), hereafter *MBA*. Where possible I have preserved Mozart's italics, punctuation, and abbreviations. Musical examples follow the *Neue Ausgabe sämtlicher Werke* (Kassel: Bärenreiter, 1955–2007), hereafter *NMA*.

Despite the many revisions to the Köchel catalog, for ease of referencing I have used the familiar first-edition Köchel numbers.

In order to ensure accessibility, I generally avoid references to secondary sources within the main text. Readers should consult the endnotes for discussion of the scholarly literature.

Theme

On paper, a musical score is an intricate but lifeless pattern of dots. But listen to the sounds that pattern encodes, or hear them in your mind's ear, and you enter an imaginary world teeming with motion. Individual notes disappear into the flow of melodies; rhythms incline toward each other as if gently magnetized; and chords take on a gravitational attraction to any harmonies that cross their tonal orbit. Such aural alchemy is magical in itself, but the musical experience goes further. Within this world we sometimes sense the organizing presence of a human mind, a consciousness whose perceived emotional states and overarching worldview bind a musical work into a coherent whole. Behind the ingenuity of Bach's Goldberg Variations, that painting of the old Kapellmeister smirks down through the ages, aware of his music's contrapuntal brilliance. Water Music rings with Handel's good humor, Haydn's sonatas exude affability, and Beethoven's late quartets seem to many listeners the very embodiment of a portentous scowl.

What presence do we encounter in Mozart's music? The question is difficult to answer—though not for lack of eligible images. Mozart's talents have been a source of endless fascination since 1762, when news of the six-year-old prodigy first swept Europe's capitals. Yet his output is so richly varied, so diverse in its expressive range and dramatic register, so thoroughly steeped in the ambiguities and ambivalences of the human experience that it seems to sustain any interpretation imaginable. For the fictionalized Salieri in *Amadeus,* Mozart was a cackling savant, a vessel who channeled divine melodies implanted in his head by God. For the early Romantics, he was a misunderstood genius who composed stormy, minor-key music before dying at thirty-five and receiving a pauper's burial in an unmarked grave. For the Victorians, he was an angelic child. He has since been seen variously as a composer of glittering but trivial minuets; a musical rebel who fathered neither the symphony nor the string quartet but who nonetheless redefined the scope of every genre he touched; a studious craftsman who composed each day until his fingers were numb; a freelancer who hustled for students and commissions in order to feed his family; a prolific and scatological letter writer; a salacious doodler; and much else besides. Although these views are couched in the straightforward language of biography, each melds an account of the man with an implicit evaluation of his music. If the divine Mozart seems worlds away from his workmanlike counterpart, both represent attempts not only to pin down the origins of his compositions but also to capture something of their essence: to say in what spirit we should approach them, which of their features merit attention, and, by extension, what meaning and significance we may ultimately derive from them.

In this book I explore one interpretive approach to Mozart and his music. Like so many accounts, mine begins in the world of biography. At the heart of this study is a single historical fact: that, whatever else might be said of him, Mozart was a virtuoso pianist and inveterate showman. For Mozart, every composition was a performance *in potentia*, to be discharged either on the concert platform or on the printed page. He often calculated his music to produce specific effects on those who consumed it—on audience members, primarily, who would witness his pianistic fireworks firsthand, but also on the amateur musicians who would purchase his published editions, the professional colleagues who would play his concertos or sing his operas, and the students for whom his sonatas or written-out cadenzas would serve as pedagogical aids. That Mozart wasted no opportunity to flaunt his talents was not only for the inherent delights of adulation; it was a matter of financial necessity. As a freelance composer, his livelihood during long stretches of his career depended not on the luxury of a secure courtly post but on an ability to win plaudits in the public marketplace. It was by enchanting his audiences that he could attract patrons, garner commissions, and build a roster of students. When Mozart pursued higher-order artistic ideals in his compositions, it was usually alongside the more basic goal of showing listeners a good time.

This view of Mozart's professional priorities seems straightforward to modern-day intuitions, yet it is the hard-earned product of nearly a century of historical investigation. Numerous scholars have worked to dispel the lore that so persistently shrouds Mozart's image—the supernatural inspiration, the flawless first drafts, the creativity that defied all practical concerns, the premonition of an early death and attendant rush to compose three final symphonies, and the poisoning, to name a few of the most tenacious myths—replacing them with the simple idea that Mozart was, like the rest of us, a human who needed to make a living. Yet while this achievement marks the culmination of a biographical enterprise spelled out over thousands of scrupulously researched pages, it represents only the starting point for the explorations I pursue here. The de-mythologized viewpoint provides a perspective from which to regard Mozart's creative practices, but it does not in itself explain how those practices shaped his artistic decision-making or what they might tell us about the nature of his style. My goal is to sketch a possible answer to such questions. I begin from the simple, biographical premise of the centrality of performance among Mozart's priorities and trace its implications throughout his oeuvre.

These implications are perhaps most evident in Mozart's piano writing, which pares down issues of communication and expression to an interaction between composer-performer and instrument. In the sonatas, variations, fantasias, and concertos, it is often possible to imagine Mozart himself seated at the instrument, his hands navigating the keyboard's jagged topography, his stage persona exuding a verve so easily lost on the printed page. Consider, for instance, the pianistic drama that unfolds in the opening phrase of the Sonata in B♭ K. 333 (ex. 0.1).

So numbing is the scrim of familiarity that, listening casually, we may hear little more than a polite cascade of sixteenth notes, the music-box melody that follows, and that most elementary chord progression, I–ii–V–I. But envision the sonata as a performative event, and it takes on a different nature. If the piece seems superficially straightforward, perhaps this is because the right hand's melody moves obediently through a series of stock gestures, exemplified by the appoggiaturas arrayed with almost dull regularity on each of the first five downbeats. At the same time, however, the left hand offers a provocative running commentary. It avoids downbeats altogether, offsetting the repetitive weight of the right hand's emphases with a series of breathless sighs like those heard in Cherubino's first aria from *Le nozze di Figaro*. These silences, and the rising shapes that emerge from them, undermine any facile notion of accompanimental decorum. Even the harmonic plan hints at unexpected depths. In the first bar, the left hand has barely finished outlining the tonic chord before F rises to G, yielding a briefly sounded minor triad. Is Mozart

Example 0.1 Piano Sonata K. 333, first movement, mm. 1–10

simply avoiding parallel fifths on the way to measure 2? Or does a shadow momentarily darken the phrase? Mozart's poker face betrays no answer.

The sonata continues, and the two hands engage in more overt sparring. Beginning in measure 5, the left hand finally deigns to join the right on the downbeat—and it does so with a sharp dissonance that sends the right hand into a tizzy of sixteenth notes. The left hand continues its wheedling until the right, exasperated, finally launches into an enraged scale all the way up to the highest note on the pianos of Mozart's time. Here, the composer-performer's puppetry is especially tangible. Beneath the veneer of *politesse* a rich pianistic drama unfolds, with each hand pitted against the other and the right hand bumping up against the outer edge of the instrument's range. In the space of ten bars, Mozart beseeches, cajoles, prods, and teases, all the while showing off his ability to draw stagey excitement from even the most conventional patterns.

The medium of the solo sonata encourages playful readings, since the pianist's expressive freedom is unhampered by the presence of other collaborators. But the same virtuosic intensity courses through Mozart's chamber and orchestral output as well. A string quartet or a symphony may not cast a spotlight on a single musician, but these genres nonetheless encode the residue of imagined dialogues, conversations, and arguments. Meanwhile, Mozart's operas bring the concept of drama beyond the realm of metaphor. The composer there serves as a theatrical director, breathing life into the characters while focusing listeners' musical attention and calibrating their moral gaze.

Such performative impulses constitute the subject of this book. In what follows I explore their presence throughout Mozart's compositions. I examine his pianistic techniques as encoded within the compendium of physical gestures that make up his keyboard sonatas, concertos, and variation sets. I also seek to recover something of Mozart's improvisations—if not the unwritten notes themselves then at least the protocols that may have guided his hands as he wove his elaborate fantasias, cadenzas, and embellishments. Ultimately, I attempt to capture the dramatic persona Mozart adopted while working: that imaginative, fictional role he stepped into whenever he sat at his writing desk or played for an audience and which turned every composition into an operatic stage. As I will argue, one of Mozart's signal achievements in crafting this persona was the evocation of the subtle ambiguities that infuse so much of his music. We have already felt a brief hesitation in that passing G-minor sonority from the first bar of K. 333, but this impulse is actualized more fully elsewhere, when the desire to write searingly beautiful phrases is tempered by an irresistible urge to fool around—or, conversely, when the need to joke manifests itself in a way that is laden with feeling. I will argue that Mozart's evocation of these ambivalences, as well as the broader expressive stance and interpretive approach they suggest, help give his music its elusive yet human quality.

This book represents, on one level, an attempt to carry forward the demythologizing impulse that has motivated so many other recent Mozart studies. I am guided throughout by the conviction that great art can be analyzed, explained, and understood. Mozart was not touched by the supernatural; his compositions are notes all the way down. Yet if many Mozartian myths have been incorrect in their factual claims, they nonetheless capture something essential about the spirit of wonder with which we should approach his music. Thus, although my goal is to examine the building blocks of his craft, I hope to do so in a way that does not diminish the value of what he produced. To lay bare even in small part the intricate machinery underpinning his music—the technical facility that gave rise to it, the aesthetic vision embedded in it—should only deepen our appreciation.

For all of the divinity and grace once attributed to him, Mozart and his music are firmly rooted in the bustling world of human activity. Unlike Bach, whose counterpoint is often spoken of in terms better suited to the abstract perfections of a mathematical theorem, Mozart created music that brims with images of earthly life and the range of experiences it entails: its joys and pains, and the many ambiguities that lie somewhere in between. In the end I hope to show that Mozart's defining musical presence is neither a smirk nor a scowl. It is the spirit of an irrepressible performer who wants, in every sense, to play.

VARIATION I

Mozart the Performer

Introducing the Composer-Performer

For Mozart, the acts of composition and performance were inextricably linked. The melodic threads that run through his works, the harmonic patterns that underpin them, the formal structures that provide a sense of overarching logic, and the sophisticated rhetorical acuity binding them together—in short, every technical and expressive dimension of his craft—were shaped by skills he cultivated as a performer during his three-decade career. In this book I trace the points at which these two domains overlapped, including the pianistic physicality of his sonatas and concertos, the improvisational aesthetic of his embellishments, and, ultimately, the dramatic complexities of his operas. To some extent, I am concerned with the historical origins of the music I examine, particularly the ways in which Mozart's experiences as a performer shaped his compositional priorities. Yet my study takes history as its starting point but not as its goal. I hope to show that performativity is not only a compelling explanation for the origins of Mozart's compositions but an interpretive principle in its own right, one that can guide the way we listen to, perform, and understand his music.[1]

The interconnectedness of composition and performance was, to be sure, an element of most music making before the twentieth century. From our present-day vantage point, the two activities seem neatly divided: clear boundaries distinguish the skills involved in each, and large communities of specialists practice one but not the other. During Mozart's lifetime, however, such compartmentalization did not exist. Virtually all composers were performers: if their music held broad, public appeal, it was often as a result of the composers' own renown as instrumentalists. Performers, too, were often practiced composers, and although their music might never plumb the depths of artistry, it nevertheless provided adequate means for the display of virtuosity before an admiring audience. This synthesis was reflected not only in the careers of countless celebrated composer-performers from Buxtehude to Busoni but in broader cultural appraisals of musical craft.[2] Although today we remember Mozart for what he wrote down, his contemporaries celebrated him primarily as a virtuoso pianist and improviser. To his earliest listeners, the notated compositions served as vehicles for acclaimed performances rather than as objects of sustained appreciation in their own right.

Such historical perspectives are uncontroversial, yet the relationship between composition and performance is more complex than these statements suggest. It is one thing to note that Mozart, along with many others over the centuries, excelled at both skills. It is altogether different to ask how, and indeed whether, each actively informed the other. Many composer-performers of the seventeenth and eighteenth centuries seem to have viewed the two crafts as distinct artistic categories and pursued both without bringing them into truly productive alignment.[3] Even those who were celebrated during their lifetimes as exemplars of both composition and performance often cultivated remarkably different habits and personae in their practice of each. This is true, for instance, of Palestrina in the sixteenth century, whose careful, almost cerebral part writing was most likely obscured beneath lavish improvised diminutions when his music was performed; of Corelli's violin sonatas in the eighteenth century, which are today praised for the Apollonian clarity of their basslines and counterpoint while his performances and improvisations were revered for their Dionysian ferocity and abandon; and of various nineteenth-century figures, including Liszt, whose public image as a superstar belied the academic rigor of his modernist style.[4] Some musicians, meanwhile, practiced both crafts but adopted an approach to composition that actively disdained the practicalities of performance. The young Beethoven, even before the onset of deafness, is famous in this regard. He blithely ignored the range limits of contemporary pianos, often preferring to exceed an instrument's compass than compromise the Platonic integrity of his music; and he produced compositions so difficult that most performances during his lifetime were destined to fail—an outcome he helped ensure by organizing concerts that were overly ambitious yet underprepared.[5]

For Mozart, such disregard for the practical would have been untenable. As a freelancer in Vienna, that bustling musical capital, Mozart depended for survival on the cachet of his public image. At times he secured an income through the sale of printed editions of his music, marketed to professional or amateur performers who could admire the intricacies of his work as captured on the page. Yet more often it was through performance that listeners would encounter his music and that he would attract audiences, build a roster of piano and composition pupils, and cultivate patrons.[6] Mozart's awareness of the practical dimensions of music making, then, had to be finely attuned to the showing each piece would receive. This in turn calls up a sequence of considerations pointing ever deeper into the rudiments of composition. His music had to engage and satisfy listeners; he therefore had to write with a sensitivity to his audience's expectations and sophistication. Comprehensibility also meant that what he wrote must be readily playable, and this, in turn, meant that he had to understand the subtleties of each instrument and voice-type, as well as the abilities of specific collaborators who would perform his music on any given occasion.

Yet Mozart's ambitions also pointed beyond the technical capacity of an instrument or performer. He shaped his music to suit colleagues and collaborators not by pandering to the limitations of those with whom he worked but by emphasizing their strengths: by seeking to capture each player's personality and predilections within the music, the better to create a dazzling and engaging public reading. Thus, Mozart's output does not only include compositions whose demands he adapted to the abilities of their recipients (such as the Piano Concerto in C K. 246, written to accommodate the modest keyboard technique of the Countess Antonia Lützow, and the easiest of his concertos) but those intended to stimulate more active pleasure on the part of the musicians who would bring them to life. In an oft-quoted letter, Mozart explained to his father that when composing operatic arias he attempted to make the music fit the singer "as accurately as a well-made suit of clothes," and this ideal certainly applied to instrumental music as well.[7] At times, such tailoring took the form of playful jibes aimed at a dedicatee. In the Piano Concerto in E♭ K. 271, written for the virtuoso Louise-Victoire Jenamy, Mozart interpolates an unexpected minuet into the last movement, a sly reference to Jenamy's father, the renowned French dancing master Jean-Georges Noverre.[8] Elsewhere, Mozart sought to evoke a deeper personal essence. He described the slow movement of the Piano Sonata K. 309 as an homage to his Mannheim pupil, the young Rosa Cannabich, whose nature he hoped to distill:

> Cannabich's daughter who is 15 years old, but the eldest child [. . .] yesterday played my sonata—exquisitely. She plays the Andante—which

> must *not be played too fast*—with all possible sensitivity. And besides, she loves to play it. You know that I had already finished the first allegro the 2nd day I came here, consequently I had seen Mad^{selle} Cannabich only once. It was then that the young Danner asked me how I would compose the andante; I want it to be entirely like the Character of Mad:^{selle} Rose. Then when I played it, it was an extraordinary success, and young Danner said afterward: it is true, she is just like the andante.[9]

Mozart's account of his evening at the Cannabich household mingles stories of compositional planning with delight at an effective performance. The satisfaction he seems to have derived from his exchange with Danner—and particularly from the boy's recognition that Rosa was "just like the andante"—is bound up not only with Mozart's own performance but with the pleasure Rosa herself derived from playing the movement. The same ethos helped to shape much other music as well, from the complex social scenarios played out in Mozart's string quartets and other chamber music to the family relations enshrined in the Concerto for Three Pianos, K. 242, and the Flute and Harp Concerto, K. 299 (both written for parent-children teams of soloists).[10]

The ideals Mozart pursued when writing for other performers also informed the music he wrote for his own use. In one particularly explicit reference to the possessiveness he felt over his compositions, Mozart exhorted his father and sister (whom he had recently sent a score of the Rondo in D K. 382) to "protect it like a *jewel*—and do not give it to anyone else to play [. . .] I wrote it *especially* for myself."[11] This statement speaks to Mozart's concerns over copyright and his fears that publishers and rival performers alike might take advantage of him if they came into possession of his manuscripts.[12] Yet it also suggests a keener sense of ownership. Mozart wrote the Rondo K. 382 for himself: for his hands, for his stage persona, and perhaps most of all, for the adulation he would earn as both the work's ingenious composer and its virtuoso performer. Although this sentiment rarely finds express voice in his correspondence, it lies behind many of his other statements—for instance, the satisfaction he describes when, during a Mannheim house concert, listeners recognized his compositional thumbprint in the Oboe Concerto, K. 314.[13] The same mindset guided the trajectory of Mozart's compositional career. It is no coincidence that he lavished so many innovations on the genre of the piano concerto, for it was here that he would show off all the facets of his creativity at once: his composerly flair, his improvised embellishments and cadenzas, and his glittering pianistic virtuosity. Applause garnered in the performance of this music would be directed wholly to him.[14]

That Mozart often anticipated such applause suggests the extent to which his creative process involved not only consideration of the musicians who would play his music but, equally, of the audiences who would hear it. In a letter to his father in 1778, Mozart describes the premiere of the "Paris" Symphony, K. 297, narrating the audience's reaction in real-time and recounting the compositional scheming that primed it:

> In the middle of the opening allegro there was a passage I knew very well was bound to please, all listeners were carried away by it—and there was loud applause—but as I knew when I wrote it what effect it would produce, I introduced it again at the end—now people wanted to have it encored.

He comments on the last movement in even greater detail:

> They also liked the andante, but especially the final allegro—because I'd heard that here all the final allegros, like opening ones, begin with all the instruments playing together and often in unison, so I began mine with 2 violins only, playing piano for 8 whole bars—followed at once by a forte—the listeners, as I expected, went "shhhh" at the piano—then came the forte—and as soon as they heard it, they started to clap.[15]

The confluence of compositional craft with an awareness of his listeners' expectations is made even more explicit in another famous letter, written while at work on *Die Entführung aus dem Serail*:

> The beginning and end [of Osmin's act 1 aria, "Solche hergelauf'ne Laffen"] are sure to be very effective—Osmin's rage is made to seem comical by the Turkish music I used here [. . .] *Drum beym Barte des Propheten* etc. is still at the same speed, but with fast notes—and as his rage grows and grows—just when you think the aria is over—the allegro assai—in a completely different meter and different key—is bound to make a tremendous effect; just as a person in such a violent rage oversteps all the bounds of order and moderation, completely forgetting himself—so the music must forget itself—but because the passions, whether violent or not, must never be expressed to the point of causing disgust, and because music, even in the most terrible situation, must never offend the ear but must give pleasure and, in other words, must always remain music, I've not chosen a key foreign to F (the key of the aria) but one

> related to it, but not the one closest to it, D minor, but the more remote A minor.—Now for Belmonte's aria in A major, O wie ängstlich, o wie feurig, do you know how it's expressed?—even his beating, loving heart is indicated—by the 2 violins in octaves [. . .] one sees the trembling—wavering—one sees his breast begin to swell—which is expressed with a crescendo—one hears the whispering and sighing—which is expressed by the first violins with mutes and a flute playing in unison with them.[16]

Both letters carry implications concerning the historical practices of concertgoing and listening. Even more, they say much about Mozart's compositional imagination. His desire to please his audience was no idle wish; rather, he attempted with exacting precision to anticipate, capture, and stimulate specific expectations on the part of his listeners. In the "Paris" Symphony letter, he calibrates musical decisions against what he assumes to be conventions of the time and place: other composers begin symphonic finales *forte*, so his must begin *piano*. In the *Entführung* letter, Mozart considers both the psychology of Osmin's character as well as the experience he wishes to provoke. He refers variously to humor that will arise from the incongruous juxtaposition of dramatized rage and the light, "Turkish" style of the music; the shattering of expectations ("just when you think the aria is over . . ."); the jolts prompted by jarring metrical shifts combined with changes of tempo; and, ultimately, that delicately measured disorientation brought on by a modulation that is neither too distant nor too routine. More broadly, the letter reveals that Mozart's performative impulse—the desire to surprise and titillate listeners—manifested itself in highly technical aspects of composition. He does not wax lyrical about a nebulous goal of confounding expectations; instead, he plots each move, maximizing the expressive weight of all musical parameters from tonality and rhythm to timbre and orchestration. Every internal feature of these compositions is bent in the service of a single, communicative end.

Such composerly decisions reflect performance in the basic sense that they consider matters of practical music making. Yet they also draw on performance more broadly in that they issue from an actively performative imagination. The decisions Mozart describes in both letters suggest that the imaginative projection of future performances was integral to his craft. The technical dimensions of his written oeuvre seem to have depended largely on performative details that would play out in his mind's ear long before any actual stage event took place. These imaginings must have encompassed anything from external considerations, such as the psychology and expectations of his listeners, to personal matters, including a highly developed model of his own performing persona—all bound together with an understanding, either explicit or not, of the communicative potency of various musical gestures. The resulting intuitions, sharpened over years of experience, would most likely have fostered a seamless integration of composition and performance, one suggested as much by the direct claims in his letters as by the casual ease with which his descriptions pass from one realm to the next. Although the letters themselves do not provide conclusive proof of Mozart's thought processes as he worked, they certainly depict a creative mindset that moved constantly between manuscript leaf and imagined stage.

Under this mindset, the blurred boundaries of performance and composition would allow for causal flow in both directions. If imagined performances helped to shape Mozart's written compositions, his written compositions would in turn both respond to and prepare the circumstances of actual performances. This fluidity is particularly evident in the alterations Mozart made to various compositions after their premieres. For Mozart, completed pieces were not fixed entities. The success or failure of performances had a direct bearing on future versions of each composition. When Mozart set about revising his music, nothing in the text was off-limits: a virtuosic solo in a concerto (alterations to which can be seen in successive drafts of the Piano Concertos K. 449, K. 450, K. 488, and K. 491) was as likely to be reworked as finer matters of accompaniment and instrumentation.[17] Elsewhere, revisions included broad changes: the occasional deletion of individual measures so as to make unexpected deceptive cadences more surprising (K. 449); the removal of entire melodies and the concurrent shifting of aural focus toward other textural elements (K. 488); or the reshaping of expressive details to alter the flow and density of melodic figuration (as when Mozart reallocated embellishments from one phrase to another in the slow movement of the Piano Sonata K. 457).[18] The junction of performative and compositional considerations is especially striking in Mozart's operatic revisions. Whenever a new production introduced changes to a cast, Mozart would thoroughly rewrite or even replace entire arias in order to accommodate the vocal characteristics and dramatic abilities of the new singers. Such changes were motivated by practicalities of performance, but they also carried far-reaching implications for the psychology of his operatic characters and thus for the dramatic scope of each stage work as a whole. It is no exaggeration to say that the voice of Francesco Morella, who played Don Ottavio in the 1788 Vienna production of *Don Giovanni*, effected a deep shift in the nature of the character by inspiring Mozart to insert the aria "Dalla sua pace," which ultimately replaced "Il mio tesoro."[19] The new aria, redolent of the Countess's music in *Le nozze di Figaro*, lends Ottavio a moral poise and compassion that, in turn, infuses the opera with a warmth largely absent from the original 1787 Prague version.[20] Such revisions serve as convenient case studies because they make Mozart's second thoughts especially transparent—and it is usually possible to trace these thoughts to practical concerns. By juxtaposing multiple versions of a composition, modern-day scholars can become forensic detectives, following the movements of Mozart's quill and reconstructing the motivations behind his decisions.

Unfortunately, no comparable source lays bare the workings of Mozart's mind during the initial stages of compositional planning. Yet circumstantial evidence suggests that performance featured centrally in his creative process. Despite his highly developed musical imagination, Mozart preferred to compose at the piano for at least the first half of his career. His mother complained, during their 1778 visit to Paris, of the apartment in which she and her son lodged: "the entrance and the stairs are so narrow that it would be impossible to bring up a Clavier. Therefore Wolfgang has to compose away from home, at Monsieur Legros', because there is a keyboard there."[21] Mozart himself made a similar statement when moving house in Vienna in 1781: "The room into which I am moving is being prepared;—now I'm going off to rent a Clavier, because, until there is one in my room, I cannot live in it because I have much to compose and not a minute to be lost."[22]

It is certainly true that, if necessary, Mozart could work away from the keyboard. It seems to have been equally true, however, that the keyboard served an important role in his compositional process. What might that role have been? For many contemporaries (even those who did not sustain careers as professional, virtuoso performers), composition often seemed to originate in an act of improvisation. Haydn, for instance, famously reported a preference "always to compose at the keyboard. I sat down [and] began to fantasize. . . . Once I had seized upon an idea, my whole effort was to develop and sustain it."[23] Mozart's widow Constanze, interviewed by the biographer Franz Niemetschek, attributed to her husband a similar process in which the piano allowed for the exploration of ideas that would later be codified on the page: "When [Mozart] received the libretto for a vocal composition, he went about for some time, concentrating on it until his imagination was fired. Then he proceeded to work out his ideas at the piano, and only then did he sit down and write."[24] Both Haydn's and Constanze's words are frustratingly vague.

They describe generic features of each composer's relationship with the keyboard without providing detail as to the musical thought involved. What did it mean for Mozart's imagination to be fired? Was his deep concentration aimed at producing the largest possible set of viable melodic ideas that he would then organize on paper? (This possibility is corroborated by a letter to his father in which Mozart hints that musical invention and revision were two distinct phases of the creative process: "you will find within [the manuscript score of *Die Entführung*] many crossings-out; that is because . . . I let my ideas run freely—and before I gave it to the copyist I first made my alterations and cuts here and there."[25]) Alternatively, might his pianistic fantasizing have taken the form of coherent but unwritten drafts, which needed only slight refinement during the subsequent act of notation? We cannot know with certainty, though surviving source material provides fuel for speculation. Mozart began and abandoned hundreds of drafts and fragments, many of which taper off after a single phrase, and this suggests that he often concocted tunes without concern for the compositions that might arise from them.[26] He might, as Constanze implies, begin in this way before setting about the more arduous task of linking those ideas into a satisfying arc. In this view the piano may have served at minimum as a flexible stand-in for notation, allowing Mozart to test ideas more quickly, and revise them more readily, than would be possible with quill and ink. Such a hypothesis would also apply to those finished compositions whose manuscripts are eerily free of corrections or revisions. Rather than assume that Mozart possessed a preternatural ability to spin flawless first drafts, we might instead suppose that the first drafts of each, along with inevitable manipulations, tinkering, and editing, arose at the keyboard rather than on paper in a process made possible by his facility as a pianist and improviser.

Composition and Improvisation

In this brief, speculative account of Mozart's compositional process, written music emerges through an act akin to improvisation. Composition, viewed thus, is not a calculated, cerebral exercise through which the writer develops and tightens phrases into a coherent narrative; it is, instead, an attempt to *discover* the elaborative potential of each idea.[27] When the medium at hand is a piano rather than a pen, such discovery is limited only by the strength of the composer-performer's imagination and memory. Within the bounds of thought, adjustments can occur continuously and on any level, from tweaks to individual melodies or harmonies to larger-scale structural changes involving the reordering of themes. This flexibility might, over years of practice, become integral to the creative process. Improvisation and composition would then fuse into an iterative task in which alternative possibilities are continuously weighed as a piece of music takes shape.[28]

Beyond analogies with composition, improvisation served Mozart as a prized musical act in its own right. It was a skill at which he excelled and which formed the basis for much of his acclaim. Eyewitness accounts of Mozart's playing celebrate the mastery, wit, and flair with which he could spin out lengthy extemporized compositions at will. In his early nineteenth-century biography of Mozart, Georg Nikolaus Nissen (second husband of Constanze) describes an extraordinary 1787 performance in Prague:

> At the end of the concert, Mozart improvised a good half hour on the pianoforte, and with this, he inspired the enthusiasm of the overwhelmed Bohemians to the highest degree. The stormy success that followed his playing prompted him to sit down at the piano once more. The flight of this fantasia captivated the audience even more strongly; they stormed him for the third time. . . . He started once more in an elevated spirit; he produced something that was never heard by anyone. Suddenly, in the dead silence a voice from the audience: "From the Figaro!" Mozart introduced the melody of the favorite aria "Non più andrai," and improvised a dozen of the most interesting and most artful variations. Roaring ovation closed this memorable event.[29]

Similar panegyrics for Mozart's improvisations are echoed in a host of other sources. "What a richness of ideas! What variety! What changes in passionate tones!" "This small man and great master twice *extemporized* on a *pedal piano*, so wonderfully! so wonderfully! that I didn't know where I was. The most difficult passages and the loveliest *themes* interwoven."[30]

Considering that Mozart's earliest listeners esteemed him more as an improviser than as a composer, it comes as no surprise that Mozart incorporated improvisation into so many of his public appearances. He improvised fantasias at the outset of performances, preludes and capriccios between works during concerts, cadenzas at the close of concerto movements, and, as described by Nissen, variation sets from themes presented or requested by his audiences. Mozart also developed an approach to compositional style that would allow him to weave improvisation into the fabric of his notated music. This occurred most often through the insertion of embellishments: those complex decorations a soloist might lavish on sparsely notated passages in concertos, arias, and sonatas. Mozart also occasionally forced his own hand, adopting a skeletal style of notation in which he would indicate the outlines of the phrases to be played that he would have no choice but to flesh out spontaneously in performance. This practice most likely served as a playful self-challenge, raising the stakes of even the most routine concerts. Perhaps it also reflected the economic realities of freelance life in Vienna: Mozart had to write fast, often without the luxury of time to polish his notation. Either way, he seems to have relished the resulting risks. In a letter to his father, he proudly described the premiere of the Violin Sonata K. 379, for which he had time to notate only the violin part and was forced to invent the keyboard part on the fly—a feat he reprised three years later with the Violin Sonata K. 454, written for the Italian virtuoso violinist Regina Strinasacchi.[31] Mozart also left unwritten significant passages in his mature piano concertos, including K. 482, K. 491, and K. 537. At times, the excitement of improvisation could even arise in more fully notated settings through the use of compositional styles that would approximate improvised genres or events. Mozart often crafted models of improvisational music for those who lacked the skill to extemporize on their own but who nonetheless wanted to capture an air of spontaneity in their performances.

No genre better combined skills associated with composition and improvised performance than the variation set. Improvised variations were staples of Mozart's life as a performer, and even among his written output the piano variations seem to embody a spontaneity unmatched by other compositions. Many of Mozart's variations originated in actual extemporized performances, and as a result they blend some of the most audaciously virtuosic technical passages in his keyboard output with a keen sense of development as each variation wrings increasingly complex material out of unassuming themes.[32] Although Mozart evidently revised them during the process of notation, the fact that the majority of these compositions survive in multiple, conflicting drafts and fragments contributes to the almost improvisatory mystique—the sense of flexibility and flightiness—surrounding the sets.

During Mozart's lifetime, variation was not only an improvisatory genre but a compositional principle that could be used to generate large swathes of material out of simple thematic ideas.[33] The transformations that often occur within variation sets—melodic divisions, harmonic variation, rhythmic and phrasal adjustments, modal shifts, textural explorations, and so forth—were precisely the techniques composers used in structuring longer pieces in almost any genre. The variation genre, then, shows the intersection between composition and improvisation at its most concretely technical. Various eighteenth-century treatises encourage beginning composers to master the skills associated with variation and, in so doing, to sidestep the challenges of creation ex nihilo.[34] Mozart himself made reference to the usefulness of variation when he described a frustrating composition lesson:

> I think I wrote to you in my last letter that the Duc de Guines, whose daughter is my composition student, [. . .] has very much talent and genius [as a performer on the flute and harp]. [. . .] But she seriously doubts whether she has any genius as a composer—especially as regards thoughts—ideas. [. . .] She's now starting to write in 3 parts. It starts well; but she soon gets bored; but I can't help her; I can't go on to the next stage yet. It's too soon, even if there really were genius here, but unfortunately there isn't—one will have to do it all with art. She simply has no ideas. Nothing comes. I've tried everything possible with her; then I had the idea of writing out a really simple minuet and seeing if she could write a variation on it—yes, it was a waste of time—Now, I thought, she simply doesn't know how she should begin—so I started to write a variation on the first bar only and told her she should continue in the same way and keep to the idea—ultimately it went fairly well.[35]

Although in Mozart's letters variation receives no other direct mention as a compositional aid, evidence of similar thought survives in the notebook chronicling his composition lessons with his English pupil Thomas Attwood. Here, simple minuets serve to demonstrate techniques such as harmonic variation and motivic expansion as well as the recombination of melodies with various alternative basslines.

Composing with Modules

The overlapping skills of composition and improvisation were natural consequences of the musical vernacular in use during Mozart's lifetime. In the late eighteenth century, musical creativity was understood as involving not the production of new, never-before-heard melodic or harmonic material but the ingenuity with which composers or improvisers could assimilate and recycle standard tropes.[36] Thus, Mozart and his contemporaries fashioned all their music from a common currency of modular building blocks.[37] Some of these

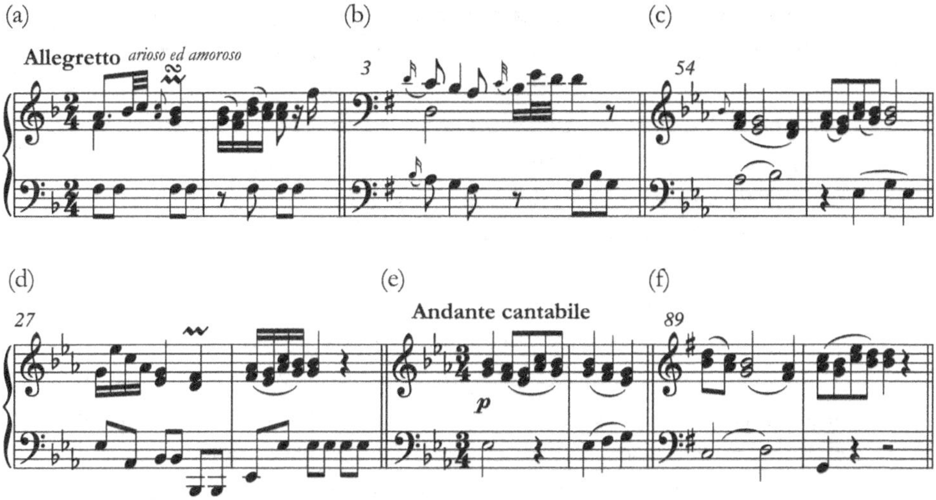

Example 1.1 *a*, C. P. E. Bach, Keyboard Sonata H. 74 (1753), third movement, mm. 1–2. *b*, Luigi Boccherini, Cello Sonata G. 5 (1766), first movement, m. 3. *c*, J. C. Bach, Piano Concerto op. 7, no. 5 (1770), first movement, mm. 54–55 (piano part). *d*, Nicolas-Joseph Hüllmandel, Violin Sonata op. 1, no. 2 (1773/74), second movement, mm. 27–28 (piano part). *e*, Mozart, Piano Sonata K. 333 (1783?), second movement, mm. 1–2. *f*, Mozart, Piano Concerto K. 453 (1784), first movement, mm. 89–90

modules consist of short, recurring melodic or harmonic patterns, deployed in a wide range of contemporaneous compositions (ex. 1.1).[38] Others include the structural segments that come together in phrases, periods, and movement-long forms. Viewed more abstractly, modules even encompass expressive devices such as "topics"—gestures or styles quoted outside their normal contexts, for instance, when a pair of violas in a string quintet evokes a horn call, when a solo piano plays a fanfare redolent of symphonic grandeur, or when a violin concerto passage suggests an opera recitative.[39] Although topics are not tied to any fixed melodic or harmonic content, they are nonetheless discreet entities that, like other modules, are distinguishable from the surrounding material and subject to imitation and reuse. All such patterns constituted a ready-made compendium of gestures laden with syntactic and rhetorical associations, which could be selected and combined so as to create a polished, coherent, expressive piece of music. In some pedagogical traditions, musical training took the form, quite literally, of systematic memorization of modules that, once absorbed, could be applied at will throughout an unfolding composition, whether improvised or notated.[40] This practice proved especially convenient for improvisers, since fluent extemporization requires total mastery over a set of simple musical procedures. That many modular gestures occur both in written-out models for improvisation and in contemporaneous compositions suggests that the vocabulary developed in the one discipline fed directly into the other, providing an elegant explanation for the transfer of creative skills between the hands and minds of late eighteenth-century composer-performers. Although the extent of Mozart's explicit engagement with these pedagogical traditions is unknown, his notated music shows clear evidence that he was conversant in modular conventions of the day.

To some extent, all music makes use of modules. As Leonard Meyer has argued, style itself is essentially a "replication of patterning" by composers of a given time and place.[41] Theorists across the ages have propounded similar views, with writings about musical modules in various guises stretching back at least to the *Musica Poetica* of the early 1600s and encompassing devices that have been referred to under a range of terms, such as the *regole* and *passaggi* of the early baroque, the *intavolature*, *partimenti*, and *solfeggi* of the Neapolitan tradition, and the ornamental *Setzmanieren* of the later eighteenth century. Despite the longevity and durability of such traditions, however, it was during Mozart's lifetime that modular structures reached their apogee. In a modular view of musical style, what defines each composer's idiom is not the local material from which individual pieces of music are built (since this is shared by contemporaries) but the unique selection process through which the gestures are combined and transformed during the act of composition or improvisation. Some uses would have been dictated by prevailing norms. For much of the eighteenth century, the module known as the Romanesca—a bassline familiar from Pachelbel's famous Canon in D—was associated with openings, and was often followed immediately by the module known as the Prinner, a scalar descent through $\hat{4}$–$\hat{3}$–$\hat{2}$–$\hat{1}$ in the bass and, a tenth above, $\hat{6}$–$\hat{5}$–$\hat{4}$–$\hat{3}$ in the treble.[42] Modern-day studies of musical modularity have emphasized the importance of formal conventions such as these, drawing comparisons across disparate repertoires and in so doing demonstrating the continuity between the practices of canonical figures and their lesser-known contemporaries.

Yet an emphasis on convention makes it easy to forget that such strictures were not only determined by tradition and passively inherited; they were also shaped and reshaped through continued application and experimentation. Each composer is not only the beneficiary of a stylistic tradition but a potential innovator whose music might help to shape that tradition's subsequent

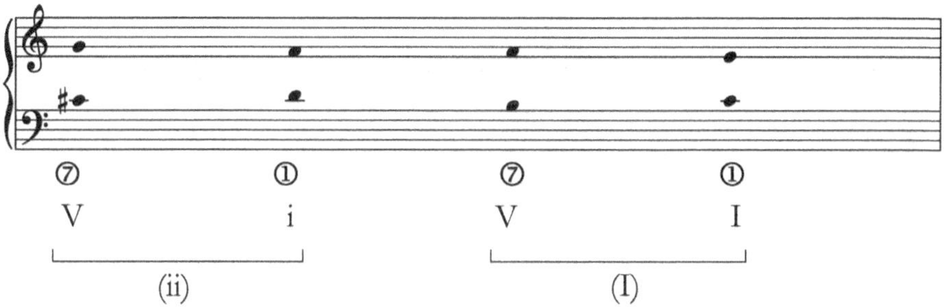

Example 1.2 Fonte schema

course. Thus, although Mozart sometimes treated modules according to contemporary norms, with Prinners duly succeeding Romanescas in the opening of many compositions, just as often his writing flouts convention. One module in particular, the Fonte, can illustrate the flexibility and wit with which Mozart approached the vocabulary of the day. The Fonte is a short, descending sequence in two parts. The first is in the minor mode and the second, one step lower, is in the major (ex. 1.2). The Fonte often places the leading tone of each dominant chord in the bass—C♯ first, and then B in the example here. However, other inversions are possible as long as this series of chords operates at some level of structure.

The Fonte is more than a sequential pattern involving a stock chord progression. Stepwise descents were routine at the time, but the Fonte also represents a rhetorical turn, combining its harmonic elements into a distinct "call and response" package that audiences would recognize and that would carry functional associations all its own. The Fonte served identifiable structural purposes and was most often used immediately following the repeat sign in binary form movements. (The term was coined, along with two related modules, the Ponte and Monte, by Joseph Riepel in the 1750s as a strategy for beginning the second half of minuets.[43]) Mozart often observes this conventional placement of the module, as in the Adagio from the Piano Sonata in E♭, K. 282, when a heavily decorated Fonte bridges the movement's two formal segments (ex. 1.3).

Yet Mozart also treats the Fonte idiosyncratically, deploying the figure in contexts where it may have sounded out of place to contemporary listeners.[44] One example occurs in the Piano Sonata in B♭ K. 281, when an unprepared Fonte begins the last movement. This is not only a violation of the module's standard transitional function; it also generates a momentary clash when the first bass note is a B♮ rather than the correct tonic, B♭. The phrase succeeds in

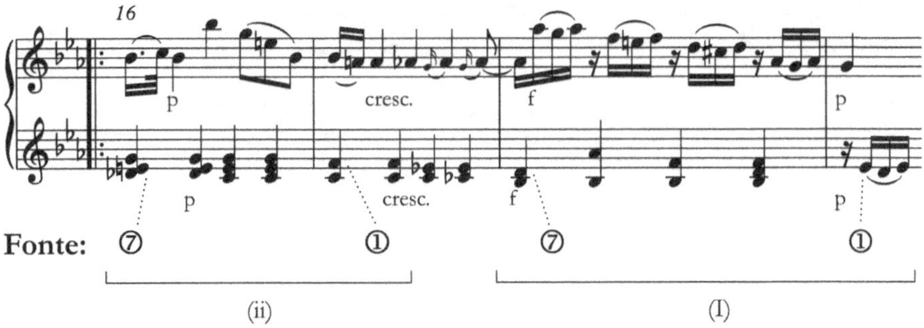

Example 1.3 Piano Sonata K. 282, first movement, mm. 16–19

part because the gesture is sufficiently familiar that it can be parsed in hindsight, in light of the soon-to-be-affirmed tonic, and in part because a touch of impropriety is acceptable given the playful feel of the movement. Elsewhere, Mozart uses the same strategy to a gloomier end, as when a Fonte (elongated and superimposed with two other modules) provides the organizing underlay for the shadowy first phrase of the "Dissonance" Quartet, K. 465.[45] Here Mozart eschews the rhetorical cohesion befitting an opening; the piece creaks painfully to life, as if unsure how to begin. The modules that features in this gambit are, taken alone, familiar elements of the eighteenth-century vernacular, but together they present a tangled series of digressive harmonic implications and chromatic wrong turns.

Mozart inserts the Fonte at unusual interstices within movements as well. These function as transitions of a kind, and thus conform in some measure to convention; yet he often harnesses them not to effect modulations back to the movement's tonic (the purpose they serve in more compact binary forms) but to modulate into new key areas. In the first movement of the Piano Sonata in C K. 279 (mm. 17–20) and the second movement of the Piano Sonata in D K. 311 (mm. 12–15), Mozart uses a Fonte to move swiftly into the dominant. In K. 279, the sudden irruption of E major, voiced with a boisterous arpeggio in the bass, can be interpreted as a comic turn, taking its place alongside other humorous features of the sonata.[46] In K. 311, the modulation is more plangent, the unprepared B-major chord and its subsequent turn to E minor briefly darkening the simpler music heard until that point.

Elsewhere, Mozart entirely abandons the transitional applications of the Fonte, embedding it within contexts that neither mark formal divisions nor bridge two phrases. One instance occurs in the Piano Sonata in B♭ K. 333, during the second theme area of the first movement. Beginning in measure 23,

Example 1.4 Piano Sonata K. 333, first movement, mm. 46–49

a tightly structured opening phrase gives way to a series of phrasal extensions and additions all meant to loosen the formal structures of the movement and increase the sense of culmination at the concerto-like cadence in measure 58. Along the way, his strategies for delaying closure and building expectation draw from standard harmonic and structural devices. He begins by writing melodies that emphasize C-major chords rather than F major, which shift metrical weight away from the tonic and toward the dominant (mm. 38–42); he then weakens the metrical thrust of each successive cadence. He introduces a deceptive progression in measure 44 that playfully recalls the left hand's antics at the start of the movement—its unexpected silences, its wheedling dissonances.[47] (Indeed, the left hand in this phrase returns to its erstwhile subversiveness: the deceptive cadence itself occurs because the left hand slyly mis-harmonizes a series of melodic half notes that might as well have closed in the tonic.) It is here, amid the persistent denial of resolution and the pulling-against of formal function, that a Fonte appears in measures 47–48 (ex. 1.4). In one sense, the module simply "kills time" by filling out a four-bar phrase that both starts and ends in F major, and thus goes nowhere new. Yet on another level its purpose is flagrantly rhetorical. It introduces a brief if abortive flash of chromaticism into a static phrase, and it does so humorously, even bunglingly, through the use of a building block that is ill placed in the context. As in the finale of K. 281, this incongruity gives the music a piquant charm. Mozart harnesses convention while putting it to idiosyncratic use.

In focusing on these unconventional applications of the Fonte, my purpose is not to sever Mozart from the mores of his day. The Fonte, like all harmonic patterns in their idealized states, is a theoretical construct. Any composer who deploys it in actual music will inevitably flesh it out, in the process translating it from its abstract form with the result that each concrete appearance must be unique to a greater or lesser extent. Although Mozart played fast and loose with some norms, therefore, the flexibility with which he treats the Fonte can be understood in part as an outgrowth of the very nature of the vernacular in which he worked. Moreover, even his idiosyncrasies are, in their way, affirmations of convention, since a "misplaced" Fonte bears rhetorical potency only by virtue of both the composer's and the audience's familiarity with the module's more decorous uses. Yet these Mozartian breaches are significant, for they suggest that a familiarity with conventional patterns is alone not enough to account for the intricacies of his compositional voice. Moreover, they make clear the extent to which his compositional voice depended on, and how sweepingly it had assimilated, the improviser's stock-in-trade. That he could misplace the Fonte at all is a sign of how far this assimilation went. The module served him not as a jigsaw piece fitted for a single formal setting and dependent on other surrounding figures but rather as a device that he could insert anywhere and in music running the expressive gamut from ominous to slapstick. The creativity he summons in his use of the Fonte helps demonstrate that Mozart the composer drew not only from the ethos and practice of improvisation but from its most essential materials.

So far I have taken a finely grained view of Mozart's modules, locating distinct, replicated patterns in the form of individual melodic or harmonic segments. However, modularity operates on other structural levels as well. The expressive unfolding of his compositions generally proceeds through discreet chunks of one, two, or four bars, with entire movements often seeming to emerge as successions of self-contained cells whose boundaries are differentiated either through changes of harmonic action, melodic shape, or rhythmic gesture as well as through affective markers such as instrumentation, texture, or topic. It is here that the historically colored analytic mode I have been exploring begins to suggest interpretive approaches, offering ways for us to hear his music. In the slow movement of the Piano Concerto in D K. 451, for instance, the orchestral opening moves through a set of four modules (ex. 1.5). From an analytic perspective, these come together to form a period composed of a two-bar antecedent and two-bar consequent. Yet they also guide our ears, inviting us to adopt a style of interpretation that depends on an awareness of modular juxtaposition.

A careful balance of similarity and difference makes transparent the shift from one module to the next. Module *a* presents a flowing line, rich with melodic chromaticism, gently oscillating between tonic and subdominant. Its drone bass (supported by cellos and horns), alongside the voicing of the

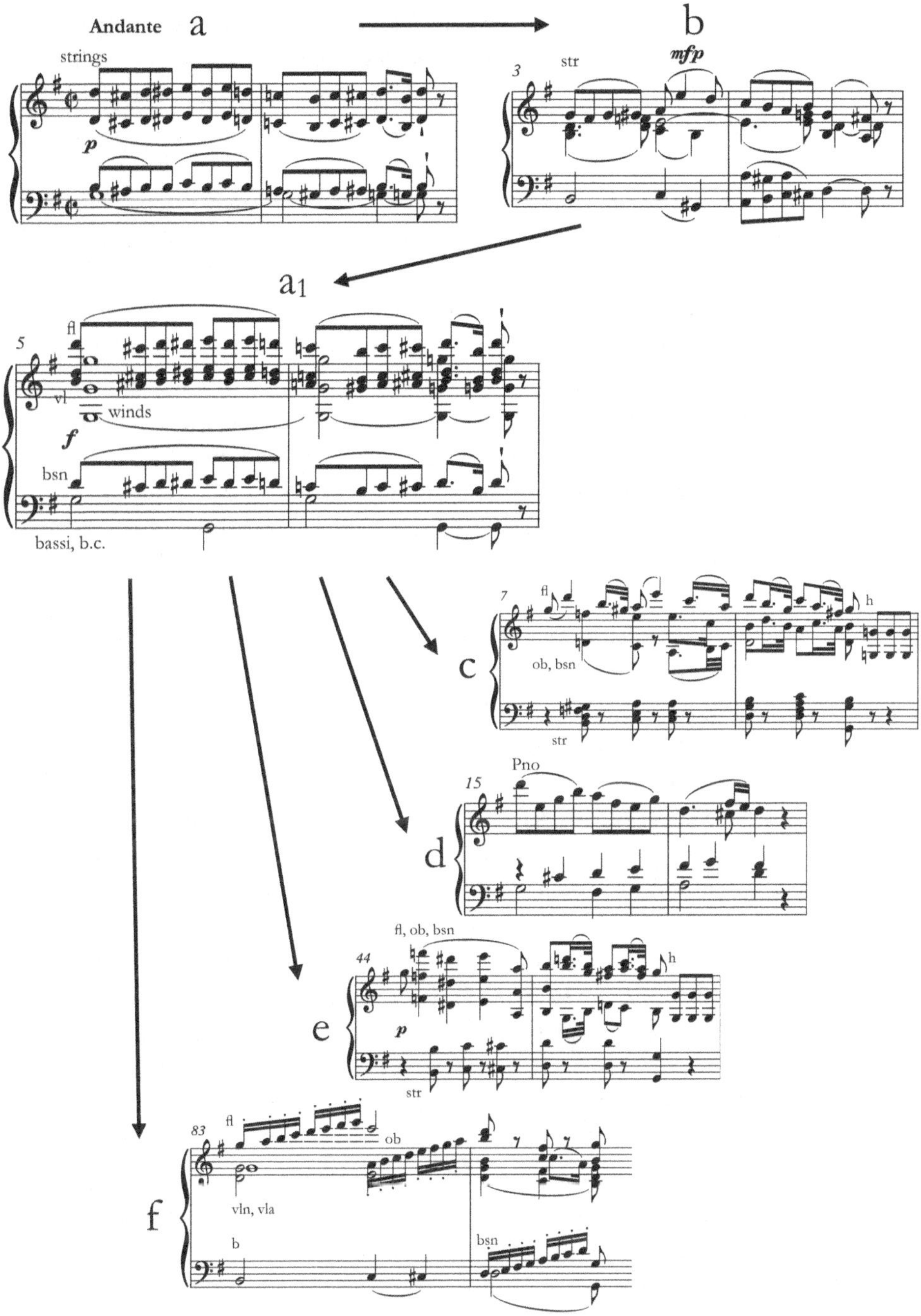

Example 1.5 Piano Concerto K. 451, second movement, modular pathways

upper strings, suggests a pastoral topic, albeit one transplanted from its usual meter of $\frac{6}{8}$. Module *b*, a contrasting idea, initially seems to follow from *a*, with a melody that echoes the chromatic line heard previously. Yet this brief repetition is glue rather than substance, an attempt to soften the discontinuities of bassline, texture, voicing, orchestration, and dynamics. We have entered the world of chorale, with four-part counterpoint. Chromaticism here serves not only to heighten the expressive melodic writing but to mark a certain muted cleverness: the G♯–A initially presented in the first violin is imitated slyly by the bassline in measure 3 and by the violas in measure 4. The melodic shape and character of the phrase changes as well, and we hear a subtle, throbbing accent as the violin rises from A to E—the first nonscalar melodic motion in the movement so far. Next comes a_1, a consequent that restates a version of the first module, this time increasing the dynamic and broadening the passage's instrumental range so as to span three octaves in the melody, four including the drone bass. Mozart introduces continuo figures into the soloist's line, an invitation for the pianist to join the orchestra's expanded texture.

Modular discontinuity comes to the surface at the close of a_1, when Mozart declines to give a straightforward restatement of *b*. Module *c* does echo some aspects of *b*: it begins with a first-inversion tonic chord, and the melody ascends once again from A to E. In this sense, *c* may be termed a variation of *b*.[48] Yet a new wave of features emphasizes rhetorical disruption rather than continuity: a focus on the winds, who carry the melody while the violins support; a formulaic cadential bassline; a metrical shift away from the *alla breve* of the first six measures toward rhythms that pulse at the quarter note; and, most of all, a melody that, despite having emerged from the violins' ascending fifth, expands this idea into a fixation in its own right.

These segments, along with their expressive identities, constitute combinatorial cells that Mozart rearranges as the movement proceeds. With every thematic return, we encounter a new route through the modules. The soloist's first entrance reprises the relationship between *a* and *b*, as do subsequent entrances in measures 38 and 77. Even the textural shift introduced by the lapse of the drone bass and the introduction of a four-part chorale texture is maintained in the solo piano line. Yet in each repetition, a_1 is followed by a new module: *d*, *e*, or *f*. *D* is entirely sui generis. The keyboard introduces sighing, melodic leaps for the first time in the movement and modulates to the dominant—the only time this period ends without confirming the original tonic of G. Modules *e* and *f*, meanwhile, resemble *b* and *c*, preserving the cadential bass motion that harkens to the opening phrase. Even so, *e* and *f* are thoroughly reimagined, first with a syncopated chromatic figure in the winds, and later with imitative writing that anticipates the enchanting trio for flute, oboe, and bassoon in Susanna's act 4 aria from *Le nozze di Figaro*.

My descriptions so far have centered on the musical content of the modules from K. 451. But what of the modular sound of the piece itself? What might it mean to listen to this movement as arising out of a series of self-contained units? For one thing, the music takes on the quality of a mosaic. The composite image retains its overarching coherence, yet at the same time a variety of smaller, interlocking components vie for aural focus. Attending to these means listening for contrasts rather than for continuity: apprehending and delighting in the shifts of expressive tone, changes of timbre and orchestration, and the range of textural states through which the music moves.[49] We track, for instance, Mozart's handling of the surface figuration through the various modifications of *a*—the piano soloist's filigree that subtly accompanies the wind melody in measure 13, as well as the full-voiced octaves the soloist assumes in measure 77.

Even more important, hearing K. 451 as a gathering of modular cells makes it possible to imagine a certain contingency within the notated composition. *This* arrangement of building blocks flowed from Mozart's pen in March of 1784—but perhaps on another occasion the same gestures might have given rise to a very different Andante. Strictly speaking, of course, such an idea is little more than an interpretive fiction. Mozart's choices were not arbitrary, and it is entirely possible that the movement would have unfolded the same way even if he had composed it under different circumstances. But such historical matters should not limit our aesthetic interests, and the notion of contingency is a powerful imaginative aid. If modules *c*, *d*, *e*, and *f* are not taken for granted as the inescapable consequence of a_1, then each arrives after a short but pointed moment of suspense as the transition from one segment to the next prompts us to wonder, *What will Mozart invent this time?* Hearing these modules as modules, we may imagine the entire Andante unfolding as an elaborate improvisation. The course of the movement no longer seems inevitable but arises anew with each hearing. Such an attitude, in turn, suggests broader considerations in our approach to Mozart's music. To focus on contingency or draw analogies with improvisation means calling into question some traditional notions of genius. No longer should we experience these compositions as fixed entities—singular, predetermined, issuing from a font of supernatural inspiration. Instead, the music seems a creation of the moment, arising through a series of imagined real-time choices that invite further analytic speculation and interpretive questioning.

To the extent that this mindset is facilitated by a sensitivity to modularity, it is not difficult to adopt it in the presence of Mozart's music, for the simple reason that discreet segments form the basis of his entire output. Much of what I have said about the Andante from K. 451 applies to the most compact of his minuets as well as to weightier movements from his mature symphonies, concertos, and chamber pieces. In some cases, the various iterations of a melody show multiple different routes through which their component modules might unfold; in larger-scale sonata-form movements, a similar sense of contingency may arise through the reordering of entire themes, which are often arrayed differently in expositions and recapitulations—a flexibility that allowed Mozart to counteract the inherent predictability of formal returns and that allows us, now, to imagine multiple paths through the most familiar pieces.[50] Yet even when thematic order remains consistent between exposition and recapitulation, and where counterfactual speculation is not fueled by a particular composition's content, Mozart still manages to differentiate and thus draw aural attention to the various modular components of recurring phrases. In the first movement of the Violin Concerto in A, K. 219, a secondary theme from the exposition (mm. 74–78) repeats in the recapitulation with its individual component gestures transposed into different registers (mm. 176–80). This change highlights the dialogic nature of the material. Mozart presents two musical "characters" whose distinction, latent in the exposition, is not fully cashed out until the phrase repeats later in the movement.

The effectiveness of Mozart's use of modules arises, in part, from the many levels on which identifiable patterns operate simultaneously, which allows him to finesse the balance of similarity and difference as each phrase unfolds. In K. 219 the modules represent expressive gestures that operate on the musical surface. We hear two different profiles in this exchange, with the first gesture's broken thirds, paired slurs, ascents, and emphatic, metrically strong line endings posing a sharp contrast to the gracious sighs of the responding idea.[51] At the same time, however, both modules begin with a pair of eighth notes in the upbeat, which, for the first three gestures, occur at the same scale degree. This carefully managed continuity and discontinuity is itself presented within a larger-scale module: the organizing scheme of an antecedent-consequent pattern, in which Mozart binds the more granular gestural shifts into a phrase that oscillates between tonic and dominant and thus proceeds through the logic of return and recurrence. These many layers of gesture, instrumental range, and character give the impression of a bustling scene held in equilibrium by the polite contours of conventional phrase structures. If Kofi Agawu has aptly described Mozart's music as presenting a compendium of figures that "convey a series of poses or stances in an almost cartoon-like fashion," these poses nonetheless merge into a coherent *tableau vivant* that derives its sense of unity in part from the larger-scale, phrase-level patterns that maintain order even as Mozart presents a barrage of local modular shifts.[52]

The vocabulary of modules constituting Mozart's musical language provided an essential ingredient in his practice of both composition and performance. Yet the explanatory import of these gestures, and the associated way of conceiving musical craft, reaches beyond the technical and artistic considerations I have already explored. Mozart lived at a time when modules of all types were familiar not only to practicing musicians but to experienced listeners; thus, his pursuit of technical facility along these lines would also have led, as a by-product, to competency with rhetorical and communicative dimensions of music making. In the letters detailing the composition of the "Paris" Symphony and *Die Entführung*, both quoted above, Mozart repeatedly describes his attempts to shock and delight listeners in terms compatible with a modular view of his style. Discussing the last movement of the "Paris" Symphony, he makes no mention of the scurrying second violins or the playfully disorienting syncopations in the first violins. Instead, he focuses on the phrasal "slots" in the composition: eight bars of *piano*, followed by a burst of *forte*, building-block proportions his listeners would intuitively understand through constant exposure to compositions that consist, in essence, of modules placed one after another. In the first movement as well, Mozart refers to a passage that he brings back unexpectedly at the end of the movement—and this ploy, of inserting a discreet segment of music in the "wrong" slot in order to surprise his listeners, speaks to a further element of audience manipulation made possible by the modular nature of contemporary style. Because many gestures were associated with either phrasal beginnings, continuations, or endings, deliberate misapplication would serve a communicative end similar to that of the dynamic shifts and tempo changes discussed in the *Entführung* letter. In the Piano Concerto K. 271, figures normally used to signal closure are placed at the outset of phrases, with the effect that the soloist seems constantly to resuscitate melodies just as they are poised to finish. In the Symphony in E♭ K. 543, the memorable tune that begins the last movement also doubles humorously as its final gesture.[53] Such hijinks will become central to my arguments about wit and improvisation in chapter 3; for now we might simply note that these cases of modular manipulation all occur in genres associated with large-scale public performance. Unlike in Mozart's piano sonatas and chamber music, where the listeners for whom he wrote were usually the score-reading players themselves (a fact that led him to explore other means of generating intrigue), those who attended the premieres of his symphonies and concertos would encounter the music without the aid of a printed score and would therefore have to rely entirely on aural clues for orientation.[54] In cases such as these, Mozart's communicative acumen was greatly facilitated by the style's inherent modularity and particularly the separability of cells, which could be reorganized in whatever way might produce the maximum effect.

Explaining Mozart

The modular understanding of Mozart's style I have defended so far is valuable in part because it elucidates the techniques practiced by eighteenth-century composer-performers, and it does so in terms compatible with those espoused in theoretical sources of the time. Modularity is also useful as a conceptual aid: the very idea provides a unified thread linking such disparate subjects as tactile keyboard technique, improvisatory methods, compositional language, expressive vocabulary, and the communicative effects featured in this repertoire. However, as I also argue, an equally important element of the modular perspective—perhaps its most important element for my purposes here—concerns the mode of explanation it entails whereby a given set of historical or biographical considerations helps shape the interpretive attitude we adopt in the presence of this music. The fact that such an explanation efficiently bridges the gap between history and modern-day listening, connecting an account of Mozart's human activities with the mindset under which we might approach his music, is remarkable indeed: it suggests a deep unity among the ideas we bring to bear in the presence of artworks. This unity, no less than the playful, performative impulse at the heart of Mozart's style, is a subject of this book. Therefore, before moving on to the next chapter, I will briefly explore the nature and workings of musical explanation, noting in particular its points of intersection with other historical and analytic pursuits.

An explanation is an account of *why* something is so rather than simply *that* it is so. The quest for explanatory understanding can take many forms; but applied to the topic of this book, seeking an explanation entails asking how a piece of music or a style emerged the way it did. We may wish to explain why a composer selected one note rather than another when crafting a phrase; why modules are arrayed in a given order in a movement; why a movement conveys a particular series of expressive stances; or indeed why a piece came to be written in the first place. Each of these questions can be addressed using a broad range of approaches. I have already discussed Mozart's decision-making in light of listeners' expectations, and in what follows I will propose further explanations involving his piano technique (chap. 2), his improvisatory showmanship (chaps. 3, 4), and his sense of theatricality (chap. 5). Taken together, these suggest a broad framework with which to conceive the whole of Mozart's artistry while also implying a more detailed, causal account of how that framework structured the minutiae of his compositional problem-solving. As we have seen, some of the associated explanatory efforts arise through assessments of Mozart's life or the culture in which he worked; others focus on musical detail. Yet all such approaches, whether rooted in history or musical style and aesthetics, ultimately lead us to speculate about the workings of Mozart's mind as we imagine the specific criteria that may have guided him during his acts of musical creation.

Many (though not all) modes of musical engagement currently practiced in the worlds of both scholarship and performance shy away from the pursuit of explanations, aiming at something more akin to description—perhaps in verbal form through close reading and analysis, or perhaps nonverbally through performance. For some readers, the very idea of investigating "Mozart's thoughts" will be cause for alarm: such thoughts, after all, can neither be observed nor verified, and to make conjectures about them puts us at risk of committing the intentional fallacy. Yet even those who avoid any outright attempts to explain Mozart's music nonetheless rely on a host of inexplicit explanatory assumptions when interacting with individual compositions.[55] When multiple musicians approach a given piece, they invariably produce interpretations that diverge widely in both outlook and substance, perhaps even to the point of mutual incompatibility—and this is so despite the fact that all such musicians engage the selfsame collection of notes and phrases. This alone suggests the large extent to which prior explanatory theories influence how and what we hear in individual artworks.[56] The passing G-minor triad in the first bar of the Sonata K. 333, discussed briefly in the Theme, can be interpreted in any number of ways. What we make of it depends primarily on whether we are predisposed to accept a flash of ambivalence on the part of Mozart's compositional persona. If we are so disposed, then the event becomes a locus of hermeneutic significance; if we are not, the meaning I ascribed to it earlier will seem implausible. The sonata does not in itself clarify which approach is best any more than it transmits a straightforward guide to the weight performers should accord each of the first four downbeat appoggiaturas or, for that matter, how the phrasal structures in the remainder of the exposition should be divvied up. (Hence, even in this familiar composition, two standard accounts of eighteenth-century musical form disagree on the question of just where the second theme area actually ends.[57]) This piece, like any other, affords countless options for interpretation, and although some may intuitively seem more compelling than others, the choice often comes down not to musical content but to explanatory preference. Such preferences can arise in any number of contexts. Even matters of practical performance—for instance, historical explanations for the phrasing of slurs—may exert a significant pull on analytic thinking about a composition.[58] At the highest levels, explanations may arise through creative conjecture or as part of ideological stances interpreters self-consciously adopt. But whatever their source, all such explanations orient scholars, performers, and listeners alike, determining their sensitivities to detail as well as shaping the broad, aesthetic attitudes to which they are sympathetic. All close readings, whether written or performed, are alike in the crucial respect that they shine a light on the explanatory preconceptions of those who carry them out.

The history of Mozart reception demonstrates the ways in which explanatory preconceptions influence engagement with styles and compositions. Every new development in Mozart interpretation over the past two centuries may be seen as issuing from just such a framework, from the proto-Romantic Mozart of the early nineteenth century to the angelic, childlike Mozart that held sway into the twentieth and, more recently, to the savvy, professionalized "working stiff" described in an influential 1994 essay by Neal Zaslaw.[59] These are only three examples of many, yet their simultaneous influence on all downstream facets of interpretation is particularly transparent. For instance, Zaslaw's workmanlike Mozart is intimately related to the module-driven Mozart of recent analytic efforts, who studiously masters a repertoire of conventional gestures and thus thrives in his bustling milieu. This view is, in turn, bound up with the ideals of the late twentieth century's historical performance movement, which began to flourish alongside the first modern-day theories of musical modularity[60] and which, according to one polemic, turned Mozart into a "mundane, if dexterous, representative of his age" precisely by emphasizing the conventional dimensions of his craft rather than his "genius" or individuality.[61] Each of these views—the Romantic, angelic, and modular Mozart—rests on a different set of implicit explanations adopted at the cultural level and applied during the acts of musical appreciation. Concepts such as genius, talent, inspiration, or hard work are all explanatory aids proposed in order to account for the existence of Mozart's music. And each in turn calls up other, related explanatory theories, which shaped their ages' intellectual climates and by extension determined the attitudes available to musicians and listeners.

If we discount the role of broad explanations in all forms of musical engagement, the confluence of aesthetic ideals in each successive Mozartian theory must seem largely coincidental. In any case, we face something of a chicken-and-egg problem: who sparks the interpretive revolution, and how? By contrast, a focus on explanation accounts neatly for the fact that trends often arise in both scholarly and performative circles at once. They do so because both are jointly symptomatic of more basic theories—in this particular case, involving changing notions of the interaction between convention and innovation or the balance of inspiration and technical craft in artistic creation.

Yet if explanation is omnipresent in our encounters with Mozart's music, not all explanations are equally plausible. The various theories of Mozart that have held sway over the centuries are strikingly dissimilar in many respects—most crucially in the number of his activities for which they can comfortably account. Many nineteenth-century appraisals fare poorly by this measure, expressing admiration for only the most brooding compositions. The early biographer Franz Niemetschek, for instance, held that the pinnacle of Mozart's output was represented by the act 2 finale of *Don Giovanni* ("sublime music, created from the depths of his genius").[62] The musical maverick Friedrich Rochlitz, in an article for the December 1805 issue of the *Allgemeine musikalische Zeitung*, gave a longer list, arguing that Mozart's style is epitomized by the overture, finales, and "main scenes" of *Don Giovanni*, several numbers from *Idomeneo*, the late symphonies and piano concertos, the late motets, and the Requiem.[63] Both authors focus almost exclusively on music that now seems exceptional in Mozart's output. A balanced representation of his style was, perhaps, of less interest than a celebration of the figure who, within a decade of his death, had already become an icon of Romanticism.

As cultural mores shifted through the nineteenth century, Mozart interpretation changed with them. The expressive and rhetorical complexities of Mozart's symphonies and concertos clashed with the burgeoning Victorian image of Mozart as an eternal child, and these pieces gradually disappeared from concert programs.[64] Mozart's operas, too, were sidelined. *Le nozze di Figaro* was so unpopular in the 1850s that the biographer Otto Jahn found it necessary to mount a broad defense of the opera in an attempt to revive public interest in it.[65] *Così fan tutte*, meanwhile, was considered irredeemable. In the rare cases when it was performed, it was extensively revised so as to prettify a plot whose alleged immorality clashed with prevailing notions of Mozartian innocence and grace.[66] From a modern-day vantage point, it would seem uncontroversial to claim that a conception of Mozart's craft, style, and aesthetic that does not embrace *Figaro* or *Così*, to say nothing of one that deems four-fifths of his concertos non-Mozartian, is missing something essential about his art. This is not to imply that every one of his compositions must slot neatly into a single, monolithic explanation. Mozart's style underwent many developments over his career, and even within individual creative periods he composed in an astonishing range of expressive styles, from comic to learned, light to dark. But far from undermining the notion of a comprehensive explanatory theory that might undergird our engagement with his music, these shifts are phenomena for which such an explanation should attempt to account.

It follows from all this that shifts in understanding of a musical style are not driven by close study of individual compositions. Instead, they occur alongside broader explanatory changes, which reorient our perceptions of that style and allow us to reimagine its implications. Such changes, in turn, bear on the more minute elements of our listening and therefore on our understanding of individual compositions. The purpose of this book is to pursue one such explanation for one artist: to propose that we hear Mozart's music as having issued from the mind, hands, and pen of a composer-performer and to ask what this might mean for musical interpretation.

So far I have discussed explanation at the cultural level. But in asking how the intersection of composition and performance might have helped shape Mozart's style, I am moving into a more exacting realm of explanation—this time aimed at asking why particular pieces of music emerged as they did or, by extension, why we might wish to approach them with one interpretive attitude rather than another. Explanatory questions along these lines can be answered, broadly, by pursuing two investigative paths: the historical and the aesthetic. Historical explanations attempt to arrive at "why" by examining the circumstances that led to the creation of a given composition or the emergence of a style, often with reference to the social backdrop against which a composer worked, the economic trends that prevailed during and before that composer's lifetime, or other topics relating to biography and cultural milieu. Aesthetic explanations, by contrast, in the sense in which I use the term, emphasize the internal workings of a given composition or style: that is, they explain a composer's choices in the light of internal, artistic considerations. Although these two modes of explanation occasionally overlap—indeed, this book is an exercise in moving between the two domains—in ends and methods they are largely distinct.

Historical explanation is currently the dominant trend in musicology and, increasingly, in music theory, a discipline whose onetime aesthetic preoccupations have given way to a historically informed approach in which theorists turn to contemporary sources to corroborate their interpretive leanings and nuance, perhaps even justify, their close readings.[67] Yet although there is much interest to be found in historical explanations, their ability to account for the specifics of individual compositions must remain incomplete unless supplemented with possible aesthetic conjectures for a composer's decision-making. As a case study, imagine investigating the origins of *Le nozze di Figaro*: how did this opera come to be written? A historical explanation might begin from contextual circumstances, referring perhaps to the rise of the monarchy and contemporary political and philosophical movements as well as the inequalities and strains that crystalized in the French Revolution. It would take account of the authorship and reception of Beaumarchais's *Le marriage de Figaro*, on which Da Ponte based the libretto, including the unease Habsburg Emperor Joseph II (brother of Marie Antoinette) felt at the prospect of an operatic adaptation of so incendiary a play. A historical explanation might also examine the consolidation of economic power that allowed Joseph II to fund operas in the first place as well as the factors in Mozart's own career and station that led him to rely on such patronage. Taken together, such investigations would indeed explain the emergence of Mozart's *Figaro*, all while saying little about the opera's music.

History may tell us why Mozart wished to write an opera and even account for the genesis of a particular opera. But what of the series of musical decisions he faced while working? It is not that his choices were insulated from broader social or cultural factors. An understanding of Mozart's style depends on an awareness of the norms he inherited. Every piece of music is the result of negotiations between one composer's voice and broader convention, and as I have already argued, in this Mozart is no exception. For instance, the choice of tonalities in the eighteenth century rested in part on the social setting in which a piece of music would be played. Orchestral trumpets and drums during Mozart's lifetime were, owing to details of instrumental construction and technique, able to play only in a small range of tonalities; thus, the use of these forces, de rigueur for large venues and grand occasions, limited composers to the keys of C, D, or E♭. It is no coincidence that each of Mozart's mature operas begins or ends in one of these keys. But such constraints are never absolute. Having undertaken to compose in C, D, or E♭, Mozart could still write in any expressive idiom. The socioeconomic circumstances leading up to the composition of *Figaro* would be compatible with countless alternative versions, including those in C major or in which the overture featured an energetic fugue. References to historical circumstances say little about why Mozart chose *that* particular note or melodic shape instead of the myriad others available to him. The same applies to other historical considerations that bore on composition. In crafting his operas, Mozart often wrote for the voices of specific singers, and as a result studies of these works' compositional histories often begin with the question of each singer's identity and abilities, framing the interpretation of the characters' actions and psychologies in light of the performers who created each role. I have already acknowledged the merits of this approach; yet here too, limitations arise. As Jessica Waldoff observes in her study of *Così fan tutte*, to pursue character analyses primarily in light of the human identities of Mozart's collaborators is akin to "[restricting] our understanding of *Romeo and Juliet* to readings that bear in mind that Juliet was first created on the stage by a boy."[68]

At some point the aesthetic mode of explanation must take over, allowing us to view Mozart's practices in light of the internal musical and dramatic world in which his operas, and compositions more generally, unfold. Even source studies—those forensic investigations of paper types, inks, and handwriting, and the onetime focus of historical musicology—ultimately rely on aesthetic modes of explanation. Careful analysis of the documentary evidence can enhance our knowledge of Mozart's working habits; but if we wish to explain why Mozart retained one draft and discarded another, the reason will involve the notes enshrined on that page and how he expected them to feature in the finished composition. Here as before, the quest for explanation leads away from historical matters of paper and ink and toward abstract, musical content. We cannot verify our assumptions concerning Mozart's thoughts; but if we want to understand how a piece came to be written, it is within the aesthetic realm that our conjectures must eventually arrive.

Addressing matters internal to pieces of music means explaining the aesthetic considerations that guided the composer's pen. It goes without saying, however, that not all aesthetic discussions are equally successful in this regard. Even the most careful analysis of the notes that make up a piece of music provide no guarantee of higher-order understanding. As Leonard Meyer reminds us in a wide-ranging study of musical explanation, "One can list and count traits—say, the frequency of *sforzandi* in Beethoven's music or the number of deceptive cadences in Wagner's operas . . . but if nothing is known about their functions (structural, processive, expressive, and so on), it will be impossible to explain why they are there, how their presence is related to other features observed. . . . Such traits may even serve as reasonably reliable 'identifiers' of Beethoven's or Wagner's style, yet contribute nothing to our understanding of how that style functions."[69] The same concerns arise in Kofi Agawu's writings on topic theory in late eighteenth-century music. Despite Agawu's pioneering and brilliant advocacy for the importance of topics in analyzing musical discourse, he admits that, no matter how comprehensive a list we create of a piece's topical universe, this alone will not help us establish a "self-regulating account" of the ordering, structure, or function of the expressive context of that composition.[70] In other words we must appeal to broader modes of explanation if we wish to understand why a piece demonstrates a particular series of rhetorical stances rather than another. Hermann Abert, occasionally criticized for his allegedly old-fashioned approach to musical biography, defended a similar view in the early twentieth century, taking other Mozart scholars to task for attempting to situate the composer's creative practices as straightforward outcomes of his immediate influences without stopping to ask the more important question of how Mozart decided which models to adopt and what steps he took in making them his own.[71] Though spanning more than a century, all these statements share a core premise: in pursuing explanations, we should avoid lapsing into mere descriptions, for these may be just as incomplete as attempts to derive musical detail from historical events.

The power and reach of aesthetic explanation has already been a touchstone in this book during the earlier discussion of modules. Although the task of identifying modules may seem an exercise in description rather than explanation, it also carries explanatory ramifications. Modules account for the evolution of particular tropes in Mozart's style, particularly in light of his joint practices as a pianist and an improviser. Indeed, the identification of modules paves the way for an understanding of his compositional mind. To identify as a Fonte the figure that occurs in measures 16–19 of the first movement of K. 282 (ex. 1.3) is not simply to label a stock chord progression. The gesture as it appears in the sonata is so complex that it would almost certainly have bewildered contemporaries encountering the piece for the first time. Yet by noting the pattern from which the progression is fashioned, we can reverse engineer the process by which Mozart created it. We can glimpse the continuity between this passage and the treatment of themes in Mozart's variations, both of which use simple phrase elements as a scaffold on which to mount other transformations—here, a descending chromatic bass, syncopations, and a melody that hints at the well-behaved repetitiveness of sequential writing while still managing to avoid predictability. These observations resonate with other ideas I have mentioned concerning Mozart's interest in the manipulation of his listeners and his attendant warping of many conventional modular gestures—a thread of explanation that will become central to my argument in later chapters. The explanatory pathway begins with the basic features of the musical language Mozart inherited but ultimately touches on the evolution of his own idiosyncratic developments. And if modules constitute that rare kind of explanatory device that simultaneously responds to historical practices of Mozart's lifetime while also encompassing many of the unique features of his idiom, we have also seen that they carry implications for the appreciation of his music. As discussed above, an emphasis on the modular nature of Mozart's style can shape the way modern-day listeners approach his compositions, prompting a move away from continuity, childlike grace, or simplicity and toward the sudden shifting of affects and the juxtaposition of disparate expressive states. The impulse to explain the content of Mozart's music leads us to a specific mode of interpretation as we attend to the kaleidoscopic image that emerges from a cluttered discontinuity of individual fragments.

However, the modular explanation is not in itself sufficient to capture Mozart's style. It leaves untouched higher-order questions concerning pacing, rhetoric, and expressive coherence. To focus on modules is to embrace reductionism, and although a sensitivity to building blocks may suggest an interpretive mindset that could otherwise prove elusive, it may all too easily distract from other equally legitimate modes of explanation. At its most granular, the modular view does not distinguish one composition from another; nor does it alone capture the difference between the artistry of one composer and another.[72] It is possible to break a style down into arbitrarily small units and still (following Meyer and Agawu) remain insensitive to the larger-scale strategies that structure and regulate the units, just as one can examine each word in a joke without grasping the humor that arises from higher-order matters of syntax, context, and associative meaning.[73] The explanations I pursue in this book, therefore, supplement their attention to modularity with an awareness of more holistic features that drive the unfolding of Mozart's compositions. These, too, have already made a brief appearance in my references to expectation, surprise, and unrest. In many cases, as we shall continue to see, the most compelling way to explain the unfolding of an individual composition is by invoking the higher-order expressive or even psychological states that give purpose to Mozart's modules, dictating the way in which they are arranged.

It is under the organizing ideal of performativity that this book synthesizes the many facets of Mozart's compositions into a unified, explanatory whole. The argument I put forth in the coming chapters is, simply, that the skills Mozart acquired as a performer are best explained not as biographical details but as a set of aesthetic strategies. These strategies account for the emergence and nature of his style. They also suggest a mindset through which modern-day performers, scholars, or listeners can interpret his music. Unlike the proto-Romantic, Victorian, or even "working stiff" theories of Mozart, the view I pursue in the remainder of this book aspires to be comprehensive: to embrace the many intricacies and complexities of his compositions, their astonishing inventiveness, their dizzying technical acuity, their wit, and their soulfulness. To give substance to these broader claims, as well as to explore their ramifications for our understanding of individual compositions, is the task of what follows. In each chapter, I focus on a different facet of Mozart's craft. Chapter 2 begins on comparatively firm historical footing with an examination of his piano technique that draws together contemporary evidence and inferences from his compositions. I then move beyond the historical mode, turning to explanations rooted in Mozart's performativity as expressed, successively, in his improvisations, his embellishments, and finally, in the dramatic nuances of his operas. Although my approach is based on a small set of premises concerning Mozart's compositional priorities and performative activities, I hope to show that from these assumptions many interpretive riches follow. And beneath it all hums the sophisticated machinery of the composer-performer's art.

VARIATION 2

Mozart the Pianist

So culturally entrenched are tales of Mozart's upbringing as a wunderkind that it is tempting to view his career as having been fated from the outset. That Mozart was raised by one of the premiere musical pedagogues of the time, that he had an elder sister whose dazzling pianistic abilities spurred his, and that he grew up in the rich culture of Salzburg all seem in hindsight to have set him on a path leading inexorably to his celebrated public image as a composer and virtuoso pianist.[1] Yet a listener encountering Wolfgang in the early 1760s would have been hard pressed to imagine how his many talents would ultimately take shape. Mozart began his performance career at age five in a theatrical vein, dancing in pantomimes and sacred plays.[2] By age seven he had become a highly competent composer, harpsichordist, clavichordist, organist (as his father reports, Wolfgang initially played the bass notes by walking along the pedals, since his legs were too short to reach down from the bench), violinist, and singer.[3] He did not maintain a neat separation between these skills but plied them alongside each other in extravagantly multifaceted performances. One memorable occasion, spread across two days in October 1769, began with the performance of a Mozart mass. Afterward, according to an eyewitness, Mozart "played for half an hour on the great organ to the astonishment of all," followed by a concert the next evening at which he "sang, and played the violin and the clavier to everyone's amazement."[4] The young virtuoso had not yet turned fourteen.

With maturity came focus, and as Mozart's abilities deepened he no longer attempted to maintain all of these skills simultaneously. His last documented performance as a singer took place in 1770. Eight years later, aged twenty-two, he resolved to cease playing the violin in public as well so that he could devote his energies to composing operas.[5] This goal even sidelined his interests in the piano. "I would rather [. . .] neglect the Clavier than Composition," he wrote to his father in 1778. "The Clavier is only a secondary thing for me, but, thank god, a very strong secondary thing."[6]

Yet if Mozart's ambitions lay in composing, he must on another level have been aware that the many strands of his budding career all centered on his activities at the keyboard. It was at the keyboard that the public would see him as a virtuoso improviser, spinning lengthy variations and fantasias. The keyboard also served Mozart as a vehicle for displaying his abilities as a serious composer, particularly through the genre of the piano concerto, that musical laboratory in which he explored with ever-increasing boldness new expressive and structural devices. The keyboard's role as a focal point for his improvisatory, technical, and compositional skills in turn fueled other facets of his career, including the acquisition of students, his publishing efforts, and his activities as an impresario, all of which were necessary to ensure financial stability. Even his desire to compose operas, which may seem far removed from the performance concerns of a non-singer, provided opportunities for instrumental showmanship through recitative continuo that would propel the stage action as well as through the occasional obbligato aria that would allow him to share the spotlight with famous divas.[7]

The keyboard also served an important offstage function in Mozart's life. As we have seen, he preferred to write at the keyboard for at least the first two-thirds of his creative career, most likely in a process akin to improvisation, testing passages and developing ideas without the hassle of reworking music already set on paper. Even when forced to compose away from the instrument, many of the skills he developed as a performer—the manipulation of schema modules, the mindset associated with variation techniques, and, more broadly, an intimate familiarity with virtuosic pianistic devices—would have remained readily available within his musical imagination.

But while it is clear that Mozart's pianistic abilities influenced his compositional working habits and career trajectory, it is less obvious what direct impact his pianism might have had on the content of his music. That there was some connection between the two is not in doubt. In some cases it is even possible to glimpse Mozart's negotiations between performative and compositional ideals, as when he revised solo passages in concertos such as K. 449, K. 450, and K. 491 in order to increase their playability and tactile elegance.

Elsewhere, though instrumental considerations featured in Mozart's compositional planning, they did not limit his musical imagination, and it is sometimes possible to safely exclude pianistic thought from a conjectured account of his priorities. (Regardless of how he created the spectacular fugal apotheosis that ends the "Jupiter" Symphony—whether at the keyboard, or directly from imagination to ink—its internal features are best explained with reference to the deft manipulation of contrapuntal lines and his rich language of topics, expressive gestures, and orchestral effects.) Even in the keyboard music, where links between instrumental technique and compositional structure are most plausible, the relationship remains ambiguous, in need of careful excavation. When piano technique featured in Mozart's compositional thinking, it would have been one factor of many.

The aim of this chapter, then, is to explore aspects of Mozart's engagement with the keyboard, examining the intersections of pianistic thought and compositional style, particularly where the keyboard may have helped him solve musical problems he encountered during the creative process. My goal is to flesh out an image of Mozart's professional persona that transcends the printed score. Because today we know Mozart only as a composer, and only through his written music, it is all too easy to conceive of his activities and innovations in terms of the intellectualism of compositional craft (or, for the "working stiff," in terms of production schedules and commissions) without taking into account his engagement with the physical dimensions of performance. As I have already implied, the point of rendering this image more concretely is not to draw deterministic links between material conditions and his music. When I invoke the mechanics of piano playing, I do not mean to suggest that Mozart played or composed by rote, through a dull or automated process. Rather, I want to show his compositional style as drawing actively and inventively on the considerations he faced as a pianist—the constraints imposed by contemporary instruments and performance methods leavened with abstract, expressive concerns that will occupy my argument in later chapters.

Evidence and Speculation

An understanding of the relationship between Mozart's performing activities and compositional habits must begin and end at the keyboard, where the many facets of his musicianship intersected. Yet owing to the lack of applicable, specific evidence, the details of his playing are frustratingly vague. To be sure, this problem is not unique to studies of Mozart. Music is an ephemeral art, and the physical habits of past performers, to say nothing of their musical imaginings, are inaccessible to most forms of modern-day investigation. Researchers with an interest in historical performance have recovered or reconstructed period instruments; mined treatises and other theoretical sources for advice; studied iconography; and developed exhaustive accountings of practical, theoretical, social, scientific, and religious texts that bear on music making. Yet despite these efforts, the resulting picture of historical practice remains patchy and inconclusive.

One problem is simply that textual sources cannot play or sing for us. Any conclusions we draw from them are necessarily filtered through our own musical and linguistic preconceptions—and these preconceptions, like the aesthetic explanations I discussed previously, reflect broad, cultural assumptions and priorities.[8] Period instruments make audible the ideas and beliefs not of their historical designers but of their living players, and antique literary documents, read by present-day minds, are easily misunderstood. Leopold Mozart's *Versuch* instructs performers to treat slurs as diminuendos, with the first note of each gesture played longer and heavier than the last note.[9] But how much stronger? How quickly do the notes taper? Even if we obtained the perfect reading of such a source, problems would remain. Many texts reflect the idiosyncratic views of their authors rather than opinions safely attributable to other musicians—even when those other musicians share a last name. Leopold's life was closely intertwined with that of his son, but it does not follow that the two held compatible preferences in the realm of musical performance.[10] Nor is it possible to sidestep these issues by reading sources en masse and forming a broad, impersonal image of contemporary practices free from the quirks of individual musicians. The resulting amalgamation is little more than a fictional abstraction, a picture that, though stripped of individual biases, probably bears little resemblance to the practices or preferences of any actual people at a given time and place. Of course, even if a reliable image of an "average" eighteenth-century musician were available, there is no reason to think that it would fare better than Leopold's advice in illuminating Mozart's compositions. Mozart's relationship both to his father's preferences and to contemporary performance convention is questionable.

Mozart's letters present similar obstacles. Although his family's voluminous correspondence contains references to countless aspects of musical life and culture, his words are often vague. At times, readers may find themselves asking questions much like those I asked of Leopold's tapered slurs. For instance,

Mozart reports in one letter that the pianist Josepha Auernhammer plays well but has the bad habit of "clipping" notes during *cantabile* passages.[11] Should we conclude that he preferred legato playing? At all times, or only in slow movements? How clipped is too clipped?

Even when Mozart discusses contemporary music making in fuller detail, he often avoids precise description of instrumental technique. He wastes no opportunity to lambaste other musicians for their shortcomings. Many of his letters contain caricatures of the performers he encountered, all described with great flair and comic acuity. Yet it is rarely easy to derive musical substance from these entertaining tales. For one thing, Mozart's words often focus on his subjects' physical deportment rather than their playing as such. When traveling through Germany in 1777, he reported an encounter in Augsburg with Maria Anna Josepha Aloysia von Hamm: "She seems to me so curiously affected—she stalks up and down the keyboard with her long bony fingers in such an odd way. [. . .] You say I should have tested her playing?—I simply couldn't, I was laughing so hard."[12] Mozart criticizes the organists Nikolaus Bayer and Anton Marxfelder for their facial expressions: "To watch these gentlemen is enough to make one die laughing. The second, when seated at the organ, is like a child on the toilet; one sees in his face what he is capable of. The first, in any case, wears glasses."[13] Even when Mozart's penchant for humor came into alignment with his exacting musical standards, and even when his letters focus on specific performative failures, it is difficult to draw broader inferences from his words. He criticized the organist Johann Franz Xaver Sterkel, describing his playing as "so fast that it was hard to follow, unclear, and not in time,"[14] and he praised the young pianist Rosa Cannabich for performing the second movement of K. 309 as a slow, rather than a fast, Andante.[15] His scathing account of Abbé Georg Joseph Vogler's halting attempts at sight-reading the Piano Concerto K. 246 brings the same point into greater relief:

> Before dinner he scrambled through my concerto [. . .] sight-reading [. . .]. The first movement went *prestissimo*, the Andante *allegro* and the Rondeau, truly, *prestississimo*. He played most of the bass differently from the way it was written, inventing now and then an entirely different harmony and even melody. Nothing else is possible at that speed. Eyes cannot see the music nor the hands play it. [. . .] The listeners [. . .] can say only that they have *seen* music and piano playing. They hear, think—and feel—as little during the performance *as the player has*. You

> can easily imagine that it was unendurable, because I could not bring myself to say to him: *far too quick*.[16]

It is tempting to imagine, as some have, that Mozart therefore preferred steady and deliberate tempos. But this conclusion sits uneasily alongside other statements in his correspondence, for instance the claim that the last movement of the "Haffner" Symphony must be played "as fast as possible."[17] All we can say is that Mozart disliked performers who played faster than they could manage—and put so plainly, this is little more than common sense.

Only rarely does Mozart turn his critical gaze toward his own playing. In one oft-quoted letter, he describes his approach to *tempo rubato*: "Everyone is amazed that I can always stay strictly in time. What they can't grasp is that in tempo rubato, in an Adagio, the left hand should go on playing in strict time. With them the left hand always follows [the right]."[18] More often, however, his letters even about himself focus on bodily movements rather than musical detail: "I do not make grimaces, and yet play with such expression that [the piano maker Johann Andreas Stein] himself confesses, no one up to the present has been able to get such good results out of his instruments."[19] Although this letter makes explicit reference only to the calmness of the face, he later suggests that the same focus and stillness should characterize the motions of the hands as well: "I beg my sister not to practice those passages *too much*, so that she will not spoil her quiet, even touch and that her hand may not lose its natural lightness, flexibility, and fluent rapidity."[20] Mozart's words recall Forkel's fabled description of J. S. Bach's clavier playing, with finger movements that were "hardly perceptible" and the rest of his body held utterly still.[21] It also directly contradicts the advice of Carl Philipp Emanuel Bach, whose treatise on keyboard playing advises performers to exaggerate their facial expressions so as to aid the audience in understanding the music.[22]

Mozart admired C. P. E. Bach's compositions but would have had none of his histrionics. Mozart's most comprehensive caricature of such issues is his description of Nanette Stein, the eight-year-old daughter of the piano builder whose instruments Mozart championed in the late 1770s. He captures in great detail the many faults of young Nanette's playing:

> Anyone who sees and hears her play and can keep from laughing must, like her father, be made of stone. [*Stein* is German for *stone*.] For instead of sitting in the middle of the clavier, she sits right up opposite the treble, as it gives her more chance of flopping about and making

> grimaces. She rolls her eyes and smirks. When a passage is repeated, she plays it more slowly the second time. If it has to be played a third time, then she plays it even more slowly. When a passage is being played, the arm must be raised as high as possible, and according as the notes in the passage are stressed, the arm, not the fingers, must do this, and that too with great emphasis in a heavy and clumsy manner. But the best joke of all is that when she comes to a passage which ought to flow like oil and which necessitates a change of finger, she does not bother her head about it, but when the moment arrives, she just leaves out the notes, raises her hand and starts off again quite comfortably—a method by which she is more likely to strike a wrong note, which often produces a curious effect. I am simply writing in order to give Papa some idea of clavier playing and clavier teaching.[23]

Even here, it is not clear how to understand Mozart's words in relation to his own playing. He fixes on Nanette's pianistic errors but is equally concerned by her general lack of discipline, so much so that his critique of her pianism seems almost incidental.[24] In his next breath he reports that he enjoined her father to maintain a stricter regimen in her piano studies: "Herr Stein is quite crazy about his daughter, who is eight and a half [. . .]. She may succeed, for she has great talent for music. But she will not make progress by this method. [. . .] Herr Stein and I had at least two hours' talk about this." The musical training Mozart underwent at the hands of his own father was, by all accounts, draconian. He is also said to have perpetuated the same strict pedagogical style when teaching his young protégé, Johann Nepomuk Hummel.[25] It is therefore tempting to understand Mozart's words as indicative of his possible preconceptions as to the way children should be treated rather than his musical ideals as such.[26] Perhaps he would have been more lenient had an older professional played just as flamboyantly. In any case, we cannot be certain that, despite his harsh assessment of Nanette, he himself adhered scrupulously to such strictures.

These problems seem inconsequential when viewed alongside larger concerns raised by aspects of Mozart's correspondence. Mozart's letters are not only vague at times and prone to misreading at others; they also force us to consider the uncertain relationship between Mozart the correspondent and Mozart the man, to say nothing of Mozart the musician. Mozart was, as is often observed, an eminently literary writer who could describe events, people, and situations with considerable ironic distance. As a result, his epistolary output is immensely entertaining but rarely useful as the basis for detailed musical inferences. To be sure, some letters (particularly those addressed to his father) are more transparent than others in their rhetorical motivations; yet in many other writings, too, Mozart hedges and obfuscates. Straightforward communication was not usually his main priority.[27]

Thus, although Mozart's letters exude a sense of personality and persona, they offer no simple entry point for understanding the nuances of his engagement with the piano, either as a virtuoso performer or as a keyboard-playing composer. The letters demonstrate a seamless interweaving of the many sides of his creative life, but they are curiously inert when probed for detailed information about his performing habits. It is at this point that attempts to investigate Mozart's playing often give up the chase, seeking refuge amid the comparatively explicit prescriptions found in contemporary treatises. We have already seen that such sources are problematic, but even so their allure is understandable: some evidence of contemporary practices, even when it is of questionable application to a particular composer, is more attractive than no evidence at all.

Yet we can approach the investigation from a different direction. Mozart's musical corpus contains the residue of the processes by which he created it not only in the form of forensic evidence, such as ink and paper types, by which scholars can piece together elements of his working habits, but in the musical notes and phrases themselves. His compositions for keyboard in particular are a rich repository of clues about his interests, preferences, and development as a pianist. Before turning to the more elusive elements of Mozart's piano technique or their ramifications for interpreting his compositions, it is worth testing this style of investigative reasoning on simpler issues in the performance of his music. Consider, for instance, that perennial problem, the proper execution of grace notes. Should they be played on the beat or before? Full length or shorter than their notated duration? Contemporary treatises diverge on these matters, yet Mozart's notational styles hint at an answer. In the Piano Variations K. 180, Mozart notates the antecedent of the first phrase in Variation 6 using full-value sixteenth notes and the consequent with an appoggiatura. Considering the norms governing phrasal balance during Mozart's lifetime as well as the fact that upper passing tones were routinely notated as grace notes, it seems likely that he intended both figures to be played in the same way, with the grace note given on the beat as a full-length sixteenth note.

This is corroborated by his notation in the second movement of the Violin Sonata in E minor, K. 304 (ex. 2.1). The minuet theme is given with three dif-

Example 2.1 Violin Sonata K. 304, second movement, mm. 1–7 (piano part)

ferent grace-note values: an eighth note on the opening downbeat, a quarter note two measures later, and a sixteenth two measures after that. The only way to make sense of these different durations is to play the grace notes on the beat and at their full value.[28] If played before the beat, it would be impossible to distinguish the eighth note from the quarter note, since both would perforce remove a similar duration from the preceding beat. Conversely, if played at less than their full values, there would be no reason to differentiate an eighth note from a sixteenth note, since the former would in practice sound similar to the latter.[29]

This type of explanation does not attempt to extrapolate historical knowledge from a close reading of Mozart's notation. Rather, it begins with conjectures about the type of thought that may have led Mozart to set the notes on paper in one way and not another. One conjecture here concerns Mozart's likely view of the relationship between antecedents and consequents; another the notational options to which he would have turned had he wished to indicate different styles of execution for grace notes. Similar processes can apply to any number of other musical issues and notational practices as well. All such reasoning views the written score not as a fixed entity from which to extract clues but as an outgrowth of a particular mindset held by its creator. That mindset is the true object of investigation; the notation simply mediates it, providing the thin evidence that it is our task to look imaginatively beyond.

The same applies to Mozart's piano technique. It is impossible to reconstruct the workings of his hands or observe their movements across the keys, just as it is impossible to view the causal relationship such movements may have held for compositional habits. Yet a close study of the keyboard compositions, and a willingness to engage in creative guesswork about the musical persona behind it, can cast light on some of these otherwise mysterious phases of his creative process. Rather than simply trying to understand implications that follow from his finished keyboard output, it is possible to ask what types of mental and physical practices may have produced that output in the first place.

Instrumental Constraints and Compositional Creativity

To say that Mozart's pianism may have influenced the content of his music entails, at minimum, that what he considered playable on contemporary instruments constrained his compositional decision-making. Some limitations would have involved the pianistic norms of his lifetime, which dictated the types of virtuosic techniques he could include in pieces destined either for publication or for individual musicians. Other constraints bore on even the music Mozart conceived for his own use, imposed not only by considerations of technical facility but by the nature of contemporary pianos themselves: their five-octave range, their timbre, the different characteristics of the various registers and octaves, and of course mechanical features such as the weight of the keys, the shallowness of the key bed, the speed of the hammers and dampers, and the precision of the action, all of which would directly shape the player's physical experience.[30]

Perhaps the strictest limitation imposed by period pianos, and the one easiest to study from a modern-day vantage, is keyboard range, since this did not vary significantly during Mozart's lifetime and could not be circumvented even by an adventurous player willing to experiment with alternative technical approaches to finger action, touch, or phrasing. As is clear from the letters quoted above, Mozart believed his own tone and pianistic style to be quite unique; and those who heard him generally concurred—yet he, like everyone else, was bound by Viennese instruments' customary five-octave range. To understand how this aspect of instrumental design may have influenced the content of his compositions, we might begin by observing that his keyboard writing could never ascend beyond f‴, the highest note on his pianos. Taken alone, this is a banal fact. Often, the limitation posed no challenge, since melodies could be shaped so as to remain within the keyboard's rich, central octaves. In some phrases, however, both the constraint and the creative problem-solving it necessitated are evident.

This is particularly true in Mozart's recapitulations. The recapitulation presented a unique problem for composers of the late eighteenth century, since melodies previously given in the dominant during the exposition needed either to be transposed down a fifth or up a fourth in order to be played in the tonic. In the majority of cases, neither choice was ideal. Melodies transposed down a fifth would often end up in a murkier portion of the keyboard, losing any timbral brilliance they may have sustained earlier in the movement. Those pushed up a fourth, meanwhile, would risk exceeding the compass of the instrument. Mozart's solution was generally to avoid straightforward transposition, instead altering recapitulated melodies to ensure their fit in the correct octave.[31] One clear example occurs in the third movement of the Piano Concerto in C minor, K. 491, during the variation in C major. Having modulated to G, the piano initially plays a broad, two-octave scale from d′ to d‴ (mm. 177–78). When the passage repeats in C, Mozart shifts the scale a fourth higher, beginning on g′ (193–94). Yet the ascent can no longer repeat verbatim, and he therefore reworks both the peak and the figuration in the initial descent so as to mask the upper limit of instrumental range. Here, the increased complexity of figuration—the sixteenth-note thirds, and later the flashy broken octaves—all ensure that the scalar flight remains busily virtuosic despite having been confined to a smaller portion of the keyboard.

A further prompt for compositional problem-solving involved the sonic balance between soloist and orchestra in piano concertos, particularly given the quiet volume of contemporary pianos, which full orchestral forces could easily overwhelm. (This issue remained a focus throughout Mozart's career. As I noted in chapter 1, he often revised the instrumentation and accompanimental voicing in his later piano concertos to allow the soloist's sound to project more efficiently through the orchestra.) The problem would have been most acute for listeners during the first solo entrance in each concerto, when the brilliance and volume of the orchestral tutti would give way to the solo pianist, unable to match the sheer dynamic force of the music just heard. In Mozart's first original keyboard concerto (K. 175 in D major, completed at age seventeen), the transitional strategy is clumsy at best. The ritornello ends with an orchestral fanfare, after which the soloist launches into a melody presented moments earlier, *forte*, by the full orchestra—a melody which now seems deflated in the softer dynamic. To make matters worse, the soloist plays this tune while doubled quietly by the orchestral violins. Mozart may have intended the doubling to diminish the sonic gap between orchestra and piano, reinforcing the sound of the melody; yet in practice (and to judge by modern-day period-instrument performances), it makes the soloist even more difficult to hear.[32] Mozart himself probably considered the transition from tutti to solo in K. 175 to be a failure, for he never repeated the procedure.

Instead, each of his early concertos explores a different solution to the problem of balance. In his next piano concerto, K. 238, Mozart once again begins the first solo with the *forte* melody that started the piece. However, he adjusts the context so as to manage the pianist's entrance more elegantly: first, by ending the ritornello quietly, the better to close the gap between the volume of orchestra and soloist, and second, by allowing the pianist to enter alone, unencumbered by the ensemble. The accompanimental sixteenth notes in the soloist's left hand, which in K. 175 were mere clutter, are now fully audible behind the melody's half notes and quarter notes—a source of excitement and momentum that distinguishes the soloist's entrance from the orchestra's more staid version of the tune. Even the harmonic makeup contributes to the sense of motion: whereas the opening theme of K. 175 moved through a series of static block chords better suited to symphonic writing, in K. 238 a constantly accelerating harmonic rhythm undergirds the theme and seems, along with the soloist's sixteenth notes, to push the music excitedly forward.

In his next solo concerto, K. 246, Mozart addresses the balance problem by inserting melodic embellishments that distinguish the pianist's version of the theme from the orchestra's. As far as embellishments go, the effort here is modest: he uses a series of chromatic grace notes, both in the initial gesture and in the melody that follows. Yet these embellishments are not superficially decorative. They transform the character of the passage. The orchestra's opening statement is assertive, a one-bar "Mannheim rocket" with symphonic pomp. The soloist's entrance, by contrast, is playful and sly. Its humor results both from the lighthearted chromaticism of the grace notes themselves and the broader incongruity that arises from their placement within what was, in the orchestra, so proud a gesture. In this way Mozart accomplishes two tasks simultaneously: he adds notes to the soloist's material (thus increasing the density of musical activity) while also creating new character associations for the soloist's phrase, in the process lessening the disparity between the strength of the two statements. This approach serves Mozart in many of his subsequent concertos, including K. 449, K. 451, and K. 537—compositions where the pianist enters with a flurry of ornamental virtuosity that more than makes up for the comparatively quiet instrument.

Mozart hits on yet another strategy, perhaps the most creative, in his next concerto, K. 271. Although much has been made of the pianist's surprise entrance in the second bar, an equally innovative turn comes at the end of the ritornello, when Mozart addresses the balance problem by freeing the pianist entirely from the orchestra's melodic material (ex. 2.2). For the first time in his keyboard concertos, Mozart does not introduce the soloist with a restatement of the opening theme, varied or otherwise. Indeed, because of the way

Example 2.2 Piano Concerto K. 271, first movement, mm. 50–60

this particular concerto begins, there is not even a clear candidate for such a theme. Instead Mozart invents a new melody for the soloist along with a new way of introducing it. He signals the end of the orchestral material with a stereotypical closing gesture: one that accomplishes this goal both rhetorically, through emphatically repeated cadences, and in the overall expressive trajectory of the orchestra's material, with a return to *forte* after two quieter, more probing melodies.[33] Thus, the end of the ritornello arrives—yet the soloist, having entered "too early" in the opening of the movement, is now absent altogether. Instead, we hear another quiet, cadence-like figure in the violins, a pattern that swings back and forth between tonic and dominant for six measures. It is during this unexpected moment of stasis that the soloist sidles in with a teasing trill. As Charles Rosen puts it, this is the soloist's *second* "dramatic" entrance in the concerto—a designation perhaps even more apt than Rosen intended, for the ensuing passage is an instrumental appropriation of the *fermata sospesa*, a mainstay of opera arias in the *seria* tradition.[34] Although Mozart explored a similar move in the Violin Concerto in A, K. 219, the pianist's entrance in K. 271 brings the technique under greater compositional control. In the violin concerto, Mozart relies on a change of tempo and an invitation for a free cadenza in order to soften the shift from orchestra to soloist. In the piano concerto, he bundles the same effects into a single, densely packed phrase without once interrupting the metrical flow.

As with the embellishments in K. 246 (his previous piano concerto), the sonic transition in K. 271 smooths the perceived shift from the orchestral bustle to the more intimate perspective of the soloist. Unlike in the previous concerto, however, K. 271 manages this aural elision not by increasing the activity and virtuosity of the soloist but through an ebb in orchestral activity. Mozart attaches a quiet closing tag that both rounds off the ritornello and allows the pianist to emerge gradually out of the newly calmed texture. This strategy becomes the rule in many of Mozart's subsequent concertos; yet despite repeated use, it never lapses into routine. In some cases, including K. 413 in F major, the soloist quite literally takes over from the orchestra, fashioning a smooth melodic "handoff" using the violins' closing motive. In others, including K. 450 and K. 467, the soloist launches into a brief improvisation, summoning the excitement of spontaneity from the very start. In still others, including the two late minor-key concertos, no elegant melodic elision occurs. The soloist simply begins with new material following the orchestra's self-contained close.[35]

These procedures allow us a glimpse into the delicate interplay of instrumental constraint and compositional problem-solving. Mozart's exploration of the structural and rhetorical techniques discussed above, whereby he could create smoother and more satisfying transitions from an orchestral ritornello to a concerto's first solo passage, most likely resulted from considerations involving the volume and tone color of the pianos available to him. Yet the compositional problem-solving that ensued soon became a locus of musical ingenuity in its own right—one that gave rise to a far more nuanced and varied relationship between soloist and orchestra than had previously existed in the concerto genre, whose earlier champions operated within different stylistic norms and, often, wrote for harpsichord and therefore faced a different set of sonic considerations. It was Mozart's relationship to the piano, both as a composer and performer of virtuoso music for the still developing instrument, that helped prompt his departures from the generic standards known in earlier repertoires.[36] Yet even so we should not overemphasize the influence of the piano in such cases. The range and comparative volume of the instruments of Mozart's time may have posed practical problems (problems facing other contemporary composers as well), but they did not predetermine simple solutions. Creative experimentation, through which Mozart's practices could evolve in new directions, was necessary. This parallels a statement about schema modules in the previous chapter: although Mozart operated within a strict set of stylistic constraints, using a musical language that, for the most part, he shared with many other figures, the fact that he inherited prefabricated musical building blocks did not restrict his ability to find new ways to stretch, mutate, and deploy them. The piano, too, presented constraints that necessitated problem-solving but did not limit the solutions Mozart could ultimately discover.

If the piano did not limit Mozart's creative problem-solving, however, it certainly provided a vehicle for the broadening of his expressive palette. At various specific points during his career, an expansion of compositional creativity coincided with mechanical innovations in the construction of pianos. The most striking of these shifts occurred in 1777, when Mozart encountered the instruments of Johann Andreas Stein (father of grimacing Nanette, above). He sent Leopold a glowing report, contrasting Stein's pianos with those he had known previously:

> Before I had seen Stein's work, I'd always preferred Späth's pianos; yet now I prefer Stein's as they dampen so much better than the Regensburg instruments. If I strike hard, then whether I keep my finger down

> or raise it the sound ceases the moment I hear it. However I attack the keys, the tone is always the same. It doesn't produce a clattering sound, it doesn't get louder or softer or fail to sound at all; in a word, it's always even. [. . .] A particular feature of his instruments is their escape action. Not one maker in a hundred bothers with this. But without escape action it's impossible for a pianoforte not to produce a clattering sound or to go on sounding after the note has been struck; when you strike the keys, his hammers fall back again the moment they hit the strings, whether you hold down the keys or release them. [. . .] I played my 6 sonatas [K. 279–284] many times from memory. I played the fifth one in G at the aristocrats' concert in the Bauernstube. The last one, in D, sounds unparalleled on *Stein's* pianoforte. The device one presses with the knee is also better made on his instruments. I hardly need to touch it and it works; and as soon as one removes one's knee even a little, one no longer hears the slightest reverberation.[37]

In this letter Mozart marks three virtues of Stein's pianos: their evenness of tone, their escapement mechanism (a device allowing the hammer to fall to its resting position after striking a note even if the player holds down the associated key), and the knee lever (precursor to the sustain pedal of later pianos). That all of these are intimately connected with the aesthetic of Mozart's mature keyboard music suggests that Stein's pianos opened up new possibilities for the expressive scope of Mozart's compositions. Such influence is clearest in his textural writing, particularly as evidenced in the variation sets he composed directly after encountering Stein, including K. 264 and K. 354, both of which date from 1778. Whereas his earlier variations take a largely conservative approach to pianistic sonority, the Stein-era sets feature an elaborate textural vocabulary, a testament to the responsiveness of the new instruments. These sets show an increase in variety of left-hand accompanimental styles, for instance in the many passages with textures in which bass notes are sustained while an inner voice moves, an effect whose clarity depends on the precision of the escapement and dampening mechanisms. (In such a low register, any reverberation from the nonsustained notes would create murkiness—yet as Mozart observes, Stein's pianos avoid this.) Mozart's melodic effects, too, become richer and more diverse. He begins to write larger, more extravagant leaps (combining legato gestures with notes inevitably cut short because of the considerable distance the hand must travel) as well as effects that depend explicitly on the piano's mechanistic evenness: doubled octaves, a host of grace notes and slurs notated with a precision not found in his earlier compositions, and long scales that, in a single run, cross more than half of the keyboard.

The piano's evenness, precision, and textural affordances are also evident in the cadenzas Mozart wrote following his encounter with Stein. In 1776 Mozart composed the Piano Concerto K. 271 along with a set of cadenzas to be performed by Louise-Victoire Jenamy, the original recipient. When he revisited K. 271 years later, after his encounter with Stein, he composed new cadenzas[38]—and although these show little change in compositional acuity, they differ considerably in pianistic profile. The earlier cadenzas, like Mozart's early variations, are conservative, featuring only short runs and standard textures. (Aside from explicitly contrapuntal passages, for instance, the melody is always safely allocated to the right hand.) The later cadenzas, meanwhile, contain long runs similar to those in his Stein-era variations. The later cadenzas also call for a varied array of accompanimental patterns (including left-hand writing with slurred eighth notes and silent downbeats resembling the opening phrases of the Sonata K. 333) and rich, four-voice textures. Because these cadenzas all draw from a single set of tunes in a single composition, they provide a highly controlled study of Mozart's changing imagination. Against the constants of register, theme, and harmonic plan, Mozart's pianistic growth is all the more evident, as is the expansion of his expressive idiom.

Mozart's Pianistic Modules

The points I have explored so far in this chapter lay the groundwork for a more thorough study of Mozart's pianistic habits. Although details of his keyboard technique are impossible to recover without speculation, we have seen that, through a careful treatment of his written music, we may develop a more nuanced picture of the pianistic problem-solving that helped shape the development of his style. Integral to this process is a mode of investigation that inverts the usual approach to score study. No longer do we treat the written text as a simple starting point on which to heap analytic observations; instead, those texts are reconceptualized as end points that emerged through a complex interplay of physical habit and creative thought. Rather than extrapolating information directly from the texts, we may begin by guessing at the processes that produced them.

Some of the intersections between Mozart's piano technique and his compositions can be glimpsed indirectly from the technical instructions he left for his students. One particularly useful source is a set of étude-like exercises he composed in which he provides fingerings for various types of sixteenth-note passagework. These exercises show that Mozart approached piano fingering through a set of consistent and identifiable precepts—for instance, that he attempted to avoid using the thumb on sharp or flat keys during melodic passages, preferring instead to stretch the second finger while maintaining the frame of the hand on the main portion of the keyboard (ex. 2.3*a*).[39] Assuming that Mozart himself adhered to these guidelines, the exercises suggest an initial point of mediation between the keyboard and his written compositions, many of which feature technical writing aligned with his fingering preferences. One example occurs in the first movement of the Piano Concerto in C minor, K. 491, when Mozart sets up a Fonte progression but alters the melodic material at the second step of the sequence. In many other sequential phrases throughout this movement (including the parallel passage in the recapitulation), Mozart does not shy away from verbatim repetition. However, restating this pattern would require a series of repeated B♭s in the beginning of measure 168, and these, given the surrounding figuration, would be awkward to play using a finger other than the thumb. Mozart's recasting of the melody for the second step of the Fonte may have been inspired by the pianistic preferences evidenced in his fingering exercises (ex. 2.3*b*)

Another investigative route, more broadly applicable, arises simply as a result of the remarkable technical consistency of Mozart's keyboard writing. Many compositions, dating both before and after his encounter with Stein's pianos, draw from a relatively limited set of technical tropes: a pianist's vocabulary of "licks" that may correspond to physical gestures Mozart found comfortable under the hands. Many of these are associated with particular tonal areas, each of which implies a unique combination of white and black keys and thus carries associations for the pianist-composer's engagement with the topography of the keyboard. Charles Rosen humorously observed that one of the hazards of playing Mozart's concertos from memory is that, owing to the density of generic passagework, the pianist can all too easily slip inadvertently from one composition into another.[40] Rosen's remark concerns the Concertos K. 450 and K. 595 and the Sonata K. 333 ("typical Mozartean virtuosity in B flat major"), though the same observation applies to other keys and other compositions, as well.[41] To take one example, the sixteenth-note patterning of a brief passage in C minor during the first movement of K. 271 (mm. 78–80) finds an echo in the finale of the "Kegelstatt" Trio, K. 498, during a similar C-minor digression (mm. 45–47). The melodic and harmonic similarities between these passages speak to the more thoroughgoing pianistic profiles

Example 2.3 *a*, Three measures from Mozart's fingering exercises showing extension of left-hand second finger (rather than thumb) onto F♯. *b*, Piano Concerto K. 491, first movement, mm. 165–68, compared with hypothetical sequential continuation

such compositions share. In each, Mozart leads the right hand across the keyboard in a strikingly consistent way.

We might fruitfully conceive of these recurring gestures through the conceptual framework of modularity. The overlap between piano technique and modularity is already immanent in theories of harmonic schemata introduced in chapter 1—those brief chord progressions which eighteenth-century keyboard players would learn by rote and which would then have been available in the hands for use in improvisation. Although I previously discussed modules as building blocks of compositional structure, they were also elements of contemporary keyboard players' tactile intuitions. So, too, were countless other physical motions that recur in music of the time and which we might consolidate, using the same explanatory approach, as "pianistic modules."[42] An Alberti bass of the type that features in so much of Mozart's accompanimental writing is not only a commonplace pattern outlining triads; it is also a set of familiar physical actions involving a rapid alternation of the left-hand thumb, middle finger, and little finger. The entirety of Mozart's keyboard output may be analyzed in the light of such motions, which connect compositional thought with the tactile dimensions of piano playing. Like the harmonic modules discussed in chapter 1, these pianistic modules open up a way of explaining the compositional decision-making that shaped Mozart's output while also bringing these familiar works into the interpretive world associated with performance, contingency, and improvisation.

Pianistic modules differ from other modules in their degree of separability from specific musical content. The harmonic patterns I have already discussed, including partimenti, are identified entirely by chordal underlay rather than by the fingerings required to play them. The Romanesca *is* a descent from the tonic through the dominant and submediant, just as a Fonte *is* a two-part descending sequential pattern that passes from the minor to the major mode. A pianistic module, by contrast, is a series of finger movements bearing no inherent relation to musical content. Consider, for instance, a simple pianistic action—the rotation of the right hand over the thumb, required when tackling the Variations K. 264, Piano Sonata K. 283, and Piano Concerto K. 467. The passages shown in example 2.4 differ musically in important respects, yet they all require the player to execute a single type of physical motion. Of course, some pianistic modules are loosely correlated with musical content, since characteristic physical actions may end up using a consistent combination of white and black keys. Other pianistic modules, meanwhile, may function independently of melody or harmony while maintaining a link to certain formal contexts. The techniques of hand crossing need not be tied to any particular local material, yet owing to its elevation of physical awkwardness to the level of a flamboyant trope ("horse-play," wrote Daniel Gottlob Türk in his 1789 treatise on keyboard playing[43]), it is in practice often reserved for a small range of situations: the final phrases of lengthy sonatas and variations (K. 455 and K. 457), virtuosic concerto passages (K. 413, K. 450), and dense, chromatic phrases whose murky harmonies find a mirror in the intensity of the pianist's bodily deportment (K. 284, K. 301). All of this suggests a continuum of musical specificity associated with these and other pianistic actions.

Example 2.4 *a,* Variations K. 264, variation 9, mm. 9–14. *b,* Piano Sonata K. 283, first movement, mm. 35–36. *c,* Piano Concerto K. 467, first movement, mm. 147–49. Editorial fingerings show the crossing of second finger over the thumb

Owing to the varying degrees to which they are linked with identifiable melodies, harmonies, keys, or contexts, their study can run alongside an examination of Mozart's compositions, crossing boundaries of form and genre and inviting comparisons of pieces usually viewed in relative isolation from each other. We can locate beneath a wide range of different phrases a small selection of gestures that help us imagine more clearly the complex negotiations between Mozart's pianistic intuitions and compositional thought.

Just as a vocabulary of pianistic modules can cross boundaries of form and genre, so, too, does it cross boundaries of ease and virtuosity. When discussing Mozart's compositional modules in the previous chapter, I observed that his characteristic use—or, at times, intentional misuse—of such modules does as much to color the language of his music as the content of the gestures themselves. The same is true of pianistic modules. It has often been observed that Mozart had two different "registers" of keyboard writing. The compositions he prepared for publication, which were intended to appeal to a broad public, are easier to play than those he wrote for his own expert hands. These judgments are true, yet they discount the broader consistency of Mozart's keyboard vocabulary. As suggested by the material in example 2.4, the physical motions required to play passages in his mature concertos do not differ in essence from those required to play his earlier or published compositions. What differs is the way Mozart deploys the motions. Mozart wrote K. 467 for himself; and it is here that the right hand sustains a constant flow of sixteenth notes while the left plays a different, equally demanding style of figuration. Thus, the passage from K. 467 is far more awkward than that from K. 264 (published during Mozart's lifetime), which grows naturally out of a simpler chord progression and whose mirroring of the hands makes the composite effect less forbidding. The varying levels of ease and difficulty mask a thoroughgoing tactile continuity between these phrases.

Piano Technique as Melodic Structure

Mozart's keyboard corpus is, therefore, amenable to the same type of modular analysis as his musical language as a whole. The purpose of this section is to provide an overview of the pianistic vocabulary at play in his compositions. The most straightforward place to begin is with those gestures associated with individual melodies, where musical concordance makes the pianistic similarities easiest to detect. I then move on to devices Mozart uses more flexibly. Taken together, these figures constitute the vocabulary that may have guided his hands and imagination during improvisations and, equally, through the process of composition.

Technical Gestures with Melodic Associations

When technical gestures carry particular melodic connotations, it is often because they outline a recurring pattern of the piano's white and black keys. The music that makes use of such gestures generally draws on identifiable combinations of notes in specific tonalities. One example is a G-minor arpeggio with chromatic neighbor tones, which appears at various points throughout Mozart's sonatas and concertos (ex. 2.5).

If K. 280 and K. 281 were the only sonatas in which he used the figure, the correspondence might simply reflect large-scale cyclic design, a structural practice Mozart often cultivated in collections of his compositions, in which small motivic or thematic repetitions would bind different pieces together

Example 2.5 *a*, Piano Concerto K. 238, third movement, mm. 125–26. *b*, Piano Sonata K. 280, first movement, mm. 23–26. *c*, Piano Sonata K. 281, third movement, mm. 25–27. *d*, Piano Sonata K. 533, first movement, mm. 179–80

into a unit.[44] However, the same triplets appear in a later sonata, K. 533, as well as in an earlier concerto, K. 238, in different contexts. In all three sonatas, the triplets precede a half cadence, decorating a ii^6 chord in F major. In the concerto, they appear at the outset of a stormy passage in G minor, decorating an ascending tonic flourish. In none of these is the melodic gesture represented by the arpeggio straightforwardly integrated with other material; instead, it gives the impression of being a new idea toward which the music suddenly turns. Each triplet arpeggio directly follows a passage in which the primary musical argument does not involve pianistic showmanship as such but rather the display of compositional prowess through daring harmonic progressions, contrapuntal imitation, or a richly textured orchestral ritornello with a surprise modulation. All at once, the triplets launch, and the pianist's right hand moves swiftly from the middle of the keyboard to the highest available note in the G-minor chord: a burst of activity that refocuses attention, setting the stage for the technical writing that ensues.

Congruences arise within longer patterns as well, for instance, in an ascending scale culminating on $\hat{3}$ and followed by a distinctive falling figure (ex. 2.6). This gesture first appears in the Variations K. 179. It then recurs unchanged through mature compositions such as the Sonata K. 283, the Concerto for Three Pianos, K. 242, the Piano Concerto K. 459, and the final variation set, K. 613. In Mozart's keyboard writing, this pattern is associated mainly with C major. It occasionally appears in G or B♭, and a variant (adjusted for

Example 2.6 *a*, Variations K. 179, variation 9, mm. 13–14. *b*, Concerto for Three Pianos K. 242, first movement, mm. 74–75. *c*, Piano Sonata K. 283, second movement, mm. 32–33. *d*, Piano Concerto K. 459, third movement, mm. 150–52. *e*, Variations K. 613, variation 7, m. 18

the different keyboard topography) is sometimes given in D. However, Mozart often allocates appearances in keys other than C to different instruments (including the violins in the first movement of the Concerto K. 450, mm. 33–35). As with the G-minor arpeggio in the previous example, the musical diversity of these passages belies their technical and contextual consistency. All such figures either herald the opening of solo sections in concertos or—as in the Sonata K. 283, the Rondo K. 494, and the Variations K. 613—serve as embellishments of earlier, simpler scales. As such, they represent moments in which the showcasing of pianistic flair becomes a compositional feature in its own right.

Technical Gestures with Broader Melodic or Textural Associations

Other gestures in Mozart's pianistic arsenal occur in various keys. These are generally associated not with specific pitch combinations but with characteristic textural writing. Many of Mozart's hand-crossing patterns, for instance, merge physical motion with a replicated style of textural figuration, generally involving quarter notes in the upper voice (played with the left hand crossed over the right) alongside a sixteenth-note accompaniment played with the right hand. This physical profile can be applied to any harmonic progression; however, the voicing, rhythm, and texture are fixed.

Mozart's music shows countless other similar consistencies. In music for

(a)

(b)

Example 2.7 *a*, Piano Sonata K. 310, first movement, mm. 33–34. *b*, Piano Concerto K. 415, first movement, mm. 269–71

piano with other players, concertos and chamber works alike, he often assigns the piano broken octaves in a high register as an accompaniment in a pattern that usually begins with a second-inversion arpeggio. Cadences in C major across multiple compositions bring identical voicing and melodic passagework (ex. 2.7). The relevance of such gestures—hand crossings, upper-voice pedals, and cadential figuration—does not derive from rhetorical significance; unlike the G-minor triplets, these are not bursts of tactile, pianistic energy calling out to be noticed. Instead, they suggest a more routine alignment of pianistic and compositional considerations that in turn speaks to the tactile intuitions on which so much of his music was based.

Stock Gestures

Other technical gestures are entirely separable not only from keyboard topography but from texture. These involve only a replicated series of finger motions that a player might execute at virtually any point along the keyboard. One example is the series of turns or trills decorating many ascending scales in Mozart's piano music (ex. 2.8), which occurs in all tonalities irrespective of any particular pattern of black and white keys. Similar, and even more pervasive, is a circling motion that begins many of Mozart's longer ascending scales (ex. 2.9). This gesture appears repeatedly in all contexts across all of Mozart's creative periods and in all keyboard genres.

So far, I have listed pianistic modules that apply to the right hand. Others,

Example 2.8 *a*, Variations K. 180, variation 5, m. 11. *b*, Violin Sonata K. 303, first movement, m. 103 (piano part). *c*, Piano Sonata K. 330, first movement, mm. 134–36. *d*, Piano Concerto K. 450, first movement, m. 224. *e*, Piano Trio K. 496, first movement mm. 61–62 (piano part). *f*, Four-Hand Piano Sonata K. 521, second movement, m. 92. *g*, Four-Hand Piano Sonata K. 521, third movement, m. 38. *h*, Piano Concerto K. 537, first movement, mm. 190–91. *i*, Piano Concerto K. 595, first movement, m. 106

however, involve left-hand writing, for instance, an ascending octave leap combined with a lower neighbor tone. Although this figure is trivially easy to play in isolation (and indeed forms the basis for routine pedal accompaniments throughout his music), in more demanding contexts it is one of the primary markers of his virtuosic style, appearing as an elaboration of scales in K. 451 and K. 475 as well as in more treacherous passagework over leaps and arpeggios in K. 284, K. 459, and K. 467 (ex. 2.10). During scalar passages, the gesture poses no challenge, since the little finger can safely measure distances from the thumb while the hand maintains contact with the keyboard. During descending arpeggios, however, the entire left hand leaps, with no pivot point,

Example 2.9 *a*, Variations K. 264, variation 8, m. 51. *b*, Variations K. 264, variation 8, m. 62. *c*, Piano Sonata K. 284, third movement, variation 11, m. 13. *d*, Variations K. 354, variation 12, m. 17. *e*, Piano Concerto K. 466, first movement, m. 316–17. *f*, Piano Concerto K. 488, first movement, m. 123. *g*, Piano Concerto K. 488, first movement, m. 197. *h*, Piano Concerto K. 503, first movement, m. 160. *i*, Piano Sonata K. 533, third movement, mm. 166–67. Mozart sometimes notates the gesture differently: *j*, Piano Concerto K. 503, first movement, m. 103. *k*, Piano Concerto K. 503, first movement, m. 106. *l*, Piano Concerto K. 537, first movement, m. 89

Example 2.10 Piano Sonata K. 284, third movement, variation 12, mm. 9–12

to a different location on the keyboard—all within the duration of a sixteenth note. In K. 284 the pianist must move confidently both up and down the keyboard while maintaining the relaxation necessary to repeat the motion over an entire phrase. Even more, because of the figure's inherent chromaticism, the pianist must constantly adjust the relationship between thumb and second finger depending on whether the thumb is placed on a white or black key.

Gestures Involving Both Hands

Some pianistic patterns involve both hands, bringing a confluence of melodic figuration, harmonic motion, and, occasionally, contrapuntal interplay. At times, there is direct correspondence among all these musical elements, for instance in passages presented above a ii^6 chord whose lowest note, when raised a half step, yields a V^6/V. This is a standard harmonic progression; however, Mozart often gives it alongside a characteristic melodic figure, as though the gesture itself constituted a tactile trope in his vocabulary (ex. 2.11).

The contrapuntal physicality of Mozart's pianism also manifests itself in voice exchanges, especially in concerto or chamber passages in which the pianist assumes an accompanimental role. Attention to counterpoint and voice leading was, of course, an element of all competent musicianship during his lifetime. Yet beyond their straightforward use in compositional technique, voice exchanges served an improvisatory function, offering a means to prolong chords without having to invent new material. An improviser could use voice exchanges to exert deliberate control over the relative lengths of phrases or even to stall for time while deciding where a coming modulation, structural cadence, or new formal section should lead.[45] There are reasons, then, to consider voice exchanges not only as a rudimentary compositional phenomenon but as an element of Mozart's keyboard arsenal. It is no accident that they feature throughout his written cadenzas, possibly as a holdover from his actual extemporized performances.[46] The alignment of voicing and keyboard technique suggested by this device would also have been reinforced through

Example 2.11 *a*, Violin Sonata K. 303, first movement, mm. 105–6 (piano part). *b*, Piano Sonata K. 309, third movement, mm. 36–37. *c*, Piano Concerto K. 413, first movement, mm. 99–102. *d*, Piano Concerto K. 450, first movement, mm. 224–25. *e*, Piano Concerto K. 467, second movement, mm. 42–44

the craft of continuo realization, a staple both of his concerto performances and his compositional pedagogy.[47]

Other contrapuntal gestures exhibit more distinctive musical character. One such style of dialogic exchange pursued in Mozart's piano music, for instance, shows each of the two hands repeatedly "interrupting" the other. The keyboard writing in example 2.12 requires a particular physical coordination between the hands, with each playing accented syncopations while the other carries melodic material. Both passages maintain a similar melodic shape, following an ascending third with a stepwise descent. Both also share a rhetorical effect. In performance, the repeated syncopations can make the passages rhythmically ambiguous; thus, Mozart may also have associated the technical dimensions of the gesture with other elements of phrasing or even a performer's physical deportment. In this example, we see most clearly the image of an inveterate showman finding excuses to work favorite pianistic tricks into his compositions.

Example 2.12 *a*, Piano Concerto K. 415, first movement, mm. 170–72.
b, Piano Sonata K. 576, first movement, mm. 111–16

One final contrapuntal device involves the mirroring of the two hands. Mirroring occurs when one hand imitates the finger actions of the other, with the result that a given musical gesture is inverted across the two hands. (Under normal circumstances, by contrast, when the hands play a single melody in octaves, the fingering is not mirrored; an ascending C-major arpeggio moves from thumb to fifth finger in the right hand but from fifth finger to thumb in the left hand.) Mirroring is a staple in Mozart's keyboard output, particularly in his mature concertos but also in the sonatas, variations, and chamber music with keyboard. All of these use mirroring in passages that are meant to sound complex and dazzling, often at the culmination of formal sections, where musical and pianistic energy must be pressed to their maximum level—even though, in reality, the physical action involves a highly intuitive use of the hands, which both perform only a single set of motions.

In addition to its appearances throughout his finished compositions, mirroring occurs in many of Mozart's drafts. In an early version of the Concerto

Example 2.13 *a*, Piano Concerto K. 467, first movement, m. 174. *b*, draft of m. 183, with left hand mirroring the right hand's figuration from m. 174. *c*, revised version of m. 183, mirroring removed

in C major K. 467, the virtuosic episode that closes the exposition calls for mirroring of the hands in two juxtaposed scalar passages (ex. 2.13). In the final version, the left hand is adjusted and the mirroring removed.[48] The autograph score of this section shows more thorough reworking than any other passage in the concerto, and it is significant that Mozart, tinkering with these phrases in an effort to get them right, falls back on pianistic intuition, generating activity for the left hand by simply repeating, verbatim, the physical motions the right has just carried out. Its presence in the draft suggests the role of the pianistic intuition in Mozart's creative process. The other compositions that make up his keyboard corpus, and for which comparable draft material does not survive, may also have contained such characteristic technical writing in their earlier stages before it was removed and reworked. The K. 467 revisions allow us to imagine the ways in which similar passages would take shape in the hands before being codified on the page.

Piano Technique in Mozart's Drafts and Fragments

As the mirroring in K. 467 suggests, Mozart's revisions often maintain traces of pianistic thought to a degree not matched by his completed, polished compositions. This is certainly true of the large body of unfinished drafts Mozart produced during the course of his career in which the piano writing tends to be raw and angular. The fragment of an Allegro in G minor, K. 312, one of Mozart's longer unfinished pieces, features figuration and arpeggios more reminiscent of his concertos than his sonatas. Arpeggios wing up and down the keyboard; sequences seem motivated by the rote repetition of technical licks rather than by developmental musical impulses. In all, K. 312 gives the impression of a rambling improvisation. The draft's meter, tempo, rhythmic makeup, and textural style have often invited comparison with the Piano Sonata in B♭ K. 570 (written at approximately the same time)[49]—and, given the overlaps between the two, it is relatively easy to imagine a counterfactual scenario in which Mozart had revised and completed K. 312, along the way making it as playable and well mannered as K. 570. Perhaps other works, too, arose through similar processes.

Although popular culture exaggerates Mozart's ability to compose flawless first drafts, he was sufficiently fluent that his manuscripts rarely make entirely transparent the process by which compositions evolved. The means by which he molded his pianistic thought into finished pieces of music is, in many cases, mysterious. Yet even the cleanest drafts may have something to reveal, especially when their pianistic content can be compared with that of his finished compositions. A passage in the unfinished sonata fragment in B♭, K. 400, for instance, anticipates a phrase in the Piano Concerto in D minor, K. 466 (ex. 2.14). Both draw on the same tactile vocabulary (rapid broken thirds in the left hand; eighth notes and trills in the right) and are similarly placed in the unfolding of each movement (elaborating on a G-minor chord just before their expositions' culminating cadence in F). The two phrases even enact the same musical content: in both, upon reaching a first-inversion G-minor triad, the left hand drops out and the right plays repeated Ds against an ascending scale. Mozart wrote the fragment at least two years before the concerto, and these overlaps probably therefore represent the residue of physical habit rather than conscious allusion.[50] It is unlikely that he held K. 400 on his desk two full years, waiting to deploy a simple cadential passage in a different composition; instead, the passage may simply be one of his standard tactile procedures that found written expression first in the draft and then, later, in the concerto.

The notion of producing a draft in which entire phrases are fashioned from stock patterning would not have been unusual for Mozart, as suggested by the many finished compositions whose earliest versions are sewn almost entirely from nondescript, "placeholder" material but whose source history (where it can be deduced) shows signs of eventual revision and integration. One of the most vivid transformations along these lines survives in early versions of the Concerto in A K. 488. During composition, Mozart inserted significant solo passagework that constituted little more than quotidian riffs which, in all likelihood, he had intended from the outset to reshape using themes better suited to the sound world of this concerto.[51] What he ultimately added is not only more linear and melodic—the removed material is essentially rudimentary harmonic sequences in broken chords—but aligns better with other elements

(a)

(b)

Example 2.14 *a*, Fragment of Piano Sonata K. 400, mm. 36–38. *b*, Piano Concerto K. 466, first movement, mm. 147–49

of the piece, allowing for interplay between piano soloist and winds and featuring shapely scales up and down the keyboard. Here, the source material shows, quite literally, a process akin to what I have proposed for K. 400 and K. 466: behind even the most innovative keyboard concertos runs a pianistic intuition that was Mozart's first recourse in the process of composition.

In other drafts, the expunged phrases are just as revealing as the material that Mozart maintained but revised. In this respect, the significant surviving draft material for the Sonata in D K. 284 is singularly illuminating. Some of Mozart's revisions to K. 284 involved routine alterations to preexisting material so as to ensure proper pacing and playability, and these have already been a subject of extensive study.[52] Other revisions, meanwhile, saw the wholesale removal of significant technical passages, often involving florid sixteenth notes—and these have received comparatively little attention. Mozart removed bars 11–18 and 47–50 of the draft entirely in the final version and preserved bars 43 and 46 but reworked them. The excised material bears a striking resemblance to the piano writing in his first original keyboard concerto, K. 175, and an equally striking dissimilarity to much of his later piano writing (ex. 2.15). The dates of the compositions, too, align: Mozart most likely began work on K. 284 in 1774, soon after the December 1773 completion of K. 175. The revisions for K. 284 were underway as late as 1777.[53]

As noted above, Mozart's pianistic style shifted after his 1777 encounter

Example 2.15 Passages removed from an early version of Piano Sonata K. 284, compared with keyboard figuration from Piano Concerto K. 175

with Stein, and it is tempting to see the expansion of his technical and expressive horizons as reflected in the K. 284 revisions. Given that he did not publish this sonata until 1784 but used it frequently as a showpiece in performance, it is likely that the changes were meant not to normalize the technical profile for broad consumption but to appeal to his own developing pianistic tastes. By eliminating the hand motions he would have relied on as composer-performer of K. 175, Mozart demonstrates—here, in negative relief—the strides his playing had made in the intervening years.

Beyond the Keyboard: Technique and Composition on Other Instruments

Although Mozart's keyboard music occupies a central position in his oeuvre, it nonetheless represents a minority of the compositions he produced over the course of his career. It is outstripped in length, complexity, and number by his symphonies and serenades (to say nothing of his operas or masses). We may wonder, then, whether it is possible to derive an understanding of his musical imagination from so small a selection of compositions. Did the modes of thought I have explored in this chapter also serve when he wrote for other instruments?

Some of the melodic figures I have discussed, especially those bound up with characteristic physical motions on the piano, are unique to Mozart's keyboard writing. The turns that precede long scales, for instance, do not occur alongside similar scales in the concertos for flute or violin, which tend to rise directly from the first note without any initial flourish. Such divergences are unsurprising considering the care with which Mozart tailored his writing for the hands and personalities of individual musicians and, by extension, their instruments—a point I discussed in chapter 1. It would be strange indeed if his pianistic vocabulary exerted too significant a pull on his music for the violin, flute, or voice. His commitment to idiomatic instrumental writing is especially evident throughout the transcriptions he made of his own works, which always resulted in substantive musical revisions as well, all meant to accommodate demands presented by the new instrumentation.[54]

On the other hand, the very nature of contemporary musical style, which thrived on melodic imitation and development, meant that some transfer of figuration from one instrument to another would be unavoidable, especially in compositions for multiple players. In the chamber music with piano, particularly the violin sonatas and piano trios, virtually every theme crosses between the piano and violin. In the mature violin sonatas, such exchanges are so pervasive and rhetorically marked that they seem to enact the dialogic style associated with soloist-orchestra relations in the piano concertos. It is no coincidence that Mozart wrote the Violin Sonata K. 454, whose final phrases stage a battle of virtuosity between the two performers, alongside the Concertos K. 449, K. 450, K. 451, and K. 453—compositions whose emphasis on dramatic dialogue has prompted repeated comparison with opera.[55] (Nor was it coincidental that he composed K. 454 for the sophisticated technique and dazzling stage persona of Regina Strinasacchi, a fine violinist and the subject of enthusiastic praise in Mozart's correspondence.) Often, instrumental exchange in this music occurs freely, regardless of which line first introduces the relevant material. A half-note motif played exclusively by the oboe in the first movement of the Piano Concerto K. 466 (mm. 33, 115, etc.) is taken up by the piano in the last movement; and of the Concertos K. 415, K. 451, K. 453,

K. 456, and K. 459, all of which begin with identical march rhythms, all but K. 415 share the various iterations of this motif among strings, winds, and soloist. Nonetheless, there are cases where the exchange of material creates technical challenges for nonpianists. In the last movement of the Piano Trio K. 548, the violin replicates the piano's embellishments even when this necessitates awkward shifts or string crossings. The demands posed by these exchanges afford the violinist the opportunity to show off mastery of the instrument, yet the writing is unforgiving in a way that the same music, played on the keyboard, is not.

From a stylistic perspective, these thematic overlaps are inevitable outgrowths of contemporary convention. Owing to the durability of Mozart's modular vocabulary, figures are routinely shared in different instrumental lines, even across different compositions. The melody from a subsidiary theme in the first movement in the Piano Trio K. 496 (m. 37) makes a transitional appearance in the first movement of the Flute and Harp Concerto, K. 299 (m. 68), and a theme from the first movement of the Violin Concerto K. 218 (mm. 12–14) recurs as an embellishment in the first movement of the Piano Quintet, K. 452 (m. 98). Even figures designed for the hand of a pianist, such as Alberti bass patterns, appear in other instrumental lines, including Mozart's clarinet writing and the solo harp part in the Flute and Harp Concerto. Such instances of exchange are telling, since in both K. 299 and the clarinet music the writing is clumsiest precisely when Mozart assumes a pianistic idiom. Clarinetists who play the variations from the "Gran Partita," K. 361, the obbligato arias from *La clemenza di Tito*, or the Alberti patterns embedded in the Clarinet Quintet, K. 581, or the Concerto K. 622 are made to navigate difficult combinations of accidentals, cross fingerings, and awkward jumps across the break (with attendant challenges for breath control, tuning, and sound).[56] When using a basset clarinet, these difficulties are exacerbated by the added weight and the presence of the more bulbous bell. The player must bring off the same types of technical passagework, all while working to support the larger, heavier instrument. Harpists playing K. 299, meanwhile, face awkward repeated notes, broken octaves, and ascending sequences whose pianistic analogs are trivially easy but that require unidiomatic pedal changes on the harps of Mozart's time.[57] Perhaps, when composing for an instrument with which he had limited familiarity, Mozart lapsed into a keyboard mindset, allowing intuition to dictate what he set on paper.

The only instruments on which Mozart's technical abilities would have approached the level of his piano playing were the violin and viola. Mozart studied the violin with his father, performing on the instrument during his earliest tours. Later in his career, he turned to the viola for recreational music making, continuing to play it in chamber settings with his colleagues long after ceasing public activities as a string player. He produced a hefty output of virtuoso writing for both instruments, consisting most famously of the violin concertos, the various serenades with solo violin parts embedded into the middle movements, and the Sinfonia Concertante for Violin and Viola, K. 364, as well as chamber music that features both instruments in various duo, trio, quartet, and quintet configurations. Often, he treats both the violin and viola as equal partners, sharing all melodic material between them in K. 364 and the chamber music. Yet even though he seems to have regarded the instruments as musical peers, the technical demands posed by his violin parts exceed those of the viola parts, whether in showpieces such as the "Haffner" Serenade, K. 250, or the later quartets.

In many respects, the considerations I have enumerated in the context of Mozart's piano writing also apply to the violin. For instance, he adjusts many recapitulated melodies in the violin concertos and string chamber music just as he does in his piano writing, for although the violin did not share the piano's strict upper-range limit, accessibility to a broad range of consumers would decrease as the hand moves further along the fingerboard. Nonetheless, whereas Mozart's compositional career developed in lockstep with his development as a virtuoso pianist, his violin writing after 1776 consists mainly of chamber rather than solo pieces. As a result, parallels between his violin playing and compositional technique are patchy, especially in the latter half of his life. Mozart's string chamber music presents ample challenges, all of which indicate the sophistication of his abilities; yet these pieces, written for small groups and often emphasizing "conversation" at the expense of individual, soloistic flights, usually eschew the type of display that would allow us to form a more detailed picture of his technique. All we know with certainty is that he took for granted skilled soloists' abilities to play confidently in the upper reaches of the fingerboard, including to c'''' in the fourth movement of the "Haffner" Serenade and e♭'''' in the final phrases of the Sinfonia Concertante.

What is clear, however, is that Mozart's attitude with respect to violin writing—particularly, the exploratory openness his music evinces—changed considerably between his earlier and later years, with the earlier string output evincing a far greater degree of tactile inventiveness than the later compositions. He shows an interest in double stops, drone open strings, and related sonic effects as early as the Symphony K. 43. In the Divertimentos K. 136

and K. 138 (most likely intended for string orchestra rather than quartet) as well as the Violin Concertos K. 211 and K. 218, extended scales are given with slurs and dots indicating the virtuoso technique now called "upbow staccato" in which the violinist articulates a rapid series of notes in a single bow stroke without lapsing into legato—a feat requiring delicate physical coordination.[58] Elsewhere, his violinistic vocabulary expands to include more complex patterns of syncopated slurs (K. 219) and, later, bariolage (a rapid, continuous alternation) over the D and A strings (K. 328). Interestingly, all of these devices involve the violinist's bow arm rather than left hand. Mozart does not push the violinist into the realm of complex counterpoint in the manner of many string-playing predecessors and successors; instead he relishes the instrument's expressive potential in a way that foreshadows both his later interest in the sonic capabilities of Stein's pianos and, more broadly, his emphasis on articulation as an essential element of musical style. (Even in the sketchiest of his first drafts, hardly a bar exists that does not contain slurs or other articulation marks, as if these were of such central importance that he notated them before even deciding whether to proceed with each piece.) His meticulous handling of the right arm in his early violin writing shows that this expressive emphasis was a lifelong preoccupation and one that carried over into the keyboard music as his career progressed.

Although Mozart's violin writing does not seem to embody the same generative significance I have attributed to his relationship with the piano, in many of his violin compositions, technique—again, often focused on the right arm—plays a highly performative role. In the Violin Concerto K. 219, he sets up a series of sixteenth-note passages that end in bars of long, drawn-out slurs (mm. 100–102). Here, the bowing pattern features as an integral element of musical drama: the exuberant sixteenths, culminating in an ascending E-major scale, collide with the flattened $\hat{7}$ and begin a searing, chromatic sigh at the same moment that the speed of arm motion changes from sixteen short bow strokes per bar to one single, drawn-out stroke. The technique required to execute the passage mirrors the musical gesture, such that Mozart's rhetorical thrust is focused as much on the physical experience of the player's right arm as on the melodic content itself.[59]

Mozart's nearly exclusive interest in right-arm technique as a vehicle for expressive violin playing in such passages seems fitting considering his abiding interests in melody and articulation. It is strange, however, in light of his broader explorations of sophisticated harmonic structures and counterpoint. Mozart's approach to playing the violin all but ignored the instrument's polyphonic capacity, and perhaps it was partly this limitation that led him ultimately to focus his compositional and performative attention on the piano. It comes as no surprise that the complexities of his harmonic language found voice in his music for keyboard.

Harmonic Structure and Keyboard Improvisation

A final point of intersection between Mozart's tactile instrumental technique and compositional abilities involves his use of harmonic patterns that would have served as structural aids during extended keyboard improvisations. We have already seen that improvisation was an essential ingredient of Mozart's career as a pianist. Even when he performed prefabricated compositions such as the piano concertos, he inserted extensive textual interventions in the form of melodic embellishments, cadenzas, and *Eingänge* (brief cadenza-like interjections at various formal interstices).[60] He also routinely improvised in a wide range of genres. He might open public performances with long, rambling fantasias that moved daringly through various tempos, keys, and affects. He inserted modulating preludes between pieces in different keys within concerts. He was known to spin music in stricter forms as well, including variations, fugues, quodlibets (contrapuntal combinations of popular tunes), and even, at times, entire sonatas. Of these genres, the fantasia, modulating prelude, and cadenza are most closely associated with flights of spontaneity and therefore most fully inhabit the liminal space between performance and composition. Mozart wrote a handful of models for improvisation in these genres, intended as aids for those unable to extemporize on their own. These, along with modules associated with the schema tradition, offer a glimpse into the harmonic precepts that guided Mozart's tactile intuitions as a keyboard performer as well as his compositional development.[61]

As discussed in chapter 1, stock harmonic patterns were staples of music pedagogy for much of the eighteenth century, carefully memorized by keyboardists in training and others who wished to master the crafts of performance, composition, or improvisation. Because these patterns constituted a vocabulary shared by virtually every competent musician of a given time and place, they differ somewhat from the melodic pianistic modules discussed above, which reflect Mozart's own idiosyncratic keyboard writing. That many of the stock harmonic patterns known to Mozart would also have featured in the music of others, however, makes it relatively easy to examine Mozart's practices by comparing his procedures to those described in theoretical sources of the time. Studies of the partimento tradition and of schema modules more broadly provide a model for this type of investigation, viewing Mozart's output as a compendium of phrases within which to detect and analyze such harmonic gestures, all with the aim of understanding the use to which Mozart puts each. In this respect, the literature on partimento is already well developed; yet if these have recently become the most familiar species of schema Mozart and his contemporaries used, they are by no means the only such devices he absorbed. In particular, many of the harmonic tactics that shaped his improvisatory models, and even his compositions, involve not individual, local gestures but protocols that operate at higher levels of structure.

The challenge facing an improviser in the late eighteenth century involved neither the creation of new musical material nor its local deployment in any particular phrase, two issues that would be minimized in a style consisting of familiar tropes that the player had already learned. Far more pressing would have been the task of managing larger-scale form and proportion while generating music extempore. For a composer working with pen and paper, the establishment of coherent formal structures presents little difficulty: the relative lengths of phrases and sections can be planned in advance and revised at any time. None of these conveniences were available to the improviser, who had instead to develop a sophisticated set of tools to manage the structures and shapes of each unpremeditated piece of music. One such tool has already featured briefly in this chapter's discussion: the use of voice exchanges as a means to prolong harmonies, a device that would allow an improviser to manage more carefully internal phrase length and formal proportion and would ensure that decisive cadences occurred at precisely the intended moment within a hypermetrical scheme. In addition to voice exchanges, Mozart's improvisatory keyboard models feature a number of other stabilizing techniques.

The first and perhaps most widespread in its use by both Mozart and his contemporaries involves basslines in scale patterns, which would serve as formal ground plans of an improvisation. Various keyboard treatises dealing with improvisation, from canonized sources such as C. P. E. Bach's *Versuch* to the more idiosyncratic writings of Abbé Vogler in the 1770s, recommend that performers become adept at the flexible harmonization of scales. Because one-octave scales both begin and end on the same pitch, they provide a ready-made map for any number of different improvisatory contexts. When harmonized diatonically, a scalar bassline may assert and explore a single key area, providing a series of intermediary chords whose functions and inversions sustain harmonic interest without risking the complications introduced when the improviser veers into unexpected harmonic terrain. Scales could also feature in more drawn-out improvisations: when the player lingers on each scale degree for longer stretches of music, the one-octave scale becomes both an efficient route away from the starting key as well as a sure path back. Of course, improvisers who used scalar basslines in this way routinely disguised them with elaborate figuration in order to dazzle listeners by masking the rudimentary origins of their art. Nonetheless, such structures are present behind even the freest of Mozart's pseudo-improvisations. Between 1776 and 1778, he composed a number of such pieces for his sister Nannerl (a point to which I return in the next chapter), including a prelude modulating from F to C via E minor. Here, the first seven structural bass notes trace a simple, descending scale from F down to G before reversing direction and settling on B in preparation for an E-minor cadence at the end of the first page (fig. 2.1).[62]

There are some exceptions to the scalar-bass style of improvisatory elaboration. In one short passage in a different prelude, for instance, Mozart follows a standard circle-of-fifths progression (another technique familiar to improvisers), with the bass descending rapidly by fifths from C all the way to E♭. Yet for the most part, the scalar bass is a staple of Mozart's improvisatory writing. The same method underpins much of the Fantasia in C minor, K. 475, written in 1785 as a model for his student Therese von Trattner. Measures 1–5 follow a descending chromatic scale from C to A♭; in measures 5–7, the alto voice takes up the descent and continues, diatonically, from A♭ to F; beginning in measure 10, the bass continues its chromatic descent from B to F♯. Later, in measures 68–82 of the same fantasia, the bass descends chromatically more than an octave and a half, touching every note along the way and moving in a single sweep from D♭ major to the dominant of B♭. Indeed, K. 475 even partakes of the scalar bass on the most macroscopic level, since the series of key areas in which the piece settles follow, in each subsequent section, the beginnings of an ascending scale: C minor at first, then D major (m. 26), E minor (36), and F major (56).

Scalar basslines were thus flexible in their improvisatory applications: they could outline entire fantasias or individual formal segments and could either assert the tonic or move into more distant areas. Other techniques, by contrast, were more closely associated with specific improvisatory tasks—for instance, those tricks used to ensure successful modulation. Many modulatory techniques proceeded through enharmonic substitution or sliding half steps, both of which allow the performer to cross easily to the opposite side

Figure 2.1 Modulating prelude, autograph, first page. National Széchényi Library, Budapest (H-Bn), Music Collection, 6.341.

of the circle of fifths. In principle, enharmonic substitution is the more efficient means by which to move into far-flung tonalities, and Mozart uses it in passages such as the opening of K. 475, when a G♭ reinterpreted as F♯ allows him to steer the music toward B minor. However, he seems to have preferred the less efficient but more distinctive technique of modulating contrapuntally using sliding half steps, whereby individual chord tones change one at a time until the music has swiveled to a new tonal center.[63] (This technique has invited comparison with the game of "word ladders," in which "cat" can be transformed to "dog" using the same method: cat–cot–cog–dog.) These modulations, too, occur frequently in Mozart's fantasias. In measure 35b of K. 475, the extended episode in D ends when Mozart raises the tonic note by a half step, yielding a dominant chord in E minor. The same technique recurs at the end of the episode in B♭ major.

A final technique that warrants mention involves the use of diminished seventh chords as harmonic pivots. C. P. E. Bach recommends that improvisers become familiar with diminished sevenths, since they offer a convenient way to reach distant keys: one simply strikes the chord and then reinterprets any of its pitches as the new leading tone.[64] Such modulations occur frequently in eighteenth-century fantasias and cadenzas—so much so that the sonority of the diminished seventh itself became a staple of the improvisatory style during Mozart's lifetime. It is no coincidence that in K. 475 the first three notes imply a diminished seventh chord, or that the second measure uses diminished sevenths to elaborate on the dominant. Equally, the opening arpeggios of the modulating prelude written for Nannerl and reproduced above, despite outlining an F-major triad, are laced with D♯s that hint at a diminished seventh sonority (A–C–D♯) before ultimately settling on an augmented sixth chord.

These devices, familiar elements of Mozart's fantasias, preludes, and cadenzas, epitomize the structural facets of the improviser's art. And, like the pianistic modules discussed earlier, they exerted a demonstrable pull on his compositional style. Scholars have occasionally noted this alignment of improvisatory technique and compositional structure;[65] yet it is most often treated in relation to Mozart's development sections—a context where the presence of chromaticism and daring modulations is unremarkable. It is the use of these techniques in contexts where we might expect to encounter more staid, harmonically routine music that reveals the extent to which Mozart had absorbed these improvisatory methods.

The techniques described above undergird Mozart's writing in virtually

Example 2.16 Piano Concerto K. 467, second movement, mm. 2–12 (1st violin part)

all genres and across the entirety of his career. Much of his darkest music—the opening of the "Dissonance" Quartet, K. 465, the *ombra* music in the overture and act 2 finale of *Don Giovanni*—is ornately layered over scalar basslines. In *Don Giovanni*, the entrance of the ghostly statue heralds a bass descent. As the scene unfolds, this scalar bass follows numerous harmonic detours, producing an effect of complexity and sophistication while building on the simplest of improvisatory tools. Of course, such tools could generate music in other expressive spheres as well, from the lamenting but largely diatonic slow movement of the String Quintet in G minor, K. 516, to the boisterous first movement of the "Haffner" Symphony, K. 385, and the regal opening of the Symphony in E♭ K. 543. Mozart even occasionally uses the same bassline strategies to lend structure and direction to his melodic writing, for instance by disguising a chromatic assent within the famous tune from the Andante of the Piano Concerto K. 467 (ex. 2.16). Throughout this movement, Mozart offsets the classical lyricism of the theme with ethereal injections of chromaticism during the solo episodes. The chromatic line he integrates as a series of gracious appoggiaturas foreshadows the mystical world into which soloist and orchestra will soon wander.[66]

Mozart uses the sliding half-step technique, too, in his written compositions. One example occurs in the slow movement of the Piano Concerto in G, K. 453, whose retransition moves from C♯ minor to the home key of C major in a mere four steps: beginning from the dominant chord (a G♯ major triad), B♯ becomes B♮, D♯ becomes D♮, and G♯ becomes G♮—and the resulting chord resolves to C. The same technique features in greater concentration in his first six piano sonatas, K. 279–284. There is a long tradition according to which these sonatas are said to resemble improvisations. Although I nuance this appraisal in chapter 3, the truth it bears arises partly from the sonatas'

Example 2.17 Piano Sonata K. 280, first movement, mm. 18–22

harmonic plans, which echo the chromatic techniques of Mozart's fantasias. In the Sonata in F K. 280, Mozart crafts a complex chromatic transition that merges the falling chromatic basses of his fantasias with the sliding half steps of his improvisatory modulations (ex. 2.17).[67] This passage's imitation of the fantasia style is so striking that, taken out of context, it would be difficult to guess the genre of the embedding piece—except, perhaps, for the fact that the progression in the sonata begins and ends in the same key, whereas in a fantasia these techniques would be used to escape the pull of tonality. Other chromatic moves from the fantasias also appear in these sonatas: for instance, an enharmonic shift in the slow movement of K. 279, measures 44–47, in which Mozart pivots out of F major by replacing a D♭ in the bass with a C♯.

Often, Mozart synthesizes all of these techniques into dazzlingly complex music. In the first-movement exposition of the stormy Piano Concerto in C minor, K. 491, he brings together chromatic basslines, enharmonic substitution, sliding half steps, and diminished seventh chords to move briskly across the circle of fifths, from E♭ major to F♯ major. The process begins in measure 220: the G from an E♭ major triad drops to G♭; next, the fifth rises from B♭ to C♭. In two steps, Mozart has moved from E♭ to an enharmonically reinterpreted B-major triad. In this case, perhaps to offset the speed of modulation, Mozart spends the next five bars reinforcing this new tonal soundscape with a descending bass (mm. 223–28). When he finally returns to E♭, his method is a series of diminished seventh chords combined with the same descending chromatic bass (232–39). This modulation, which draws on virtually every tool in the improviser's arsenal, has inspired awe among critics, some of whom sense a profound "psychic tension" that must have gripped Mozart while he crafted such "unsettling," "disturbed" music.[68] This assessment certainly captures the piece's turbulence; yet we might also see the passage as a straightforward application of techniques Mozart had known as an improviser for the previous two and a half decades. The same applies to countless other audacious chromatic phrases in his output. An extended parenthetical in the opening movement of the String Quintet K. 515 (mm. 42–56) floats across a series of parallel tonal worlds, never truly modulating away from the tonic C major yet hinting at F minor, D♭ major, and, in the recapitulated version, C♯ minor, all using only a diminished seventh chord pivot and enharmonic respelling.[69] This piece, like K. 491, has been the subject of repeated praise over the past two centuries. Beethoven considered K. 515 the most beautiful of Mozart's quintets, and Charles Rosen described it as the most daring of all Mozart's compositions.[70] Although such admiration is often directed toward other virtuosic features of the movement (its protracted form, its mercurial thematic structures, and the fugal writing in the development section), chromatic digressions such as the one described here are just as thoroughly bound up with the intrepid technical assurance that permeates the quintet and which originated in rudimentary elements of the improviser's art.

The explanation for Mozart's facility with such devices is to be found not only in the improvisatory harmonic techniques themselves but in the way he integrated them into his language. Of particular import are the tools associated with variation, which allowed him to weave these harmonic devices throughout his music, adapting each to suit any phrase where it might prove useful. It is through variation procedures that Mozart converts the scalar basses underpinning his fantasias from an inert, idealized sequence of tones into a coherent musical statement. Even the sliding half-step modulations are outgrowths of variation, since the individual harmonic shifts often apply to motives that recur, altered, two or three times in succession. The same is true, more broadly, of the schema modules that featured in contemporary pianistic thinking. The mere conversion of a schema from its Platonic form into a gesture suited to any one musical phrase is an act of variation by which the progression is clothed in new melodic and rhythmic material. Viewed from the perspective of harmonic modules and pianistic intuition, Mozart's entire compositional output begins to resemble an infinitely complex, infinitely diverse set of variations on simple protocols rather than a repertoire whose heavenly design resists any attempt at explication.

On another level, too, Mozart's use of simple tools depended on variation techniques: not only when he placed the familiar modules within individual phrases but when he then masked his handiwork by heaping intricacy after intricacy on them. It was only in Mozart's earliest years that he made use of standard modules in their more straightforward incarnations. As his abilities developed, he frequently attempted to play up his own inventiveness. In the first movement of K. 282, Mozart inserts a Fonte in its usual place, immediately following a double bar, but he modifies every parameter of the progression (shown in ex. 1.3). He transplants the standard Fonte bass into an inner voice; he varies the melody between one sequential step and the next; and, most important for our present purposes, he bridges the F minor chord to the subsequent B♭ chord with a pseudo-improvisatory, chromatic descent. He carries the same techniques further in the last movement of his next sonata, K. 283 (mm. 77–78). Here, Mozart once again relegates a Fonte to a middle voice; however, instead of observing the convention whereby the leading tone of ii (here, G♯) should resolve up, he converts the next chord into a dominant seventh, lowers G♯ to G♮, and once again crafts a multivoice chromatic descent that recalls parallel passages in his fantasias and, no doubt, in his actual extemporizations. In these and other cases, such transformations are best explained through the lens of variation—in terms both of the ease with which Mozart departs from convention and the specific tools he summons in the act.

Mozart's wish to show off his powers of invention would have been most pressing when the vocabulary of a composition was most conventional. It is therefore unsurprising that standard harmonic patterns, the most recognizable modules, received such unwaveringly ornate treatment at his hands. Yet similar complexities also arise in his use of the other devices discussed here, which underwent parallel transformations as Mozart's style evolved. By his final months—the period of the motet Ave Verum Corpus and the Requiem—his music had become so freighted with chromatic sophistication that these techniques, which originated in his fantasias and which seemed complex in his earlier compositions, began to feature in more routine phrases. Even at this late stage, Mozart retained his characteristic experimental zeal. In the Confutatis from the Requiem, he establishes a progression that draws on both the sliding half steps and diminished seventh chords of his earlier, improvisatory music. Diminished sevenths often occur before dominant harmonies, since lowering any of the notes by a half step yields a dominant seventh—a remarkable effect in which harmonic ambiguity gives way to clarity. In the Confutatis, Mozart presents just such a diminished seventh on E♭ (m. 26), poised to resolve into a dominant seventh. However, instead of lowering the bass to D, he sustains the E♭, shifting all three upper voices one half step higher (m. 27). This creates a chilling instance of word-painting. The E♭, like the soul, is moored within the hellish depths of the texture and seems to sink while the world around it rises.[71] That this and countless other expressive effects were available within Mozart's technical reach is a reminder of the continued influence wielded by his practice of keyboard improvisation. Although it is widely accepted that his late style represents not so much a culmination of his previous aesthetic but a musical reinvention cut short by an early death, it is equally true that the harmonic techniques Mozart sustained into his final days represent the crowning height of practices he had long known as a performing pianist, for which he continued to find creative new use.

VARIATION 3

Mozart the Improviser

The tropes that make up the fabric of Mozart's keyboard writing are the residue of musical thought that occurred at the intersections of composition and performance. Viewing the compendium of pianistic gestures in the previous chapter, it is easy to imagine Mozart's keyboard music as having arisen as the direct product of performative spontaneity. Melodic or harmonic patterns, familiar from a lifetime of tactile practice, seem to have exerted as much pull on the shapes his compositions ultimately took as did the more careful planning made possible by written notation. In this view the skills associated with composition and those arising through Mozart's experience as a performer would have been mutually reinforcing, a synthesis made all the more immediate by the centrality of improvisation within his musical life, in which these two facets of his career came into constant alignment.

So far I have treated improvisation primarily as a mode of performance. Mozart sits down at the piano, music begins to flow through his hands, and listeners marvel at the immediacy with which coherent phrases crystallize, moment by moment, through the medium of the keyboard. This, in any case, is how contemporary audiences seemed to view his many feats of extemporization to judge by the many laudatory accounts recorded by those who heard him play. With a small shift of perspective, however, it becomes clear that, far from being a matter of untrammeled pianistic intuition, improvisation is also a distinctly compositional pursuit. True, the improviser plays music instead of writing it down. But even at its most unalloyed, improvisation is a process in which melodies are generated, phrases assembled, and entire pieces created.

We may go still further: in the eighteenth century, improvisation was understood not simply as a method of musical creation but as a stylistic ideal in its own right, and one to which even written music could aspire. We have already seen evidence of the porous boundaries between composition and improvisation in the form of the many fantasias, preludes, and cadenzas Mozart set on paper for his sister or students.

Although I argued that the technical elements of Mozart's craft as a pianist can reveal something of the mindset with which he produced both improvisations and finished compositions, it is equally likely that causation flowed in the other direction as well: that is, that his explorations and technical developments as a composer would have fed back into his improvisatory abilities, influencing not only the content of his extemporized performances but their stylistic thrust as well as the flair and theatrical assurance with which he could bring them off. This adds a dimension to the mode of explanation I adopted in the previous chapter. Rather than simply trying to understand Mozart's compositions as outgrowths of his tactile engagement with the keyboard, I now wish to ask how composition might mimic acts of improvised performance, capturing the theatricality, excitement—and of course the risks and volatility—of spontaneous creation.

We have already seen that on a purely technical level improvisation and composition in the eighteenth century shared a significant number of musical rudiments. Both depended on familiarity with harmonic and melodic modules and stock gestures; both drew from techniques associated with variation; and both were bound up with an understanding of musical creativity that emphasized the skillful recombination of standard tropes. Yet despite these many points of technical alignment, their aesthetic associations were (and remain) strikingly divergent, with improvisation often framed as the antithesis of composition. Improvisation is flighty, haphazard, digressive; the word itself, in modern parlance, suggests something makeshift and insufficient—"an improvised shelter," in an example from philosopher Gary Peters.[1] Even when viewed favorably, as a liberation from the constraints of a codified text, improvisation may imply disorder, since it allows neither for revision nor, at its most extreme, for forethought and planning. Although such appraisals do not primarily concern improvised music as much as "improvisation" in the abstract, the distinction they imply between the planned and the spontaneous is an idée fixe within musicological discourse. Four decades ago, Leonard Ratner suggested that it is owing to the unpremeditated nature of improvisation that its associated genres often thrust against normative conventions.[2]

Richard Kramer, in an essay on sincerity in late eighteenth-century music, places improvisation in direct opposition to composition, arguing that a performer carried freely from one whim to the next may achieve expressive authenticity but will in the process "rule out [music's] efficacy to embody . . . the rational mode of grammar and syntax" associated with compositional planning.[3] Charles Rosen, too, viewed improvisations as inherently volatile. He lamented what for him seemed a fatal lack of planning in those C. P. E. Bach fantasias that depict a player's spontaneous, mercurial impulses while giving up intelligibility as collateral damage: "C.P.E. Bach's horizon is wider harmonically [than J.C. Bach's or the young Mozart's], but his practice is incoherent: he is more interested in local effects—he delights in harmonic shock, as did Haydn; but Haydn knew how to weld his effects together, and his most disparate harmonies are not only reconciled but even explained by what follows as well as implied by what precedes."[4] What Rosen finds laudable in Haydn is a sense of structural control in which entire compositions seem to have been tightened through a revisionary process necessarily at odds with the ostensible moment by moment unfolding of improvisations. Dana Gooley's account of historical improvisatory practices has provided a corrective to the dichotomies plaguing earlier appraisals, yet even he adopts a similar stance when describing the precepts furthered in some eighteenth-century improvisation treatises as "positively anarchic," demonstrating an "untrammeled, antisystematic proliferation" of harmonic turns that defy the more "rational" techniques associated with written composition.[5] Nor do such judgments emerge only among modern-day critics. Mozart's contemporaries voiced similar perspectives in theoretical and amateur writings alike.[6] Daniel Türk, whose 1789 treatise remains central to the study of historical keyboard technique, describes the fantasia, that flagship improvisatory genre, as a piece in which the performer "holds neither to a certain main subject (theme) nor to meter or rhythm (although for some thoughts a meter could be used), when he roams around in his modulations, when he expresses various and often contrasting characters, in short, when he follows his whims completely without attempting to work out a specific plan."[7]

All such accounts, old and new, confuse means with ends. Türk's words, arrayed in a single sentence, give the impression of homogeneity; yet his observations are of two distinct types. One concerns the mode by which the improvisation is created (the player "follows his whims," proceeding without a fixed plan), the other the content of the resulting piece (lacking in melodic consistency or rhythmic stability, full of contrasting characters). Considering the many overlapping techniques underpinning both composition and improvisation in the eighteenth century, there is no reason to assume that method and style were necessarily correlated in the way such descriptions imply. Improvisations may well have been haphazard—and indeed, as we have seen, Mozart himself drew from harmonic and modulatory techniques that would allow him to evade the standard chord progressions associated with compositional propriety. However, as we have also seen, Mozart used the same techniques even in written music that was not intended to conjure the flightiness associated with improvisation. This suggests that the technical elements of improvisation were separable from the style of the music they would be used to create. A composer could marshal all available modes of planning and yet eschew any semblance of stability, instead aiming to evoke what Gooley refers to as the "aestheticized 'improvisatoriness'" arising from unexpected turns of phrase and abrupt expressive and rhetorical shifts.[8] Conversely, a sufficiently skilled improviser could certainly generate music in a more deliberate, "compositional" style, as Mozart himself did when he extemporized sonatas or piano parts in chamber music. (As Maximilian Stadler recalls in his *Autobiography*, "[Mozart's] improvisations were as well-ordered as if he had had them lying written out before him."[9]) That Stadler and other contemporaries viewed such feats with a measure of awe suggests how deep-seated were their expectations for a more capricious style in improvised music. Yet the fact remains that if improvisations called up particular aesthetic associations, it must have been a result of at least some deliberate choice on the part of their creators, who wished not only to carry out the act of improvisation but to partake in a set of stylistic moves associated with spontaneity.

Variation and Improvisatory Structure

To what extent might musicians have exercised deliberate choice in shaping the musical and stylistic content of their improvisations? One way to approach the issue is by reconsidering some of the structural protocols used during both composition and improvisation. Variation techniques in particular would have offered Mozart and his contemporaries a number of highly ordered alternatives to the stormy, volatile world of the fantasia. Variation sets were, in the eighteenth century, often associated with the public display of improvisatory prowess. However, as we saw in the two previous chapters, they were also vehicles for the development of compositional ability. Musical composition is an art of tightly controlled repetition, and the practice of composing variations—a genre in which some elements of a theme or phrase are held constant while others change—would have offered improvisers a highly focused arena within which to practice both the development of individual phrases and the successive unfolding of larger-scale segments.

We have already seen examples demonstrating the relevance of variation for the improviser's art—for instance, in the integration of stock figures or scalar basslines into a range of musical contexts. We can extrapolate additional points of significance from improvisatory passages in Mozart's written compositions. The piano concertos are a rich source of phrases in which accompanying voices establish stock chord progressions while the soloist explores shifting melodic figuration in a way that suggests free, exploratory riffing. One short example occurs in the C-minor Concerto, K. 491, when a simple tonic-dominant oscillation repeats while the right hand tinkers with the melody, testing and recasting its contours (ex. 3.1*a*).[10] Elsewhere, the same technique appears in more protracted form, binding together a series of phrases in the Concerto in E♭ K. 482 (ex. 3.1*b*). Following the tutti fanfare that begins the first movement, the winds initiate a descending sequence that repeats four times. Although the phrase structure remains unchanged, the soloist noodles differently during each subsequent recurrence: once with cascading arpeggios of the kind that might introduce a free fantasia, and later with scales up and down the higher octaves of the keyboard. It is easy to imagine contemporary listeners encountering the concertos for the first time, hearing these variation-like passages, and not knowing whether the soloist were conforming to notes already set on paper or spontaneously injecting new material.

Variations also served a generative purpose in the crafting of full-length compositions, and this utility, too, would have been available to improvisers. Through the careful management of varied repetition, whereby a small amount of material can be expanded into lengthier compositions, an improviser can proceed with confidence, knowing that a minimum number of musical ideas are in place and available for development should inspiration fail. Although this skill would serve the improviser in any context, from the conversion of concerto themes into cadenzas or the structuring of harmonic material during fantasias, it would have been particularly useful when an improviser wished to play in stricter forms, approximating the sound and feel of prefabricated music. Here, the need to maintain a steady flow of meter would be of paramount importance, as, too, would be the availability of ideas. Although the bulk of Mozart's improvisations are lost to time and cannot serve as case studies in the use of large-scale variation techniques, structural features

Example 3.1 Riffing on repeated chord progressions. *a*, Piano Concerto K. 491, first movement, mm. 241–44. *b*, Piano Concerto K. 482, first movement, mm. 3–6, 96–99, and 102–5

Example 3.2 Variation as structure in Piano Concerto K. 271, first and second movements

of his notated compositions hint at the centrality of these methods in his musical craft. For instance, many of the melodies in the Piano Concerto K. 271 derive from a single thematic unit (ex. 3.2). This gesture, presented during the soloist's initial entrance, forms the basis for at least three other tunes heard in the first and second movements, all of which ascend from B♭ up through E♭, F, and G before peaking on B♭ one octave higher. In such compositions, short musical cells take on a significant load-bearing function in the act of musical invention.

Thematic cross-referencing is still more evident in Mozart's solo keyboard music, a reminder that the structural conveniences of variation devices would have derived some familiarity from Mozart's activities as a performing pianist. Often, these cross-references involve not only melodic or harmonic content but accompanimental style and even technical pianistic associations. In the Piano Sonata K. 333, both the first and last movements begin with two versions of the same phrase. The opening bar of the finale even acknowledges and absorbs the left hand's initial silent downbeat from the first movement. In the earlier B♭ Sonata K. 281, an *Eingang* written out in the last movement recalls the retransition from the first movement. And, finally, in the Piano Sonata in C minor, K. 457, various elements of the closing theme of the first movement reappear in the voicing and melodic style of a parallel melody in the last movement.

Composition and Improvisation

The techniques associated with variation, as well as the other organizing devices I have discussed, exist partly because performers wanted to bring aspects of their improvisations under a greater degree of conscious, structural mastery. Given proper training, they could use these tools to close the gap between their spontaneous playing and the compositions they crafted through more deliberate processes. This may seem straightforward, yet it introduces a strange twist of argument. Perhaps improvisers could approximate compositional norms in their performances—yet judging by contemporary accounts, they often elected not to do so. Rather, the stereotypes surrounding improvisation proved remarkably durable, so much so that when composers set about to write fantasias, preludes, cadenzas, or other types of pseudo-improvisatory music, they continued to assume aesthetic goals very different from those used in their tamer compositions. The same was true of performers. Eighteenth-century improvisations may in some cases have been haphazard as a result of a performer's lack of skill; yet just as often, improvisers had available to them numerous tools to keep their extemporizations on track. An improviser who focuses intently on a single gesture will be guaranteed a reserve of ideas that can later be used to ensure coherence. If such a performer dispensed with these techniques, adopting a more capricious style, it must have been for a reason.

Often, the reason is not difficult to guess. Mozart's audiences placed an enormous premium on improvisation, which, through its combination of technical mastery and expressive authenticity, was a sine qua non of the virtuoso's art. Precisely because improvisation did not admit of revision, contemporaries described it as capturing a performer's deepest personal core, which passes innocently through a contrasting series of charged phrases. Thus, in Annette Richards's words, audiences of the time held a widespread belief that to improvise was "to expose naked consciousness," laying bare the recesses of a musician's mind and heart.[11] Performers who had gained the relevant skills were positioned to capitalize on the resulting confluence of ability and enthusiastic demand—and those who did not could study prefabricated "improvisatory" pieces, memorizing them and passing them off as improvisations. For this reason alone, composers had a strong incentive to create music that, even if the product of significant deliberation, would appear to have been invented on the fly.[12] Mozart himself participated in this practice by writing cadenzas, preludes, fantasias, and embellishments, many of which were intended as crutches for pupils, colleagues, and even his sister Nannerl, who in her correspondence with Mozart asked him to "please be so good as to send me soon a short prelude, only this time one going from C to B flat, so that I can gradually learn it by heart."[13] She even occasionally tested this ruse on their father, who, in an amusing 1778 letter, reports, "Your sister thanks you for the prelude, which is excellent, and she is going to write you herself. It arrived at four o'clock. I came home after five [. . .]. She began to play the first page of your prelude from memory. I stared and said, 'Where the devil did you get these ideas?' She laughed and pulled the letters out of her pocket."[14]

In order to fulfill the intended function, such compositions would need to advertise their "spontaneous" origins using every means available, conforming to popularly held stereotypes regarding the nature of unpremeditated music. Nor was the need to signal improvisation felt only by those who lacked genuine ability. Even seasoned virtuosos occasionally wished to prove their improvisatory mettle since cynical listeners were all too keen to put famed soloists' abilities to the test. In an 1829 reminiscence reported in the somewhat unreliable but always entertaining diaries of Vincent and Mary Novello, Mozart's friend and colleague Maximilian Stadler recalls that Mozart himself was forced to defend the legitimacy of his improvisations:

> [Mozart] usually played *extemporaneously*, but his imagination was so inexhaustible and at the same time his ideas were so symmetrical and regularly treated that Albrechtsberger could not be persuaded but that they were regular pieces that had been studied beforehand—One evening when Mozart, the Abbé Stadler and Albrechtsberger were together, the latter asked Mozart to sit down to the Instrument and play something. Mozart directly complied, but instead of taking a subject of his own, he told Albrechtsberger to give him a theme. Albrechtsberger accordingly invented a subject on the spot, and which he was quite certain that Mozart could not possibly have heard before; he also selected the most trivial features he could think of in order to put Mozart's ingenuity, invention and creative powers to the severest test. The extraordinary Genius immediately took the theme that had been given him thus unexpectedly, and played for upwards of an hour upon it, treating it in all possible variety of form—fugue, Canon, and from the most simple to the most elaborate Counterpoint—until Albrechtsberger could hold out no longer, but exclaimed in transport, "I am now perfectly convinced that your extemporaneous playing is really the thought of the moment and that you fully deserve all the fame you have acquired from this wonderful talent."[15]

The value of such signaling even applied when a performer's abilities were not in question, a phenomenon that, centuries later, has lost none of its relevance. Those modern-day musicians who weave fluent improvisation into their performances of eighteenth- and nineteenth-century music—Robert Levin is the best known, though others have begun to follow his example—often generate a unique aura of energy and excitement. As Levin himself has pointed out, each improvised piece is unique, available only to those present at the moment of creation.[16] Moreover, improvisation is risky. Improvisers constantly confront the possibility of a lapse—and those who witness spontaneity in action are, as a result, more easily compelled into a state of rapt engagement.[17] Audiences crave thrills, and improvisation, then and now, is among the most efficient means by which a skilled performer can deliver.

If the signaling of spontaneity seems a straightforward goal, however, its execution would have presented composers and performers alike with a challenge. As we have already seen, the methods by which a composition is created are distinct from its aesthetic features. In this respect, improvisation is perhaps best understood as a method of musical notation—albeit one in which notes are not actually set on paper. The designation of improvisation is, strictly speaking, neutral with regard to the content of what it produces: it simply indicates the process by which music is created and recorded. As such it sits on a continuum of notational styles whose other nodes encompass both alternate degrees of specificity (from skeletal jazz charts to more constrictive notation that specifies expressive parameters alongside the notes) as well as alternate means of creating that notation (the use of pencil, quill, modern-day computer software, or a piano keyboard). Improvisation bears the same relationship to style as do any other notational methods a composer might use. There is no question that each offers comparative advantages or disadvantages during the creative process, and such affordances may influence aspects of the finished piece. A composer who writes in pencil rather than pen may be emboldened to experiment with complexities certain to require revision, just as one who eschews notation altogether is free to employ a degree of rhythmic nuance not easily rendered on the page. Even so, each notational method is less decisive in shaping the music than are the composer's stylistic priorities. A pencil may facilitate revision, but how that pencil is wielded—what is attempted, what retained, and what erased—involves abstract considerations from musical preference and stylistic inheritance to explicit calculations concerning professional standing, economic needs, beliefs about listeners' interests, and so forth. There is no aesthetics of music written in pencil versus ink, and there is likewise no aesthetic essence of improvisation.[18]

Playing Dumb: Improvisation as Theatrical Fiction

What options, then, were available to a composer who hoped to simulate improvisation? One possibility was to exploit musical or formal context as established by convention. Inserting embellishments in repeated themes in a slow movement; playing modulating preludes between pieces in a concert; conjuring volatile fantasias at the start of performances; and launching into a cadenza at the end of a concerto movement—these would prime listeners of the time to hear the ensuing music as being improvised regardless of whether it had actually been planned. Yet if these clues were necessary for the suggestion of improvisation, they were not sufficient to distinguish it from music that had been learned in advance. Mozart, like his contemporaries, often had to enhance the plausibility of written-out "improvisations" by other means as well. The cadenzas nested within the piano variations are exceedingly light on thematic content, often sharing no material with the embedding set. They seem a series of exaggerated technical riffs: quick scalar runs, flashy arpeggios, and even at one point in K. 264 a glissando in sixths executed by dragging the right hand across the keyboard. The emphasis on sheer pianistic display at the expense of thematic integration was probably calculated to draw attention toward the performer's flair, in the process downplaying any semblance of planning. In combination with the contextual formal signal that a cadenza was taking place, such lack of integration might plausibly suggest spontaneity among contemporary listeners.

In the majority of cases, however, no contextual clues were available that could assist in such signaling. Cadenzas (and other genre devices that often fell within the ambit of improvisation) are the exception in Mozart's written output. A more effective way to signal the onset of "improvisation" would have been for Mozart to play into the audience's hands by validating the intuitive dichotomy between composition and improvisation. If composition was thought to be deliberate and well structured and improvisation haphazard, then improvisation could be suggested by exaggerating certain rough qualities: clumsiness, lack of polish, and structural shortcomings. The task, when attempting to signal spontaneity, would have been to write music just imperfect enough that it might seem the product of a moment's thought even if in reality it arose through more careful processes. Mozart would have to "play dumb," simulating an apparent lack of planning, foresight, and in some cases even basic compositional ability, the better to heighten suspense and sell the fiction of real-time musical creation.[19] Previously, I argued that elements of performing experience fed directly into Mozart's compositional habits, most concretely through his tactile engagement with the piano. Now, I am beginning to augment this explanation, arguing that composition can itself become an exercise in performative plotting and mis-plotting when the composer both envisions the content of fictionalized improvisatory excursions and wrests those images into music that will send the appropriate message to a listening public. In order to achieve this aim, the composer's efforts must remain focused on performance—but performance as projected in the theatrical imagination. The composer adopts a dramaturgic role, shaping as many musical elements as possible in order to convey the desired effect. Mozart remains a composer-performer, but his compositions now prefigure, rather than emerge from, a mode of performance and its associated techniques.

The theatrical fiction of simulated improvisation implies a further fiction: that of an improvisatory persona whose musicianship appears to shape the piece during the act of performance. To hear any of Mozart's compositions as being improvisatory, we should also hear within them the virtual presence of a fictionalized composer-performer, for it is ultimately to this entity that our attention is drawn.[20] The leanings and predilections of this persona, and the nuanced theatricality to which it gives rise, will be my focus in chapter 5. Here, it is enough to recognize the first hint that Mozart's dual career as a composer and performer is more than a historical explanation for the origins of his style or the techniques that underlie it—more even than the aesthetic stance and "ways of listening" I have been exploring in these pages. The notion of performative composition, we are beginning to see, also suggests a certain type of human presence: in this case, a trickster keenly aware of his audience's beliefs, and who possesses both the technical capacity and the psychological acuity to fold those beliefs into music that will create suspense and eventually release it, his displays of improvisatory imperfection synthesized into satisfying arcs. This stance retains elements of reductionism associated with the focus on modular building blocks (whose interlocking contrasts will continue to facilitate the analyses I undertake in the remainder of the chapter). Yet it also introduces a holistic interpretive attitude in the form of the complex, human persona stirring up the dramas and carefully regulating their musical progress.

In generating theatrics and fictions such as these—indeed, in adopting and fashioning this persona—Mozart would have been well served by his penchant for jokes, stage antics, and caricature. His first foray into public performance was as a pantomime dancer in a tradition closely linked to commedia dell'arte, with its stock characters and improvised plots.[21] This interest continued through adulthood: Mozart is said to have relished hamming up the comic role of commedia's Harlequin well into the 1780s.[22] His abiding love of games (both musical and verbal) is well documented and has been offered as an explanation for the serenade "Ein musikalischer Spass" (A Musical Joke), K. 522, some elements of the Piano Sonata K. 279, and the wordplay and humor throughout his correspondence.[23] Even beyond what we can surmise of his personal leanings, the many technical overlaps between composition and improvisation would also have helped him play dumb in written music. One such overlap arose from the inherent modularity of his style, which made it easy to juxtapose incongruous passages or misuse standard tropes and in so doing simulate momentary lapses that would further the theatrical fiction. Mozart could interrupt established patterns with new material, suggesting an improviser distracted by an insufficiently developed musical idea—a manifestation of improvisation's characteristic stance of "problem-finding" (as opposed to compositional "problem-solving").[24] He could also present modules in the wrong order during thematic recurrences and thus evoke an improviser who could not quite keep track of syntactic structures in the unfolding performance. Modularity would allow Mozart to render even in composed music a distractibility that would seem to conjure the vicissitudes of improvisation at either its most or least successful.

In his concertos, a genre closely associated with improvisation both real and feigned, the interstices between phrases or formal segments offer an ideal location for simulating improvisatory play. At such points, particularly when the focus passes from orchestra to soloist, we should not necessarily expect straightforward melodic continuity, since convention allows for the presentation of a new, contrasting theme. However, the soloist in Mozart's concertos often enters by building on materials used in the orchestra's preceding gesture. In one sense, this phenomenon speaks to the malleability of Mozart's modules: whereas many stylistic building blocks were clearly associated with either phrasal beginnings, middles, or endings (and were generally misused only for comic effect), Mozart often stripped such gestures of their syntactic resonances, blurring phrasal boundaries with far greater frequency than many contemporaries.[25] But in another sense, Mozart's frequent mixing of opening and closing gestures in his concertante works serves a dramatic purpose. During improvisation, performers often draw material from other collaborators on stage, building on gestures played by fellow soloists or accompanists. This process is suggested in the first movement of the Piano Concerto in A K. 414, when the pianist begins one solo as if improvising a fantasia on the orchestra's closing gesture (ex. 3.3)—a ploy Mozart was to repeat in the first-movement development of the Concerto in B♭ K. 450.[26] Nor does this effect depend on the presence of a second musical entity such as an accompanying orchestra. Even in solo keyboard music, the gesture that closes the exposition (rather than the opening phrase) often provides fuel for the development section, as if the pianist, searching for inspiration, drew on the nearest musical idea available.[27] This occurs briefly in the first movements of the Sonatas K. 545 and K. 576 and in the second movement of K. 283, but is most pronounced in the first movement of K. 311. Here, the gracious gesture that brings the exposition to its final cadence becomes the focus of the musical argument over the next fifteen measures. This developmental flight unfolds in the manner of a fantasia, with tortured chromaticism and stormy figuration in the right hand—and, all the while, no thematic connection to the rest of the movement. It seems an interpolated, improvisatory digression rather than the product of careful planning.

Mozart's attempts to signal spontaneity meet with particular success in the first movement of the Piano Sonata in C major K. 279. Critics have consistently heard this sonata, more than any of his others, as a pseudo-improvisation. Nearly a century ago, Alfred Einstein described K. 279 in precisely such terms, holding that "the tones of the instrument sound in direct response to Mozart's imagination; this is how he must have played when he was in the vein and improvised a sonata."[28] Others concur with Einstein's judgment, though they often do so with a tinge of regret. Owing to its alleged lack of thematic integration, K. 279 has been deemed the "least interesting" of Mozart's first six piano sonatas.[29] It apparently strings together "an additive, improvisatory series" of tropes "not welded into the distinctive artistic synthesis" we expect from the mature composer.[30] This framing recalls that problematic if intuitive dichotomy between the apparent randomness of improvisation and the structural clarities of written compositions.

In one sense, these criticisms are apt. The sonata is certainly fashioned from stock figuration (although detractors fail to note the organizing presence of variation principles and meticulous motivic development that offset its haphazard qualities), and familiar modules are indeed deployed without attention to rhetorical coherence as the music courses from one phrase to the next.[31] Yet the same is also true of many of Mozart's other compositions. The opening piano solo from the Concerto in E♭ K. 482, one of the grandest of his later concertos, is little more than a series of ornamental gestures that bear less relation to the movement as a whole than does the material used in K. 279.

Example 3.3 Piano Concerto K. 414, first movement, mm. 83–91

The point is not simply that such pieces use stock figuration or standard modules, since this describes virtually all of Mozart's music. The relevant issue is that K. 279 and K. 482 *display* their reliance on this basic vocabulary. As I showed in chapter 2, Mozart tends to disguise conventional material, subjecting it to such a complex series of transformations that his phrases' simpler underpinnings become virtually inaudible. In K. 279 and K. 482, by contrast, Mozart plays up the modularity, which is so clear-cut as to seem an aesthetic end in its own right. The opening solo of K. 482 does not pretend to balance out its thematic blandness with any further invention; it simply moves through its array of formulas, following one pianistic lick with another until the orchestra intervenes and the movement continues. Likewise, in the first movement of K. 279 Mozart does little to mask the cloying regularity of the formulaic gestures as they come and go. The reason, here as before, lies in the invisibility of the music's improvisatory origins. A composer attempting to simulate improvisation cannot simply draw techniques from the improviser's tool kit, since these form the basis for better-behaved compositions as well. Instead, the composer must caricature crude features so as to send the proper signal to the audience. In K. 279 Mozart does precisely this, and the critics who have lamented this sonata's incoherence while also recognizing its improvisatory flair are probably reacting just as Mozart would have hoped. Because the finer points of structure were not necessarily transparent to all contemporary listeners, the best way to achieve this communicative goal would have been to create asymmetries and gaffes so glaring that they could not go unnoticed. It is worth considering, along these lines, that unlike the sonatas Mozart created for his students, K. 279 is a piece that he himself frequently performed in situations resembling piano recitals, even playing it from memory during his travels in Mannheim in late 1777 and early 1778.[32] The improvisatory effects encoded in the music, therefore, could be amplified by the theatrical image he projected while seated at the keyboard.

Three Modes of Simulated Failure

Performing Incoherence

Improvisation is a game with stakes: a journey into the unknown in which the player risks taking wrong turns. When Mozart depicts improvisation in his written output, he does so by imitating moment to moment musical decision-making at its least successful. The near lapses he dramatizes allow him both to suggest the workings of musical thought and to make daring rescues, all the while showing off like a virtuoso escape artist. These theatrics depend primarily on his ability to reach a heroic recovery by efficient and unexpected means. Yet in the moments before recovery occurs, the playing up of failure can take a number of forms, depicting the various risks associated with improvisation.

Of these, the most straightforward is the depiction of incoherence. In compositions that engage in such theatrics, local material is unproblematic. The persona of the composer-performer is essentially competent, neither misusing chords nor flubbing individual phrases. Each module could, taken in isolation, provide a legitimate building block for a musical composition—and yet their deployment throughout the piece does not quite add up. This type of simulated lapse provides an entry point into Mozart's aesthetics of improvisation because it encompasses fantasias, preludes, cadenzas, and other familiar products of the improviser's art. The eighteenth-century theorists who understood these genres as standing in opposition to stricter, "compositional" styles were, in their way, articulating what I have just described. Individual segments of music within fantasias are often well structured and stable, yet they are strung together so as to suggest a spontaneity incompatible with deliberate forethought. In the *Versuch*, C. P. E. Bach teaches the performer how to move freely between remote key areas precisely so that such digressions could be summoned at the spur of the moment without consideration of an overarching trajectory. Yet within those remote key areas, in passages played out between the daring modulations and quicksilver affective shifts, standard local structures generally applied. This is certainly clear in Mozart's fantasias and cadenzas, whose flightier episodes alternate with staid passages in recognizable molds such as binary form.

Also in this category are compositions including the Piano Sonata K. 279 and, to a lesser extent, the first solo from the Concerto K. 482, discussed in the previous section with reference to stock figuration. Both display gaffes that seem to suggest a lack of improvisatory competence on the part of the solo pianist. In K. 279, the litany of errors includes the haphazard reshuffling of thematic order between exposition and recapitulation in each movement, as though the improviser could not quite recall how things unfolded the first time through.[33] The reshuffling is particularly pronounced in the first movement, where the themes arise in a bewilderingly different order in the recapitulation than in the exposition. Some are "accidentally" omitted from their proper place but reinserted afterward, as though the fictional improviser, barely keeping pace, realized the error too late but attempted a recovery nonetheless. Others are introduced earlier than would be appropriate under more decorous circumstances, as though they were the only melodies within reach of the improviser's flagging memory. Various explanations have been proffered for this phenomenon—that Mozart is testing the boundaries of composerly propriety and taste by deliberately misusing structurally loaded modules, or that he is playing syntactic games similar to the linguistic jests found in his most comical letters (including one to his father that ends: "warefell, I gish you nood-wight. sound sleeply. next time I'll sensibly more writely;").[34] But another plausible explanation is that Mozart is pointing to a hazard of actual improvisation, dramatizing the possibility that the player, caught up in the moment, might have forgotten how a series of modules were initially arrayed. It is of note that the reordering of recapitulated themes occurs more often in his solo keyboard music than in a large-ensemble genre such as the symphony, perhaps because it is in the context of solo performance that he could most readily simulate improvisation.[35]

The Sonata K. 279 does not represent the most flamboyant use of this particular effect, though it is the sonata most often singled out for its improvisatory character. Even more haphazard is the first movement of the Sonata in D K. 311, a piece which, in Julian Rushton's words, suffers from Mozart's experimental tendencies.[36] K. 311 dispenses entirely with a proper recapitulation, arriving at the home key with the return of a secondary theme rather than the "correct," principal theme.[37] Here, the reference to improvisatory incoherence is transparent. The development section, described above, issues from the closing material of the exposition. In both figuration and harmonic structure it seems more fitting for a fantasia than a sonata. As is Mozart's usual practice, he arrives on an augmented sixth chord midway through the development, ushering in a cadence in the submediant (B minor). From there, however, no proper return to the home key takes place. Instead, a short series of block chords effects a quick move to G major, with a verbatim restatement of a subsidiary theme from the exposition. The fictional improviser then embarks on a sixteenth-note passage built entirely from stock figuration which, after various false hints at other local tonalities, returns to the home key of D major but bypasses the first theme. The improviser has been swept into a moto perpetuo spiral, and, unable to bring about a satisfactory close, is forced into the half cadence that leads directly to the second theme. These misadventures are capped by the reappearance of the omitted melody at the very end of the movement, a last-ditch attempt to rectify this error of form.

Needless to say, in all such works, the apparent mistakes are placed alongside music so assured and so masterful in its technical dimensions that it is clear at all times that a joke is in progress—that the persona is playing at failure rather than truly experiencing it. The first solo of K. 482 is able to create pleasurable suspense through its inane, melodic emptiness only because the opening ritornello is brilliantly sophisticated at every turn. The same is true of K. 279, where the sheer pianistic flamboyance is such that any eyewitnesses taken in by Mozart's artful feigning must also have been dazzled by his keyboard prowess. In these cases, Mozart probably intended for the audience to be in on the trick, suspending disbelief so as to appreciate the fictional scenario he presents while nonetheless retaining perspective and recognizing the performance for what it was.

Very occasionally, similar structural tools evoke improvisation without the accompanying suggestion of precarity. The first movement of the Piano Sonata K. 282 follows a formal model like that of K. 311 but inhabits a tamer expressive sphere. In K. 282, as in K. 311, the return of the tonic coincides with the reappearance of a subsidiary melody rather than the melody that began the piece. But whereas in K. 311 the pianist is lost in a tangle of sixteenth notes, unable to control the unfolding of the retransition, in K. 282 this seems the result of conscious choice. The arrival on the dominant in measure 21 could easily presage any number of themes, including the opening melody—and given both the slow tempo of the movement and the gentle halting of time at the end of the brief "development," the implied improviser has ample opportunity to weigh the options. In this case, although it is difficult to hear a dramatized failure of any type, the music nonetheless suggests aspects of improvisation. The opening theme, that phrase bypassed in measure 22, is itself a simple spinning out of a scalar bassline, a device used routinely in improvisations, here spanning an entire octave.[38] By omitting this melody from the recapitulation, Mozart deepens the impression that the first phrase was but a preamble: an exploration of the sonorities of E♭ major and a gentle meditation on the fifth scale degree, all meant as a prelude to the movement's "real" beginning in measure 4. For Mozart to recall the first gesture at the moment of recapitulation would be dramatically inept, undermining the illusion of spontaneity with which the piece began. When the opening material makes a brief reappearance in the three-bar coda, it is repeated only in the loosest sense. More properly, it is recollected—half conjured but clothed in new figuration and reshaped so as to steer the movement to its peaceful close.[39]

The Sonata K. 282 is, however, an outlier. As an instance of feigned improvisation, it is remarkably earnest, its improvisatory associations used to enhance the dreamlike quality with which the movement both begins and ends rather than to play up irreverent theatricality. In this respect it differs from the first movements of K. 279, K. 311, K. 482, and other simulated improvisations, whose many pratfalls and idiosyncrasies keep them resolutely comic. One reason for this bias toward humor is the simple fact that to warp convention in a highly ordered syntactic system is always to risk clumsiness. Better to play at failure preemptively, through intentionally crafted theatrics, than to risk suggesting it as an accidental by-product of other choices. A second reason is that, as Wye J. Allanbrook has suggested, Mozart's musical vision is fundamentally comic, with the darker reaches of expression featuring only as points of contrast—a stance I develop further in chapter 5.[40] But perhaps the most important reason involves the challenge of communication and dramatic representation. The mere reshuffling of themes may go entirely unnoticed except by the most attentive of listeners, since members of a general public could not be counted on to recall the original order in which melodies were presented. If Mozart hoped to make these structural moves obvious to the widest range of listeners, he had to do so in a way that would not result in too neat a synthesis of the new thematic order. Rather, he would have to fashion the melodic surface in the most ungainly way possible. This idea, of playing simultaneously to multiple audiences with different levels of musical understanding, is one Mozart invoked throughout his correspondence.[41] Although such references were usually aimed at making music comprehensible while also keeping it sophisticated and interesting, his improvisatory dumb shows suggest another side of the same pursuit. Mozart recognizes the needs of both expert and lay listeners, and he seeks to communicate elements of risk to both groups.

Hence the hijinks of K. 279 and K. 311. These sonatas' dramatized failures are effective in part because they are so blatantly overdetermined. In K. 279, the reordering of modules does not occur in formal isolation but involves the addition of various rhythmic and metrical errors by which Mozart extends, compresses, or playfully alters themes so that they jut out of their phrasal slots. The transitional material initially presented in measure 16 is, at first, correctly aligned to the downbeat; however, recapitulatory reordering throws off the gestures, which must be lengthened to fit the meter. The result is, late in the movement, a four-and-a-half-bar phrase of a type that might be found in "Ein musikalischer Spass." In K. 311, likewise, Mozart does not simply omit the first theme in the recapitulation—a formal move by no means unprecedented in earlier keyboard music (including the sonatas of Domenico Scarlatti).[42] Instead, he piles on other surprises: first by leaving out the usual thematic return, then by interpolating an unprepared digression into the parallel minor during the second theme, then by reworking the octave distribution so as to keep listeners guessing about the range and voicing of each subsequent, boisterous melody, and finally by introducing the first theme at the end of the movement just when the expectation of closure is strongest. These missteps add up. Contemporary listeners, whatever their level of know-how, would sense that something was amiss while also marveling at the ingenuity with which the music ultimately comes together.

Caricatures of Incompetence

In K. 279 and K. 311, the implied improviser is not, on the whole, incompetent. The individual modules are more or less well formed, the figuration is sophisticated, the harmonic progressions are sensible, and the melodies pleasing. The pianistic dimension, too, is impressive. Suggestions of improvisatory lapse occur only on the highest level, through issues of structure, memory, and narrative. The fictional improviser's fundamental ability is not in doubt; he is simply having a bad day.

Other cases of simulated improvisation suggest more thoroughgoing pseudofailure on the part of the persona, whose basic competence is called into question. Here, Mozart engages in musical caricature and parody, typified by that exemplary depiction of incompetence (both improvisatory and otherwise), the serenade "Ein musikalischer Spass." Although some of the work's pratfalls depict aspects of incompetent performing (as in the chromatic writing that imitates out of tune horn playing in the second movement and the disastrous chords that close the finale), many of the errors Mozart lampoons are simple, compositional missteps—three-bar phrases, inept modulations, poor voice leading, flat-footed melodies, too-short fugue subjects, and so forth.[43] (Gretchen Wheelock has argued that, for all of the work's humorous dimensions, its purpose seems to have been to poke fun at poor compositional technique rather than poor performance.[44]) Yet some of the errors involve suggestions of improvisation. The most overt instance of simulated improvisatory failure in K. 522 is found in the violin cadenza. The putative improviser seems to possess reasonable intentions for the short improvisation but lacks the basic abilities to realize them. To begin, this is perhaps the most harmonically static cadenza Mozart wrote. Unlike the cadenzas he provided for concertos, which eschew tonal stability in favor of excitement and propulsion, the soloist here sits docilely in C major, doing little more than venturing polite alternations between I and V. Although a single sequence glances briefly toward other keys, the soloist immediately settles back into the tonic. Here, ironically, the simulated failure arises because the soloist does *not* manage to achieve the overt harmonic or modular haphazardness that, elsewhere, would convey an apparent lack of compositional planning. Instead, we hear music whose stability is well suited to nonimprovisatory genres but that falls flat in the context of a cadenza.

Subtler failures, too, occur throughout the serenade, such as the consistent misapplication of embellishment gestures in repeated passages in both fast and slow movements. Mozart often tailored embellishments to the technical affordances of each instrument. Although the musical considerations governing Mozart's embellishments remain largely consistent across all of his output (a point I explore in the next chapter), the specific selection of figures he inserts into his string music often differs from those used in his keyboard concertos, opera arias, or wind music. In "Ein musikalischer Spass," he routinely ignores these conventions. The most glaring misstep occurs in the trio of the minuet, when the violinist attempts a style of elaboration found throughout Mozart's oeuvre only in his writing for solo flute (e.g., in the Flute Concerto K. 313, third movement, mm. 158–61). Although the large leaps and repeated notes are comparatively easy on a wind instrument, they are highly unidiomatic on the violin. Because embellishments are themselves emblematic of an improvisatory act, their misapplication suggests a failure of decorum going beyond the formal humor of K. 279 and K. 311. Here, the soloist has not simply suffered a momentary lapse of memory; rather, it is the basic intention depicted in this improvisation that badly misfires.

Of course not even the wittiest concerto movements can match the flamboyant slapstick of "Ein musikalischer Spass"—and, as a result, its usefulness in casting direct light on dramatized improvisatory failures in Mozart's other music is limited. Even so, some of his compositions contain similar, if subtler, depictions of improvisatory incompetence. These passages tend to highlight expressive or technical incongruities, suggesting an improviser who, when challenged to create music in real time, fails to produce the appropriate kind of gesture. One example featured in my discussion of harmonic techniques associated with improvisation. Near the opening of the Piano Sonata K. 280, Mozart crafts a complex chromatic passage with a series of sliding descents in all four implied voices (shown in ex. 2.17). Previously, I argued that the passage achieves its sophistication by borrowing from the sound world of the fantasia. Heard differently, however, this complex descent becomes a failure of invention. The putative improviser has adopted the goal of producing a grand sonata (suggested by the breadth of the opening chords and the sixteenth-note flourishes) and even succeeds, for a time. But ingenuity soon slows. The initial bustle gives way to stasis in measure 13, with an unchanging triplet pattern that oscillates between the tonic and dominant as if unable to proceed to its next goal. Melodic invention declines further in measure 18, where the player, grasping, adopts a stock improvisatory trope whose extreme chromaticism, so deeply ingrained from the performance of fantasias, becomes a five-bar rut through which the music cannot steer free. In this interpretation, the highly ordered technical underpinning of the passage is almost incidental. What matters is the maladroit intrusion of fantasia chromaticism among the more stately phrases that launch the movement. This failure may not bear obvious resemblance to the absurdities of "Ein musikalischer Spass," but it is, in essence, of the same type. In both, the slip of propriety arises through the fictional improviser's inability to produce the right kind of music at the right time.

When viewed in this light, any number of incongruous juxtapositions take on the flavor of improvisatory failure. In many piano concerto slow movements, for instance, Mozart juxtaposes grace and banality in such a way as to suggest a soloist who, despite showing some melodic ability, is unable to carry the skill through an entire concertante episode.

The opening of the Andante from the Piano Concerto in C minor, K. 491, is one of the most exalted passages in Mozart's output. The hymnlike atmosphere and the delicately balanced shifts between melodic and chorale textures—implied by the soloist and consummated by the orchestration during the first tutti, which alternates between string and wind sections—all contribute to a sense of serene profundity. Yet the solo entrance in measure 9 sits uneasily alongside the previous eight measures. Following the expressive riches of the opening phrase and its orchestral echo, the soloist's reentrance is comparatively plain. The melody, an unadorned ascending scale, that most mundane of building blocks, fails to live up to the movement's lyrical promise. The orchestral accompaniment places no limitation on the figuration the soloist might, in principle, conjure; it is of a piece with the steady, eighth-note accompaniments found beneath the more florid passages in other concertos. Unlike in those concertos, however, here we find no hints of decorative fancy, just a trudging ascent through the scale degrees until a brief hint at the dominant brings us back to the original, graceful theme.

The same occurs in the slow movement of the Concerto in D K. 537, though the irony, such as it is, takes on different colors. Whereas the Andante of K. 491 alternates between searching chorale gestures and march rhythms harnessed within more elegant melodies, the Andante of K. 537 opens with a phrase in which invention is, from the outset, in short supply. The movement's theme unfolds first through four repeated quarter notes on a single pitch. These are neutral in their first appearance, and we wonder what beauties they will yield. But repetitiveness soon gives rise to gentle irritation. The arpeggiated eighth-note gesture that follows becomes a fixation, recurring verbatim eight times in the opening solo. Although this theme, unlike the parallel passage in K. 491, does not build anticipation for an effusive riposte from the pianist, the banality of the subsequent phrase is still jarring. In bar 17, after the orchestra's thematic restatement, the soloist enters with a simple scale, even more straightforward than that of K. 491. When the gesture repeats two bars later, Mozart includes modest embellishments—yet these simply emphasize the drabness of both the original gesture and its slightly elaborated recurrence. We once again witness a seeming lapse of invention. If we feel no immediate comical clash between this lapse and the comparatively wry outlook of the movement as a whole, some tension remains within the scope of the entire concerto, against whose grandeur the terse and ironic slow movement is all the more strange.

Faking an Inability to Improvise Anything at All

The slow movements of K. 491 and K. 537 subtly dramatize failure on the part of a fictional improviser, who cannot quite conjure a melody befitting each movement's expressive world. But how severe is this failure? In the reading I have offered, these movements maintain a delicate balance between, on the one hand, a skillful meditation on simple modules and, on the other, an inability to move beyond those modules, suggestive of a lapse of invention itself. This possibility brings us to the final, and most extreme, category of dramatized improvisatory risk. If the theatrical signaling of improvisation relies on the pretense of feigned ineptitude, then its most vivid manifestation must be a seeming inability to produce music altogether.

Here, as before, simulated failures of this type often occur in solo or concertante music, since the theatrical fiction of improvisation is most believable in compositions for an individual performer. Mozart's piano concertos serve once again as the vehicle in which these dramas play out, with the Concerto in C K. 503, constituting a vivid example. The orchestral opening of K. 503

is not only among the longest ritornellos in Mozart's output; it is perhaps the most brilliantly complex. It represents an apogee of Mozart's virtuosic use of variation devices, with a small selection of themes subjected repeatedly to an array of transformations and expansions all meant to highlight the composer's inventive panache.[45] The concerto exudes monumentality: from the grandeur of the orchestration (complete not only with the full complement of winds but with trumpets and drums) to the learned counterpoint and brooding digressions into the minor, Mozart uses every means to emphasize breadth and power. This is partly an end in itself for a composition of such scope—but it also serves a rhetorical purpose, helping to build excitement for the impending solo entrance. To some extent, anticipation is a feature of any concerto. As Charles Rosen remarked, "the most important fact about the concerto form is that the audience waits for the soloist to enter, and when he stops playing they wait for him to begin again."[46] But the inventive profligacy of this ninety-bar ritornello in particular primes listeners to expect nothing less than vaunted mastery when the soloist finally begins.

It comes as a surprise when the ritornello ends but the soloist remains silent. As we saw in chapter 2, it became Mozart's practice to end his grandest ritornellos with a new, quiet transition, so as to minimize the sonic disparity between orchestra and piano. However, whereas concertos such as K. 413, K. 450, and K. 467 solve this problem by quietly eliding the ritornello with the soloist's entrance, the K. 503 ritornello simply grinds to a halt after its final cadence. The pianist declines to pick up the thread. As if to cover for this unexpected absence, the orchestra sets up a simple V–I vamp, swinging back and forth between the two polar harmonies. The soloist appears at last—but immediately seems to get tangled in the harmonic vortex, proffering only hesitating elaborations of the underlying progression, as if experiencing a memory lapse and stalling for time (ex. 3.4). After six iterations of the V–I pattern, the soloist finally pulls free, and a more independent scalar melody ensues. But this, too, fails to get off the ground, and the soloist is left with no recourse but to repeat the gesture, this time piling on embellishments. As in K. 537, these embellishments do not propel the music forward. On the contrary, they ironically emphasize the awkwardness of the stasis. The pianist is spinning his wheels, trying to invent a way out but remaining stuck in place.[47] An escape does eventually present itself, but the reprieve is temporary: every phrase ventured in the soloist's opening proves abortive, with melodies that either evaporate into the upper reaches of the keyboard or lapse into deceptive cadences, prompting repetitions that seem almost an attempt at

Example 3.4 Piano Concerto K. 503, first movement, mm. 91–99

extemporized revision. It is not unusual in Mozart's concertos for the soloist to enter with a brief, improvised lead-in, and K. 503 evokes a soloist who fails to meet this challenge—who is either unwilling or unable to improvise out of a tight spot.[48]

In this example, Mozart does not simply suggest a failed improvisation. He also creates a brilliant and well calculated performative effect. Few events are as terrifying for performer and audience alike as a concerto soloist who flubs the first entrance. The signaling of improvisation always depends on the creation of a theatrical fiction that suggests a degree of lapse, and this opening dramatizes its most extreme form. Having already used the ritornello to show off his compositional ingenuity, Mozart ventriloquizes through the solo line to give his listeners the musical analog of a thrill ride.[49]

From Playing Dumb to Playing Chicken: Mozart's Retransitions

It goes without saying that the thrill rides Mozart creates through simulated improvisatory failures are effective only because they are fictional. A concerto soloist truly unable to improvise a lead-in makes for neither an amusing nor a pleasurable concertgoing experience. Thus, any enjoyment listeners derive from these moments of suspense depends as much on the soloist's speedy recovery as on the effectiveness of the ruse itself. In the passages from K. 491, K. 503, and K. 537 described above, it is clear that Mozart has not actually run out of ideas. We temporarily accept the fiction because, on some level, we know it to be false. And in all of these cases, our willingness to wait out the simulated lapse is rewarded. The soloist in K. 503 arrives at the edge of a breakdown but then rescues the situation, and the concerto proceeds not only without further incident but with some of the most expert musical and pianistic displays in Mozart's output. The slow movements of K. 491 and K. 537, too, go on to present ravishing passages of precisely the kind we are momentarily denied.

Perhaps Mozart began to explore dramatized lapses of invention as a way to approximate the excitement and inherent riskiness of improvisation. In the process, however, he would certainly have discovered that simulated precarity was so effective in its theatrical potential that it could be used in other contexts as well. This applies as much to his compositional persona as it does to the figure he hoped to cut on the concert stage. Even when viewed in abstract remove from their performance manifestations, much of Mozart's music still participates in the aesthetics of lapse and recovery—for instance, by moving through a succession of phrases and topics so irregular that they seem to have been thrown together gesture by gesture with little attention to form or integration. In such cases the act of composition itself takes on the quality of an improvisatory display, the finished music exuding a freedom whose challenges, stakes, and rewards are heightened by the theatrical situations Mozart evokes.

Just as Mozart's notated improvisations often drew on techniques used by actual performers when they played extemporaneously, so, too, could compositions be fashioned using methods that would prevent the application of significant structural planning or forethought. In the eighteenth century, randomizers such as dice games and spinning tops were a popular way for people with all levels of experience to generate music, and the resulting compositions could range in length from short minuets to entire sonatas.[50] Although the relevant attributions are unclear, Mozart is even thought to have invented at least one algorithmic, minuet-generating dice game himself, in May 1787 (K. 516f).[51] Yet as was the case with improvised performances, the method by which a composition is created is a separate matter from the composition's style. The expressive and rhetorical qualities associated with randomized or improvisatory processes were also available in carefully planned music to create a vivid air of spontaneity. Here, as before, the dramatized risk of failure provides the surest point of entry for a composer wishing to pursue this goal.

A composer simulating failure on the level of a composition as a whole does not face a fundamentally different aesthetic task from one simulating the momentary failure of a concerto soloist. In both, the excitement of the apparent near breakdown must balance the ultimate need for compositional integration and satisfaction on the part of listeners. The two acts diverge on a technical level in the question of which parameters to involve in the apparent failure. In the concertante music described above, Mozart focuses on the solo line, limiting himself to those passages with minimal orchestral involvement. When the purported failure occurs on the level of the entire work, however, its implications must transcend individual instrumental parts, instead implicating the entire musical image. It is the composer's own coherence and planning that must be cast in doubt.

Retransitions are the ideal context in which to explore this interpretive inquiry because they are inherently goal oriented and time sensitive. They signal to an experienced listener the music's immanent arrival at the recapitulation, and they do so with a rhetorical urgency unmatched by most other formal archetypes. As we have seen, the modulatory techniques underpinning Mozart's fantasias, cadenzas, and other improvisatory music derive their utility partly from their malleability. They may be applied in any number of contexts and at nearly any length. The retransition, by contrast, is less flexible. The length of Mozart's retransitions is often delimited by processes set in motion at the very beginning of the move toward the recapitulation—and this means that the ultimate moment of arrival is strongly implied in advance. Many of Mozart's retransitions begin, for instance, with circle-of-fifths progressions or other sequential patterns that dictate the point at which the recapitulation will occur. The strength of these sequences is such that even when he breaks the surface-level patterns during the course of the retransition, he places the recapitulation precisely where it would be had the pattern continued. In the first movement of the Wind Serenade in C minor, K. 388, for instance, a circle of fifths begins in measure 115, and although the process ruptures at 122, the tonic still arrives at 130—just as if the circle of fifths had proceeded as originally implied.[52] The consistency with which Mozart adheres to these strictures of implication, process, timing, and arrival, especially in compositions dating from after 1782, suggests his sensitivity to the rhetorical import of this formal function.

This would have made the retransition the ideal context in which to both tempt and confound listeners' expectations. In many cases, Mozart does this using techniques similar to those associated with his simulated improvisatory failures. If Mozart "plays dumb" in the first movement of the Piano Concerto K. 503, he uses the retransition of the second movement as an opportunity to revisit such theatrics (ex. 3.5). After a formal cadence in the dominant (m. 59), Mozart begins a retransition that resembles, in both its sound world and its rhythmic progress, retransitions from other concerto slow movements.[53] Although he has within three bars laid the groundwork for a successful return to the movement's tonic, he declines to resolve the progression, instead turning to an unexpected dominant pedal and prolonging it for a further eleven bars. Perhaps the most remarkable feature of this passage is its brazen lack of developmental logic. Mozart presents a series of disconnected riffs on the dominant—first, stately arpeggios in the bass beneath sustained notes in the treble, then a canon between piano and winds, and finally a series of flashy arpeggios from the pianist. At any moment, the music could easily return to F major. Yet he repeatedly denies the decisive cadence, and the composite effect is one of teasing. Such lengthy prolongations sit uneasily alongside the teleologic nature of the retransition, whose function, at least in typical cases, is to push forward to the recapitulation rather than to delay its onset. Here, it seems that Mozart is not so much "playing dumb" as "playing chicken," putting off the anticipated arrival until the last possible moment.[54] With each passing bar his taunting takes on a higher pitch of intensity as we wonder when the long-awaited tonic will materialize.

The retransition from the slow movement of K. 503 strikes a delicate affective balance. On the one hand, the passage's length is incongruous, as is its subtle thumbing of the nose at listeners who expect an easy return to F major. On the other hand, these qualities are offset by the sheer pleasure that attends the virtuosic, figural play in the solo part. Decorative invention is at its absolute maximum, and listeners oblivious to the passage's length or rhetorical implications may simply revel in the sonic glitter that shimmers through these eleven bars. In most other retransitions, however, Mozart's propensity for playing chicken meant eschewing the inventive lyricism of K. 503 and instead feigning the same clumsiness that we found in more straightforward simu-

Example 3.5 Piano Concerto K. 503, second movement, mm. 59–74

lated improvisations. When formal and contextual clues make it clear that a recapitulation is approaching, Mozart often apes an inability to effect the requisite modulations. In the first movement of the Piano Sonata K. 332 (ex. 3.6), the development reaches its point of crisis on an A-major chord, which Mozart sustains for four bars, long enough to slow the harmonic pace of the previous fantasia-like section and sever the chord rhetorically if not functionally from its role as dominant of D minor. This winding down heralds the

Example 3.6 Piano Sonata K. 332, first movement, mm. 123–32

impending recapitulation. The musical flow seems to stop, as if the composer-improviser's persona is spent from the modulatory exertions of the previous 14 bars. What follows is, in one sense, a straightforward move back to F major using the sliding half-step technique discussed in the previous chapter—a progression from vi to I so endemic that Hepokoski and Darcy refer to it as a "default" for retransitions of the time, one also enacted in Mozart's two other F-major piano sonatas (K. 280 and K. 533).[55] Yet although the harmonies underlying this progression were among Mozart's standard operating procedures for F-major retransitions, the particulars of K. 332 help set this passage off from its cousins. The comedic substance of K. 332's retransition arises in part from the caesuras that follow each tentative harmonic step. Even using a much-tested modulatory technique, the composer-improviser seems uncertain how to proceed, and must therefore try the chords, pausing afterward to reflect as well as to devise the next tactic. The dynamics, too, exaggerate this effect: the move through A minor hangs in the air like an unanswered question, after which the sudden *forte* arrival on the correct dominant is a jolting, heaved exhalation. So theatrically effective is this passage that its guise of hesitancy masks a subtle, organizational logic. We realize only in hindsight that E—the leading tone of F major—has featured prominently all along, and that the entire progression was premeditated from the start.[56] We hear, all at once, the fictional improviser's affectedly naive self-satisfaction at having brought off the needed modulation as well as Mozart's own jibe at listeners taken in by the ploy.

We can find similar plots in countless other retransitions throughout Mozart's oeuvre. Rondo movements often feature inventive retransitions or retransition-like passages, perhaps to offset the high risk of predictability posed by the repetitive nature of the form and attendant familiarity of the theme. In the rondo-finale of the Flute Quartet in D, K. 285, a return that occurs midway through the movement is beset by humorous digressions and elongations (mm. 133–60). The preceding episode, in G, ends with a relatively straightforward move back into D, the global tonic. We hear, first, a familiar secondary motif from the rondo theme, and by measure 136 Mozart has reintroduced C♯. The destination is clear—yet this attempt to modulate is undermined by an "inadvertent" arrival in the minor. Mozart initiates a dominant pedal—a standard element of his retransitions—above which the minor tonic chord alternates with a diminished seventh. This goes on for four bars, after which a listener might reasonably expect a quick shift to the major and the reappearance of the theme. Instead, he lingers, reasserting D minor with a decisive augmented sixth chord. At this point, it is difficult to predict the next move. Is the episode still underway, with more development to come? Or is this simply an implausibly long extension of the transition from episode to rondo theme, a slapstick version of the process played out in the slow movement of K. 503? The question is soon resolved—or so we think. After the augmented sixth, the upper voices manage a return to the major, initiating a sixteenth-note passage that seems first to gather momentum before slowing into another series of static dominant chords, delaying arrival yet again. The promise of propulsion wanes; sixteenth notes become eighth notes, and the fleet diatonic scales give way to a labored chromatic ascent that slows progress even further. It is only then that the rondo theme sidles in—quietly, without ceremony, perhaps as one final dig at our exhausted expectations.

On a technical level, there is nothing untoward about this passage: no incorrect chords, no ungrammatical progressions, and certainly no pratfalls that suggest an incompetence such as we find in "Ein musikalischer Spass." Yet the music is carefully calibrated so as to toy with listeners' desires in every way possible, from the placement of significant developmental material *after* the arrival of the dominant pedal to the cheeky rhetorical resistance we meet as the section unfolds. The fact that the flute and violin try to wriggle free of the expected harmonic progression and that the ultimate arrival is prepared by an extended chromatic scale, which might leave listeners in the dark as to where the center of tonal gravitation actually lies, suggest both a sensitivity to listeners' expectations and a confident ability to play against them. It is significant that the way in which Mozart accomplishes this is of a piece with the other examples discussed in this chapter. He shows off by presenting the threat of spectacular failure, in this case by feigning an inability to move the music into the correct harmonic areas, and then pretends, just when hope of recovery vanishes, to invent a dazzling way out. By dramatizing the process of failure and delaying the moment of recovery as long as possible, he flaunts his powers of "improvisatory" invention even within the world of premeditated composition. Mozart displays these skills by pretending, for one carefully calculated passage, that they have betrayed him.

Such techniques retain their potency outside of retransitions. Although it is comparatively rare to find phrases that follow such firmly established constraints of timing and arrival, examples do exist. One of these is a decisive, formal cadence that occurs at the end of both the expositions and recapitulations in the first movements of Mozart's concertos and is heralded by an accumulation of sixteenth-note passagework for the soloist, all capped by a measure-long trill. In these cases, the underlying logic is the same as that of the retransition: conventional clues alert listeners to the impending arrival, and Mozart capitalizes on them by either confirming or flouting the resulting expectations. Most often, he yields to expectation, since too-frequent violation of norms might prove frustrating rather than satisfying. But occasionally he toys with these moments of arrival as well. In the first movement of the Piano Concerto K. 467, we reach the culminating passage at the end of the recapitulation, but Mozart does not proceed to the expected trill (ex. 3.7). Instead, he prolongs the cadential six-four, bar after bar. To be sure, this chord is usually longer than the ensuing V, yet in general the relative disparity of length brings no uncertainty as to the ultimate point of arrival since the melody usually launches toward the trill, either through a bold scale (his most common formula) or through ascending arpeggiation of the kind heard in the exposition of this movement. Here, however, the gesture that should by all stylistic rights culminate in the trill does not do so but leads instead to yet another bar of six-four, followed by yet another. The melodic shape varies each time, and any could plausibly give way to the trill—but instead, Mozart goads listeners, delaying the cadence as long as possible.

Owing to the presence of the orchestra, this passage gives rise to little improvisatory fiction. We recognize that Mozart is playing chicken, but we also know his antics to be planned.[57] The solo keyboard music, however, suffers no limitations of theatricality. In the final phrases of the Sonata in C minor, K. 457—a composition closely entangled with the contexts and occasions

Example 3.7 Piano Concerto K. 467, first movement, mm. 378–84

of improvisation through its pairing with the Fantasia K. 475—the pianist seems to get lost in a similar precadential digression. The closing theme of the recapitulation, familiar from the exposition, signals that the end is in sight. Yet instead of moving through the necessary cadential steps, the pianist slips through a series of liminal chords—first briefly glancing toward the subdominant, then getting lost in farther-flung harmonies. Even when the left hand (crossed over into the treble) strikes C and E♭, the notes needed to form a cadential six-four, the right resists the tonic's attraction, instead turning to a series of evasive chromatic steps before, finally, drawing to a cadence. The passage dramatizes a compositional and performative failure, this time going beyond the abstract issue of structure and expectation. It encompasses not only the usual risks but caricatures a pianistic failing as well. Mozart plays up the disorientations of hand crossing, which reverses tactile intuitions about the relationship between fingers and keyboard topography and can plausibly result in unexpected wrong turns by a player insufficiently versed in the technique. The passage synthesizes feigned confusion on every available level: through the implication of improvisatory distraction, compositional incompetence, and even pianistic clumsiness—all bound together in a moment of display that remains propulsive and engaging.

This example brings us full circle, from the improvisatory risks dramatized in Mozart's compositions to the careful choreographing of keyboard techniques that underpins so much of his written music. We find ourselves once again viewing a sonata and seeking, behind the notes, a residue of the direct interaction between tactile pianism and compositional ideals. But we have also moved significantly beyond the mode of explanation adopted in chapter 2. There I argued that Mozart's compositions crystalized out of performative techniques and experiences. It is now becoming clear that Mozart's compositional voice is itself a species of performative persona, one that would have emerged through the theatrical imagination, shaping the notes and structures so as to capture the maximum excitement and volatility available within written music. Mozart's decades of practical experience—of piano technique, of modulatory protocols, and of stage performing—constitute an important part of his arsenal, yet they are not in themselves sufficient to account for the dramas that course through the music I have explored in this chapter. Mozart does not simply draw from past experience; he also envisions and evokes fictional performances, and in so doing brings the risks and rewards of performance into the ambit of compositional control. Such a view recasts the relationship between composer and performer, but it also expands to include imaginative triangulation with the audience as well. The listeners for whom Mozart writes are not only those actual, living consumers whom he hoped to please when playing his compositions or preparing texts for publication. Instead, his audiences, too, become a fictional construct whose desires, beliefs, and expectations are projected in the mind's ear of the composer-performer. The theatricality and thrills evoked by Mozart's simulated failures, implausible delays, and recapitulatory fake-outs reflect his carefully honed conception of these fictional listeners. They provide the model alongside which his compositional craft evolved.

This chapter has outlined one facet of the performative, theatrical Mozart, the subject of this book. In the next, I examine Mozart's notated embellishments, a melodic device that sits at the intersection between composition and imagined performance. I have already briefly discussed the musical function of embellishment in the context of "Ein musikalischer Spass" and in the dramatized lapse from the first movement of the Piano Concerto K. 503. However, as I will now argue, embellishments are implicated in other performative effects as well, from the showmanship of Mozart's concerto soloists to the psychology and desires of his operatic characters.

VARIATION 4

Mozart the Decorator

The picture of Mozart I developed in the previous two chapters is that of an inveterate showman. Whether through the inclusion of virtuosic passagework in his concertos or the carefully conceived hijinks that beset his written-out improvisations, Mozart constantly sought ways to imbue his music with a theatrical flair that would capture the spontaneity, risks, and, ultimately, the excitement of actual improvised performances. As we have seen, one strategy he adopted in pursuing this goal involved the use of fictionalized lapses. By feigning risk and distraction, he could send a pointed, rhetorical message to listeners while showing off his compositional mastery.

Contemporary culture provided another option for melding improvisation and composition: performers could incorporate actual improvisation into a written piece of music. It was standard practice for composers of the time to leave significant portions of their music in a seminotated state with the expectation that performers would flesh them out spontaneously through the addition of improvised embellishments. Mozart actively participated in this practice as evidenced both by his creation of model embellishments for students and colleagues who were unable to invent their own and by the sketchy notational state of the compositions he penned for his own performances. In the eighteenth century, musical texts were not fixed entities codified in advance and studied slavishly by those who played them; rather, texts served as starting points for spirited public showings. When the situation demanded—and it often did—performers would depart from the written score, making elaborate interventions into the contours and affective style of melodies.

These interventions, whether improvised or premeditated, bring composition and performance into closer alignment than any of the individual subjects I tackle in this book. Embellishment was the prerogative of improvising performers, yet it was also an act through which such a performer could become a revisionary composer, inserting notes and reshaping melodies, and in the process lending each phrase a new rhetorical thrust, a new expressive scope, and perhaps a new meaning. When truly improvised, these revisionary impulses would arise through a tactile intuition delicately balanced against an intellectual understanding of stylistic grammar. However, the close alignment between composition and performance persists even when the interventions are planned in advance. In such cases the embellishing performer takes on a more careful compositional presence; or, alternatively, an embellishing composer steps briefly into the role of the improvising performer, projecting a vision of what will unfold on stage.

As a focus of modern-day inquiry, Mozartian embellishment has most thoroughly been considered in the practical context of the early music movement. Many proponents of historical performance examine Mozart's embellishments in order to revive the practice of florid, improvised decoration in their own readings of this repertoire.[1] Others, meanwhile—some of whom have called into question the basic value of such "reconstructionist" pursuits—have focused not so much on the musical content of Mozart's embellishments as on the ethical issue of whether modern-day performers should depart from Mozart's texts.[2] These skeptics have speculated that advances in knowledge of Mozart's embellishment habits might give rise to a moralizing prescriptivism that would unduly limit the freedom of modern-day interpreters, fearing that if we know how Mozart embellished, we will dismiss those who choose not to adopt his style.[3] Such questions slot neatly alongside broader philosophical problems raised by the very notion of historical performance concerning the nature of composerly intention, the relevance of historical practices to modern-day aesthetic inquiry, and the responsibility of living performers to dead composers.

Over the past two decades these debates have subsided, leaving behind a widespread view that we should settle matters of performance and embellishment primarily through recourse to historical practices—that is, by heeding the artistic priorities of the composer's lifetime (or some approximation of those priorities) rather than those intuitively favored by modern-day performers and listeners. Often, this assumption is warranted: many questions about embellishment do indeed reduce to issues of history. For instance, Mozart's expectations concerning the abilities of the performers for whom he wrote demonstrably shaped his notational practices. Understanding this helps us know whether to view a given text as being highly prescriptive—and by extension, to know whether we, like the intended recipient, should adhere to it studiously. We have already seen that Mozart dabbled in musical portraiture, attempting to enshrine the personalities of friends and students in his compositions. As discussed in chapter 1, the most celebrated instance of this is the Andante from the Piano Sonata K. 309, which depicts Mozart's pupil Rosa Cannabich. This movement does not only include a high density of expressive indications such as dynamics and articulation marks but also a rich layer of prescribed embellishments, all intended to help the young Rosa develop an understanding of nuanced performance. Mozart adopted similarly thick notation in published pieces such as the Piano Sonatas K. 284, K. 332, and K. 457, all of which contain extensive, written-out embellishments meant to aid the broad base of consumers who would purchase the scores.[4] Meanwhile, the music Mozart wrote for his own use gives a very different picture of notational specificity. He leaves significant solo passages in mature concertos such as K. 482, K. 491, and K. 537 largely unnotated, implying but not delineating accompaniment figuration, virtuosic passagework, and even some melodic shapes. In all of these examples, our basic ability to make sense of these texts depends on an understanding of Mozart's priorities and the conventions in place during his lifetime.

Yet if the historical perspective is essential for understanding aspects of Mozartian embellishment, it also leaves crucial questions unanswered. It is one thing to point out that he used varying levels of notational specificity when writing for different musicians; yet this in itself does not settle the problem of how to interpret his texts. Notational specificity is often a matter of perspective. The autograph manuscripts of K. 284 and K. 332 (which lack the written-out embellishments added in the published editions) are not self-evidently "empty." Had Mozart not prepared versions for publication, we might never have come to believe that these sonatas' melodies require further elaboration. A comparison of the unembellished autographs and the final publications shows that Mozart applies embellishments even in passages that, originally, were already highly ornate and that therefore do not call out for additions. If we hope to discern his stylistic rudiments, and especially if we hope to intelligently imitate them, we must supplement pure historicism with more pointed attempts at analysis and, especially, explanation.

There are other reasons, too, that the insights gleaned from a historical study of Mozart's embellishments might fall short of those afforded by analysis. The most pressing is simply that what Mozart expected performers to do is not necessarily what he might have wished they would do—or indeed, what we might today deem appropriate based on the detailed understanding of Mozart's style we have attained over the past two centuries. Although critics of historical performance often rehearse this argument to debunk what they see as a hype for period instruments and antiquated playing styles ("time-travel nostalgia," in one of Richard Taruskin's biting polemics),[5] it can also be cast in a positive light, asserting that although embellishments are necessary additions to Mozart's music, the most appropriate way to deploy them may not be through a simplistic pursuit of practices in use during his lifetime. Judging by the many idiosyncratic decorations penned by eighteenth-century soloists, it seems that Mozart's contemporaries paid little heed to the compositional vocabulary of the pieces they embellished. In many cases, then, the adoption of an embellishment idiom aligned with the style and aesthetic of Mozart's music may be categorically incompatible with a reconstruction of any actual embellishment practices that he witnessed. The model embellishments he penned may represent not only his attempt to cater to the needs of less skilled collaborators but to limit musicians' freedom in deviating from his written texts and from the essence of his language.[6]

In this chapter I examine the aesthetic priorities encoded in Mozart's notated embellishments—and, from there, suggest ways in which those priorities align both with his broader interests as an improvising performer and his compositional vision on the whole. It is through the act of embellishment that the many facets of Mozart's career interacted most productively, and it is therefore in the context of embellishment that we encounter in clearest focus the expressive, rhetorical, and performative dimensions of his craft.

Mozart's Model Embellishments

The usual starting point for investigations of Mozartian embellishment is the set of models he created between approximately 1773 and 1785. These include decorated variants of three contemporary arias (two of his own and one by Johann Christian Bach); insertions for the Piano Concerto K. 451 (ex. 4.1; composed for Nannerl) and the Piano Sonata K. 457 (for his pupil Therese von Trattner), both of which survive in manuscript; published variants for the Piano Sonatas K. 284 and K. 332; and, possibly, handwritten embellishments for an as yet unidentified Adagio in F major. With the possible exception

Example 4.1 Mozart's model embellishments for Piano Concerto K. 451, second movement, mm. 56–62

of this last specimen, whose origins remain mysterious, and the published variants, whose pedagogical status remains unclear, Mozart intended these models to aid performers who lacked the skills to improvise decorations of their own.[7]

The literature on embellishment accords these models significant weight, yet their textual histories, particularly those of the keyboard models, suggests that they offer a less reliable picture of Mozart's practices than is often assumed. One problem involves the provenance and date of the sources. Although the keyboard music that formed the basis for these models spans nearly a decade, dating between 1775 and 1784, all of the embellished variants originated in 1784–85.[8] They therefore offer a snapshot of Mozart's style at a single moment in his development but say little about long-term trends. Mozart's earlier embellishments, for voice, would seem to balance the documentary record, but these introduce complications of their own, particularly considering the many conventions governing the setting of Italian prosody. (Whether these conventions influenced Mozart's instrumental style is not clear, especially considering the difficulty of establishing just what "the singing style" might entail in the context of instrumental composition.[9]) A further problem is that all of these models decorate only slow movements and are therefore of uncertain relevance to movements in other tempos. Finally, the instrumental models generally apply only to isolated portions of movements—a mere seven bars in the case of K. 451. The decorations he provided for K. 457 sidestep this problem somewhat, since they demonstrate progressive elaborations that become more complex with each recurrence of the theme. Yet even these amount to little more than twenty bars of material applied to only one of the movement's many melodies. If they shed some light on the types of free variation performers might conjure within a recurring theme, they say little about Mozart's expectations for other passages in the movement, or indeed for pieces in other tempos, forms, or genres.

The musical content of these models, too, is enigmatic. On the one hand, they suggest something of the extravagance with which Mozart expected performers to depart from his texts. In the embellishments for K. 451, the departures reshape the melody, altering the intervallic span of leaps and obscuring the original material beneath added scales and arpeggios (even while preserving sol–fa–mi schema underpinning the melody and embellishments).[10] On the other hand, this decorative freedom makes it difficult to identify consistent relationships between the embellishments and the tune they adorn—and this in turn complicates the process of extrapolating stylistic protocols from the passage. In some cases, the K. 451 embellishments conform to the shape and scope of the original, departing only modestly. This is true, at least, for the first two bars. Yet beginning the following bar, Mozart's departures become more daring. What originated as a leap of a sixth is embellished as an ascending octave, overshooting the notated melody before returning to dovetail with the phrase's original shape. In the next ascent, he converts an arpeggio into a decorated scale whose sixteenth notes mask the drawn-out syncopation of the original. The embellishments then briefly track the melody again before diverging further when a simple descending third is replaced by an extravagant upward leap. Though this seven-bar model has often been touted as an important piece of evidence in understanding Mozart's improvisatory practices, its significance may lie more in the general sense of creativity and imagination its decorations evince than in any specific aspect of their content.[11]

As for the embellishments included in the first editions of the Piano Sonatas K. 284 and K. 332, it is not certain whether these constitute pedagogical models in the same respect as K. 451 and K. 457, or whether they represent self-contained compositional variants. Whereas Nannerl, or the pupils and colleagues who worked directly with Mozart, would have had the luxury of comparing the embellished variants to the sparse notations in the original texts and may therefore have been able to analyze the relationship between original melody and embellished version, those members of the public who purchased editions of K. 284 and K. 332 would have enjoyed no such convenience. From the perspective of contemporary consumers, the decorated variants would seem by default the only version of the text. It is therefore doubtful that in composing them Mozart's aspirations could have been fully pedagogical. By 1784 Mozart was poised to see numerous compositions in print, and the communicative acumen that informed his public concerts would certainly have extended to his published editions as well.[12] If he intended the embellishments in the first editions of K. 284 and K. 332 in part to guide the performances of those who bought and played these pieces, he probably also wished to show off his composerly ingenuity, and he may therefore have prepared the embellishments using criteria other than performative instruction.

Sources in which we can more reliably glimpse Mozart's preferences for embellishment include the many slow movements and rondos in which he introduces progressive elaborations during repeated themes. Examples include the slow movements of the Piano Sonata K. 309, the "Dissonance" String Quartet, K. 465, and the Violin Sonata K. 481, as well as standalone rondos K. 494 (later repurposed and expanded as the finale of the Piano Sonata K. 533) and K. 511. It is not clear whether Mozart considered these embellishments as fulfilling the same pedagogical function as his more explicit models; but whatever his intentions, such pieces do hold pedagogical import far exceeding that of the published variants. By presenting the unembellished theme at the outset and then moving through a series of decorated versions, Mozart makes it easy to compare and analyze the different iterations of each melody.

Mozart's oeuvre contains countless other compositions, too, whose repeated themes undergo elaboration—not within the formal plan of a rondo, but simply during the routine unfolding of musical argument. Although Mozart does not mark off these from the surrounding material, they follow the same contextual logic as the models. By introducing melodic variation into already familiar tunes, they play out precisely the act undertaken by embellishing performers: namely, adding notes to phrases that have already been codified and notated in advance. Such instances of melodic variation occur in all possible contexts in Mozart's output, most often in solo keyboard music but also in genres that include no simulation of performed embellishment (e.g., in symphonic phrases played by an entire violin section). These decorations suggest some of the criteria Mozart would have used in the course of notating and improvising his embellishments.

Example 4.2 *a*, Variations K. 264, variation 8, mm. 1–3 and 9–11. *b*, Piano Sonata K. 330, first movement, mm. 1–10

Broadly speaking, such embellishments occur in two contexts: either across large-scale formal repetitions (including the return of a rondo theme or, more often, when a melody introduced during an exposition receives variation during the recapitulation) or on a more local level (when themes or thematic cells recur in juxtaposed phrases or periods). Both types of embellishment can be found in pieces of all genres and over the entire course of Mozart's career, from his earliest minuets through his late operas. These local embellishments demonstrate the full range of his art as a decorator, from the elaborate figuration nested within the Adagio from the Piano Variations K. 264 to the more modest interventions peppered throughout the first movement of the Piano Sonata K. 330 (ex. 4.2).

All of Mozart's notated embellishments—those composed into his models as well as those distributed throughout his other compositions—provide a highly consistent picture of his practices. Even so, it is clear that the formal context in which each figure occurs has some bearing on its rhetorical function. Embellishments are, ultimately, vehicles for the display of virtuosity either by a soloist, whose elaborate interventions show off both technical prowess and improvisatory wit, or by a composer, who demonstrates an inventive capacity to coax melodic riches out of even the simplest tunes. For either a performer or a composer to show off by embellishing, however, listeners must be able to recognize the decorations as being added.[13] This in turn means that Mozart's expectations concerning his audiences' sophistication would most likely have played a role in the crafting of embellishments. During thematic returns in rondos, listeners even casually familiar with contemporary norms would probably be aware when Mozart had reintroduced a familiar theme; however, it is unlikely that on a first hearing they would reliably recall the theme's precise contours. As a result, the embellishments added in rondos would need to compensate by advertising their presence through density and extravagance. Conversely, when embellishments occur in closely juxtaposed phrases, the increase in melodic complexity would be more readily apparent, and the embellishments could explore subtler thematic alterations. In the first movement of the Sonata K. 330, varied repetitions of individual modules are so frequent and occur in such close succession that, although the added figures themselves are slight, the cumulative effect is one of a constantly shifting musical foreground in which each idea is barely presented before it begins to transform. (Perhaps it was as a result of this mutability that the nineteenth-century music theorist A. B. Marx likened Mozart to a butterfly flitting ecstatically from one flowerlike melodic idea to the next.[14]) The same is true even in themes Mozart presents at slightly further remove, so long as they remain plausibly within the range of casual memory. In the first movement of the Sonata K. 332, Mozart gives nearly every melody from the exposition in a simpler form before restating them in more ornate versions.

That Mozart was aware of the potency of these juxtaposed variants is clear from the fact that he developed them at the earliest stages of compositional planning. From a modern-day perspective, this may seem counterintuitive. Because embellishments are associated with performance and improvisation, it is tempting to think of them as being afterthoughts in the creative process, established only once the structural aspects of a passage had been concocted. Yet the presence of embellishments throughout Mozart's surviving drafts, sketches, and fragments reveals that he weighed the implications of melodic decoration at the same time that he shaped other elements of his compositions. Local embellishments are present in many of the drafts that Mozart left unfinished, including the divertimento fragment K. 288; the violin sonata movements K. 372, K. 403, and K. 404; the string quintet movement K. 514a; and an insertion aria for soprano, K. 580. Some fragments consist of only two or three partly notated phrases, yet even the most abortive efforts often contain elaborate embellishments. Mozart also included embellishments in many discarded sketches for pieces he did eventually finish, such as false starts for movements within various piano concertos as well as in drafted versions of opera arias. It seems that embellishments formed an important element in his initial conception of each melody even before it was clear just how—or indeed whether—those melodies would fit in a finished composition.[15]

Because a fragment represents only a segment of a movement, Mozart's sketches rarely allow the comparison of embellishments across large-scale formal sections. Even the unfinished sonata movement K. 400, one of his longest, includes only an exposition and development, trailing off just as the recapitulation begins, at the very moment when we might hope to set later melodies alongside their earlier appearances. But Mozart's fragments do contain a large number of embellishments within juxtaposed phrases. In a discarded sketch for the first solo in the Piano Concerto K. 503, one phrase is repeated with elaborate chromatic divisions, sighing appoggiaturas, expressive leaps, repeated notes, and syncopations. Mozart ultimately removed this melody, along with its decorations, perhaps to accommodate the dramatized memory lapse discussed in the previous chapter (whose effect depends on a more timid entrance from the soloist). Another sketch, whose work of origin is unclear but which resembles passages from the Piano Concerto K. 537, contains a straightforward diatonic melody that, when repeated, is embellished with elaborate divisions.[16]

Generally, the notational style of these fragments with embellishments is no different from the notational style of Mozart's other fragments or indeed from the notational style of those sketches that grew into finished compositions. In all cases Mozart followed the same practice, producing a *particella*—a rendering of the melodic line, along with a partial bass line and sparse, if any, inner-voice writing. He adopted this method to maximize the speed at which he could record ideas and ensure that, should a new, lucrative commission arise, he could stop work on a draft without losing his place in the piece's development. Hence, in many drafts—and, by extension, in many finished compositions as well—he committed embellishments to paper before settling details of accompaniment, texture, voice distribution, and form. Nonetheless, changes to the embellishments would still often occur later in the compositional process. In the Concerto K. 503, although the final version removes the drafted melody and embellishments, it also introduces the embellishments discussed in chapter 3. Elsewhere, Mozart did not only add embellishments as a piece evolved but revised them as well, as in the variants written for the slow movement of the Sonata K. 457, which underwent extensive reordering between the stages of drafting.[17] In general, this meant that embellishments originally placed early in the movement were subsequently relegated to later phrases: for instance, Mozart moved a turn-and-appoggiatura figure from bar 22 to bar 46. Such changes resulted in a slower unfolding of the embellishment figures and suggest that he tried consciously to control the pacing of melodic rhetoric—specifically, to avoid generating too much expressive activity too soon. Perhaps his first sweep through a movement reflected spur-of-the-moment performative thinking, after which he would return and redistribute the embellishments so as to suggest a more considered structure.

A Musical Profile of Mozart's Embellishments

Some aspects of Mozart's embellishment practices evolved over the course of his career, and many of the gestures making up individual embellishments are tailored to the movements in which they occur. Even so, it is possible to locate a number of features that remain consistent across embellishment gestures in every major genre in which he worked.

First, Mozart's embellishments are highly circuitous in their melodic shapes. Embellishments do not simply fill intervallic gaps between two pitches; instead, they meander, changing direction multiple times while passing from one note of the original melody to the next. This indirection occurs on multiple levels of structure.[18] It can be seen most simply in the elaboration of individual intervals—for instance, when the ascending scale that begins the Adagio variation of K. 264 (ex. 2*a*) is embellished with a gesture that changes direction twice, leaping down first to c′ and then to g′ before arriving at the end point of the original scale.[19] Melodic indirection also applies at the level of entire phrases, when embellishments move against the composite shape of a given melody. Mozart's use of melodic indirection is generally consistent across all of his creative periods, a point noteworthy not only for what it suggests of his art of embellishment, which remained stable for much of his career, but as a departure from practices espoused in contemporary treatises, most of which instruct performers to fill large melodic gaps by moving directly from one note to another without introducing further digressions along the way.

A second unifying feature of Mozart's embellishments is the liberal use of expressive chromaticism. This represents one of the ways in which embellishments align with and amplify his musical language as a whole, which is habitually and pervasively chromatic. In some cases, the chromatic alterations are slight, absorbed into the gestural deployment of turns, trills, and grace notes. Elsewhere, however, his chromaticism is deliberate and marked.

Chromaticism is often linked to the affective profile of a passage, which he redefines through the insertion of local dissonances that add color and alter a phrase's scope either by suggesting its light, comic character (as in the flippant chromatic grace notes in the last movement of the Piano Sonata K. 279) or by imbuing it with a depth and complexity more usually found in lyrical slow movements.

The third consistent feature of Mozart's embellishments is the use of measured divisions rather than free runs, unmeasured scales, and other Italianate graces found in many earlier eighteenth-century embellishments (familiar from diminutions attributed to Arcangelo Corelli, Giuseppe Tartini, and Pietro Nardini). In other words Mozart often wove his embellishments from the same types of rhythms found throughout his compositions more generally. Although he does occasionally break free of this measured regularity, his departures are exceptions to an otherwise consistent norm, and they generally occur only when the flow of metrical time slackens: within *Eingänge*, for instance, or during broad, sweeping scales under a fermata. Aside from such free passages, Mozart's notated embellishments are so rhythmically staid that they tend to avoid even simple combinations of duplets and triplets within individual gestures, a device both Haydn and Beethoven used to heighten the rhapsodic freedom of their soloistic passages in sonatas and concertos.

I have described these features of Mozart's embellishments in strictly technical terms. Yet each carries implications for broader issues of expression and rhetoric. Mozart calibrates his use of all three features to maximize each passage's theatrical effect. This is perhaps most apparent in the case of melodic indirection. By introducing flamboyant changes of shape into his melodies, Mozart evokes a compositional and performative persona whose creative ingenuity seems virtually limitless. The series of repeated upbeats in the slow movement of the Violin Sonata K. 481 (ex. 4.3) exemplifies this decorative alchemy, showing off a dazzling succession of ways that the opening gesture—a rudimentary descending triad—can be constantly reinvented and reshaped, yielding complexities that would be unavailable were the sole purpose of the embellishments to connect notes by efficient and direct means. Although some of the decorated upbeats from K. 481 do precisely this, accomplishing the task with only one or two isolated changes of direction, the most characteristic introduce multiple digressions within the melodic foreground. In many respects, these draw from the aesthetic of improvisation discussed in the previous chapter, seeming to flirt with unrecoverable distraction and threaten failure—in this case, failure to maintain the broad, structural shape of the

Example 4.3 Violin Sonata K. 481, second movement, upbeats to mm. 1, 5, 13, 35, 39, 65, 69, 76, 80, and 88

melody they adorn. In the final iteration of the K. 481 theme, the upbeat sustains a "wrong" note a seventh higher than the original melody before, at the last moment, scrambling down to the intended point of arrival. Mozart successfully maneuvers the embellishment to its destination but only after playing up the delay and relishing a moment of suspense.

The other technical elements of Mozart's decorations, too, contribute to this air of showmanship. The use of chromaticism does so by blurring the structural functions of each note and as a result creating a complex haze that loosens the relation between original melody and embellishment and between embellishment and harmonic structure.[20] Even Mozart's metrical regularity contributes to his aesthetics of display, since against the constraints of timing and rhythmic evenness the on-time arrival of embellishment gestures on the correct metrical pulse seems all the more impressive, especially if an audience believes that the performer is improvising. The introduction of new melodic direction and complex chromaticism occurs without undermining each phrase's metrical integrity.

Pacing of Embellishments within Individual Phrases

The import of embellishment also reaches beyond these local considerations. The effectiveness of each gesture is not determined by the content of that gesture alone. Equally critical is the way Mozart deploys the embellishments alongside each other, within individual phrases, and over the course of each movement as a whole.

In many rondos and rondo-like slow movements, the unfolding of embellishments follows the expected trajectory, with the density of figuration increasing with each thematic iteration. There are some exceptions: in the Rondo in A minor, K. 511, one statement of the theme dispenses not only with embellishments but even with the turns that adorn the melody on its first appearance. A similar stripping away of figuration occurs in the final thematic statement in the rondo-finale of the Sonata K. 533. For the most part, however, figuration increases when Mozart reintroduces a theme.

Yet within individual phrases, Mozart's practices are more complex. Although each iteration of a rondo theme does generally bring embellishments, these are rarely distributed evenly throughout each melody. Generally, Mozart adds new embellishments to only a portion of each phrase at a time. In the slow movement of the Sonata K. 457, the melodic material of measures 1–2 repeats in measures 4–5; however, he adds embellishments only in measure 4, while measure 5 simply restates material from measure 2 (ex. 4.4). The embellishments added in measure 4, meanwhile, are striking for their density and variety. Over a mere four beats, Mozart draws on a range of different techniques, including melodic indirection, divisions, repeated notes, changes of articulation, local graces (here, a turn), and an added upbeat. He condenses this variety into the smallest possible space: despite ample room for further elaboration in the next bar, Mozart retains the plainer contours from the theme's earlier appearance. The same holds in the remainder of the move-

Example 4.4 Piano Sonata K. 457, second movement, mm. 1–2 and 4–5

ment. In measures 20–21, the material presented in measures 4–5 repeats with embellishments. This time the decorations apply to gestures originally appearing in measure 5 rather than to the material from measure 4, whose original embellishments recur verbatim. This pattern does eventually break down, since the figuration, constantly accumulating, inevitably spills into other portions of each phrase. Nonetheless, in most repetitions here and elsewhere, Mozart introduces new embellishments only in one portion of a phrase.

Which portion receives the embellishments is itself subject to variation. In K. 457, Mozart applies decorations both to the first and the second halves of each phrase, in alternation. In the Rondos K. 494 and K. 511, the earliest embellished reprises focus not on the first measures of the theme, but on the second or third. The underlying logic is not entirely apparent, but one possible correlation involves tempo. Rondos K. 494 and K. 511 are faster than the Adagio from K. 457, and the themes therefore derive some forward momentum from their rhythmic gestures. Excessive embellishment in the first bar might obscure the emblematic rhythm of the rondo themes and with it each movement's structural rhetoric. In K. 457, on the other hand, the very concept of momentum seems at odds with the slow tempo and gentler expressive profile. Here it is embellishments rather than rhythmic propulsion that establish qualities of lyricism and grace, and it is perhaps for this reason that Mozart front-loads them in thematic returns. In any case, the pattern of embellishing only one portion of a phrase at a time persists in movements such as these. Mozart summons maximum variety within the smallest feasible subsection of each phrase.

This pattern does not, however, hold during closely juxtaposed motivic repetitions woven throughout the musical fabric of other compositions. In these cases, embellishment occurs throughout each phrase as a whole rather than in only a portion of each phrase. This approach can even be seen in rondo movements such as K. 457 and K. 511 in embellished versions of melodies *other* than the movements' primary themes. Here, Mozart inserts variants wherever the texture allows with little sense of deliberate pacing. As with the question of which half of a phrase to decorate, this decision may not have followed any particular principle—or perhaps it may be linked to the rhetorical functions of juxtaposed embellishments briefly described above. In a formal thematic return, the repetitions are marked, and the purpose of decoration is to impress listeners with florid density, a goal most readily achieved by squeezing as many gestures as possible into a small portion of each phrase. In closely juxtaposed repetitions the task is not to obscure phrasal contours with a superfluity of embellishment but to sustain a more gradual increase of density.

Motivic Unity within Embellished Passages

In Mozart's variation sets, each variation tends to draw on a particular technical or musical device: hand crossing, melodic divisions, arpeggios, characteristic rhythms, modal shifts, harmonic elaboration, and so forth. The same logic occasionally applies to embellishments in rondos and slow movements. The Andante from the Piano Sonata K. 309 demonstrates the variation-like distribution of embellishments throughout a nonvariation movement. With every thematic return Mozart applies a different style of decoration: first grace notes (m. 17), then melodic divisions (m. 20), then triplets (m. 28), then rhythmic elaborations and added scales (m. 45), then doubled octaves in the right hand (m. 48). Subsequent repetitions introduce divisions in both the right and left hands, voice exchanges between the hands, and broken octaves. Mozart confines each of these to its own phrase: for instance, he does not mix grace notes and doubled octaves in a single reprise.

Yet the slow movement of K. 309 is unusually strict in the organization of its embellishments. Few of Mozart's other embellishments evince a comparable degree of planning. Nonetheless, a developmental logic is present in the melodic surface even where the composer seems to eschew explicit figural unity. In the Rondo K. 494, one iteration of the theme initially replaces a descending stepwise figure with leaps and then embellishes a further, internal repetition of the same figure with sixteenth-note divisions (ex. 4.5). The decorations here represent an instance of internal, progressive elaboration. The faster embellishments are not decorations of the original figure so much as decorations of the decorations presented in the previous measure. A glance at the rondo as a whole shows that such nested embellishments amount to a developmental principle throughout the piece, with similar juxtapositions and increases of local density occurring in three subsequent phrases. What seems at first glance a haphazard accretion of elaborative complexity is in fact

Example 4.5 Rondo K. 494, mm. 1–3, 45–47, and 89–91

a series of internal increases that unfold with a careful logic. This suggests yet another point of divergence from the variation genre, an environment whose increases of complexity are comparatively methodical, with most elaborative alterations sustained across a theme that lasts anywhere from eight measures (K. 455) to forty-four (K. 613). In contrast, the increase of density in embellishments is surprisingly rapid—yet it is largely as a result of these internal intensifications that Mozart is able to ratchet up gestural density so quickly without sacrificing the coherence that attends each movement as a whole. Embellished returns begin by drawing on rhythmic values that are already familiar from previous phrases while simultaneously preparing the ear for the incremental increase of speed in subsequent passagework.

Comparable organizing principles operate not only on the level of the individual phrase but at the level of the period (ex. 4.6). The clearest is a chiasmus pattern that links the embellishments introduced at the outset of a period to those introduced at the end while taking a different approach in the middle where the two phrases meet.[21] In K. 494, one thematic appearance presents tied syncopations followed by chromatic divisions; answering this is a phrase that introduces chromatic divisions, followed by tied syncopations. Similar structures occur in K. 511. The final thematic return begins with leaps and turns followed by stepwise, portato divisions. The next phrase reverses the pattern, beginning with stepwise divisions before returning to leaps and turns. Such patterning suggests the tightly controlled balance of unity and contrast that also structured many of Mozart's simulated improvisations. On the one hand, Mozart maximizes local variety through juxtapositions of disparate embellishment styles—a rhetorical effect he may have valued particularly for its approximation of the improvisatory freedom described in chapter 3 as the

Example 4.6 Embellishment chiasmus. *a*, Rondo K. 494, mm. 83–93. *b*, Rondo K. 511, mm. 151–57

player, initially setting out to embellish in one style, seems to follow a momentary whim by pursuing a different mode of elaboration. Having introduced a hint of digressiveness into the embellishments, however, Mozart counterbalances this impulse with a return to the original decorative strategy. He thus lends coherence to each period, if only in hindsight.

The same attention to detail connects motivic structures within embellishments to other gestures throughout the movements in which they arise. Studies of these relationships are complicated by the fact that the musical language of Mozart's embellishments does not differ essentially from that of his melodies as a whole, with the result that it is rarely clear when to ascribe meaning to overlaps between embellishments and their embedding movements. Nonetheless, some cases are comparatively unproblematic. In the Andante Amoroso from the Piano Sonata K. 281, sixteenth-note triplets form an important rhythmic presence in the first half of the movement. That the embellishments added in repeated themes in the second half are all set in sixteenth-note triplets may represent an instance of deliberate integration. Indeed, even the general (though not the precise) melodic shapes of some of the movement's triplet melodies echo within embellishments presented later in the movement. This integration is relatively loose, but other movements bring the same relationships into more precise focus. In the slow movement of the Sonata K. 309, an ascending gesture initially presented in measure 7 recurs almost exactly in the embellishments in measure 20, and then again, inverted, in the embellishments two bars later. Variants of the same motif appear at least four more times in subsequent repetitions. The same process occasionally moves in the other direction as well, when embellishment gestures seem to prefigure unembellished melodies that occur later in a movement or piece. In the Piano Concerto K. 415, the dotted-rhythm embellishments for an ascending scale in the second movement (m. 36) foreshadow a melody in the last movement (m. 56).

Pacing over Multiple Phrases

In compositions with a repeating theme, embellishments from the first repetition tend to form the backdrop for all subsequent repetitions. The turn that graces the first two notes of K. 494, the divisions added to the first two notes in the Adagio from K. 457, and the turn presented in measures 10 and 14 of the slow movement of the Piano Concerto K. 466—these originate in the first embellished recurrences of their movements' themes, yet they also recur in most if not all subsequent reprises regardless of other figuration added along the way. Likewise, in the slow movement of the Violin Sonata K. 481, the gestures presented in measures 13–14 are elaborations of the embellishments in measures 5–6 rather than of the originals in measures 1–2. The same even describes the embellishments in measures 84–87, which are related in melody, structure, and rhythm to those in measures 11–12 rather than to the simpler originals in measures 9–10. In such cases it is tempting to consider the first-time melodies as being "de-embellished" themes whose more fully decorated identity is actualized only upon repetition.[22] Considering the length of the K. 457 and K. 481 slow movements, it is striking that the pattern is sustained to the end of each, with even the final embellishments maintaining their structural and stylistic ties to the first variants rather than to the myriad other possibilities Mozart might instead have conjured along the way. Here, as before, the rhetorical effect of decorative variety is carefully offset by a more deliberate progression from one repetition to the next.

This structural protocol, by which Mozart develops subsequent embellishments out of those presented in the first repetition of a theme, is not limited to rondos but also governs the use of embellishments in some binary and sonata-form movements. In the Sonata K. 330, for instance, the first measure of the second theme contains an eighth note with a chromatic grace note. One beat later, Mozart embellishes the figure as two sixteenth notes. When the theme repeats in the next phrase, he gives the sixteenth-note version first, before presenting further elaborations. Such pacing is also evident in the published embellishments for the Sonata K. 332. He embellishes the descending arpeggio in measure 29 one bar later with a descending scale. When the theme returns in measure 33, he repeats the embellished version before introducing further decoration. The same applies to his compositions for other instruments and in other genres. In the Andante from the "Haffner" Symphony, K. 385, a descending arpeggio in sixteenth notes (m. 23) is embellished four bars later with thirty-second notes, and when the passage recurs at the end of the movement, Mozart proceeds directly to the thirty-second notes (mm. 72, 76) rather than restating the original arpeggio first.

Virtuosity and Character

For Mozart the structural precepts that guided embellishment served a high-order communicative function. We have already seen ways in which the deployment and pacing of embellishments might hold rhetorical significance, shaping listeners' experiences of the music. We can now explore the nature of this significance in more detail and follow its implications through a wider range of interpretive issues.

The first point of significance, one I have already introduced, involves the function of embellishments as a signal of virtuosity. This is perhaps clearest in concertante settings, where the decorative profligacy of the soloist must outstrip that of the accompanying orchestra. The different types of embellishment Mozart uses in both his keyboard and vocal models seem to affirm this emphasis on the virtuosic. In the keyboard models, Mozart fills large melodic leaps with detailed scalar filigree, whereas in the vocal models, large melodic leaps (sometimes of two octaves) go unadorned.[23] The logic is clear. For a pianist, playing a two-octave leap in a slow movement is trivially easy, and Mozart fills the gaps so as to increase the technical difficulty on display. For a singer, by contrast, the execution of such large leaps is itself a significant technical achievement, one that might, paradoxically, be diminished were Mozart to bridge the distance with intervening notes. The same principles can be extended to cast light on passages for which Mozart did not prescribe embellishments. The type of figuration Mozart expected his soloists to add is often clear from the decorations given in the accompanying orchestral lines, which imply a minimum density necessary in order to maintain the proper balance of virtuosity. In the Piano Concerto K. 466, orchestral embellishments take the form of local turns, and the soloist's florid contributions must surpass these simple additions. Likewise, the elaborate interjections contributed by the first horn in Fiordiligi's act 2 aria from *Così fan tutte* suggest something of what Mozart probably imagined, or hoped, the soprano would conjure—and, even more, they do so through a medium that, through its topical markedness, draws attention to the struggle taking place within the character's heart.[24] Embellishment in both cases is bound up with the very nature of the soloist's role. It provides an occasion for the type of inventive display that audiences would expect of any operatic diva or instrumental virtuoso.

The function of embellishments in concertante music also points beyond the evocation of virtuosity and toward the expressive character the soloist embodies. Embellishments do not only add notes; they also alter the affect of the soloist's line and, in doing so, suggest a degree of expressive autonomy that outstrips that of the ensemble. In the Piano Concerto K. 453, the first violins present the initial theme in measures 1–4, which then repeats one step higher, but otherwise unaltered, in measures 5–8. When the soloist enters, the structure of the phrase is maintained, but the added decorations—both as a lead-in to the theme and during the thematic repetition itself (79–82)—immediately mark off the soloist as an individual musical agent who operates in collaboration with the ensemble but remains expressively distinct. The motive presented in the violins at the outset of the movement is ambiguous in its expressive profile; it is not yet clear whether the gentle stabs of melodic chromaticism are playful, beseeching, or searing. For the soloist, however, the passage is firmly entrenched in the comic, a designation that arises almost entirely through the embellishment gestures, those circling *gruppetti* that poke fun during what was previously a more neutral utterance.

As already noted, however, display is not only the province of soloists. It also suggests a virtuosic compositional presence embedded within the music. This presence has little to do with instrumental or vocal ability as such and instead flaunts the composer's creativity, imagination, and powers of melodic invention. Embellishment is an act through which the composer lavishes expressive riches on a melody and reveals the depths concealed even within the simplest of tunes. In some cases, the embellishments themselves define the nature of the persona, whose attempts to impress listeners through sheer melodic technique become the primary locus of expression. This is particularly true where embellishments draw attention to themselves, either through flamboyance during formal repetitions or through the constant shifting of melodic substance during more closely juxtaposed passages. When the presence of embellishments becomes sufficiently regular as to be predictable, then with every thematic recurrence Mozart dares his listeners to predict just what inventive bounty he will spin out this time. The thematic returns in the Rondos K. 494 and K. 511, and the phrase-by-phrase motifs decorated incessantly throughout the first movements of K. 330 and K. 332, all show Mozart displaying a restlessness inseparable from the compositional voice more broadly.

The musical persona I have attributed to Mozart in this case is indicative of a general interpretive attitude associated with embellishment. To hear the thrust of a piece of music as arising through the use of embellishments is to hear in it a more thoroughgoing sense of restlessness than might otherwise be apparent. Mozart does not wait for a performer to improvise additions after the composition is complete. Instead, he actively probes the melodic foreground, tinkering with its shapes and exploring the ever-shifting relationship between melody and expression. The result is not simply a sensitivity to the variety of the surface; it is also a more deeply embedded sense of musical process and progress. Embellishments provide a forward propulsion by means of which each bar, each motif, each thematic repetition is like the previous one, only *more* so: more ornate, clearer in affect, and more elaborately laden with melodic significance.[25] This sense of linearity and progress complements the directional "arrow" sometimes sensed in other parameters of Mozart's style—for instance, the jagged harmonic accelerations that occur within many of his phrases as well as the relative strength and weakness of the various cadences arrayed one after the other in his larger formal plans.[26] Yet whereas such nonmelodic devices are located on a deep level of structure and may elude some casual listeners, embellishment operates within a parameter of the music that closely defines the trajectory of a piece of music in the ears of listeners—and, not coincidentally, in the formal planning of many eighteenth-century composers.[27] All of this means that embellishments, far from being superficial afterthoughts, provide the affective layering that gives each iteration of a melody its unique expressive character while also serving as rhetorical anchors for a composition's path from first phrase to last.

In chapter 3 I suggested that Mozart's compositional persona is a type of fictional character. Although I have invoked the concept of character primarily as a metaphorical expedient, the use of embellishment also calls up other manifestations of the idea. The designation of musical character is, of course, at its most concrete in the realm of opera—and here, embellishments often serve in both the evocation of musical personae and the depiction of various dramatic situations, particularly those involving spontaneity or improvisation among the figures on stage. In both the act 1 and act 2 finales of *Die Zauberflöte*, Papageno's attempts to play his magic glockenspiel are animated by virtuosic divisions. So profligate are the glockenspiel's embellishments in the act 2 finale that they spill over the boundaries of melody and give rise to a variation in which the wind instruments carry the tune. Tamino's titular flute, too, embellishes in the act 1 finale, though its decorations are not as extensive as those of Papageno's glockenspiel. Embellishment also serves as a signifier of playacting and invention in *Così fan tutte*. When Despina dons her disguise as a notary in the act 2 finale and improvises a marriage ceremony, each of her phrases is set against a background of orchestral embellishment during which a single chord progression repeats with increasingly complex figuration. Here it is not only the onstage character who participates in the feigned improvisation but the orchestra as well. Every facet of the musical texture is angled toward the display of dramatized spontaneity, the embellishments serving as its rhetorical marker as well as the primary vehicle for development and motion.

Elsewhere, embellishments serve a more distinctly psychological purpose in Mozart's depiction of operatic characters. This function most clearly manifests itself through the use of dramatically marked imitation. The embellishments added during the luminous act 3 duet from *Le nozze di Figaro* occur, significantly, in a number in which Mozart and Da Ponte depict the friendship of Susanna and the Countess as transcending barriers of social class and convention. Embellishment holds a mirror to the camaraderie of these two extraordinary women. In *Don Giovanni* prescribed, imitative embellishment serves a slightly different purpose. Two ascending chromatic half steps, a trademark embellishment of Donna Anna (heard clearly during her entrance in the act 1 quartet), is repeatedly imitated by Ottavio, for instance in his aria "Il mio tesoro." Considering that Ottavio spends much of the opera soliciting Anna's affections, his imitation may signify sexual pursuit. The use of embellishments in *Così fan tutte* merges these two approaches. Fiordiligi's and Ferrando's duet in act 2 is a rich source of embellishments, most notably in the rapturous Andante that follows Fiordiligi's fall (ex. 4.7). Beginning in measure 112, the two characters sing identical, intricately sculpted embellishments for the remainder of the number, a musical manifestation of their long-delayed romantic union.

Example 4.7 Così fan tutte, no. 29 ("Fra gli amplessi"), mm. 121–24 and mm. 126–29

One reason for the confluence of embellishment and dramatic significance in Mozart's operas is that embellishment is one of the few compositional devices that is both structurally significant and also readily available to singers. Unlike the other more deeply textural variation techniques available to keyboardists, embellishment operates solely within the melodic realm in which Mozart's operatic characters give voice to their desires. It is therefore unsurprising that embellishment would become a tool with which Mozart could manage both the psychological dimensions of his characters and the expressive performances of the singers who portrayed them, all the while using such melodic variations to intensify the music and text that give rise to these dramas. To the extent that Mozart's instrumental music incorporates techniques he honed as a composer of operas—an idea I explore more fully in the following chapter—it is no accident that the crafting of embellishments became a career-long pursuit.

Plot and Playfulness in Mozart's Embellishments

In addition to serving Mozart as a signifier for musical characters and dramatic situations, embellishment is also implicated in various forms of narrative. We have already seen that, on a purely technical level, embellishments suggest an arrow of time by which iterations of a theme become successive and additive rather than parallel. Yet the plot-like unfolding of compositions and embellishments need not arise only across successive phrases in the large-scale development of a movement but may also occur within the contours of individual lines. For instance, embellishments might disrupt expectation by introducing deviations into familiar melodies. The fundamental linearity of melody—that sense of internal causation whereby each note seems to "move toward" the next and which binds each phrase into a coherent whole—is itself a phenomenon that Mozart exploits and disrupts through the digressiveness of embellishments. It is interesting to note that this facet of embellishment mirrors his chronological development as a melodist more generally. Mozart's early compositions feature numerous passages such as the drawn-out ascent from the Symphony K. 22, where the eight-year-old composer establishes a consistent pattern and follows it, unchanged, for a significant stretch of musical time. By 1775, however, he had begun to cultivate a more circuitous language, and the fabric of his melodic writing as a whole absorbs the attributes of his indirect, chromatic embellishments. This development is epitomized by a parallel passage in the overture to *Il re pastore*, whose superficial similarity to K. 22 makes the differences all the more striking (ex. 4.8).

Both gestures occur at the outsets of their compositions, both ascend at least an octave and a half, and both rely on a similar orchestral effect—a coordinated crescendo, characteristic of the so-called Mannheim school, which inspired more excitement than perhaps any other gesture used by virtuoso eighteenth-century orchestras.[28] Yet against these constants, an aesthetic gulf separates the two passages. The symphony is diatonic, whereas the overture is chromatic. The symphony is rhythmically regular, whereas the overture is uneven and varied. In the overture, after three iterations of the initial eighth-note pattern, Mozart simultaneously alters the length of the cellular unit and introduces chromaticism by lowering the leading tone. He maintains the new, quicker version for another octave, until, just as the scale nears its peak, he lengthens the pattern once again and introduces a change of melodic direction, further delaying the anticipated arrival. Such passages are of a piece with Mozart's embellishments, which wend their way through melodies by introducing a tangle of new shapes and subshapes and meander through a series of harmonic implications and expressive shadings on the way to their destination. Although it has become a cliché of Mozart scholarship to praise the simplicity of his tunefulness, with Scott Burnham even comparing his melodies with the "lines of grace and beauty" developed by William Hogarth,[29] Mozart's devious and digressive melodic style seems rather more of a piece with the famous plotline diagram from Laurence Sterne's *Tristram*

(a)

(b)

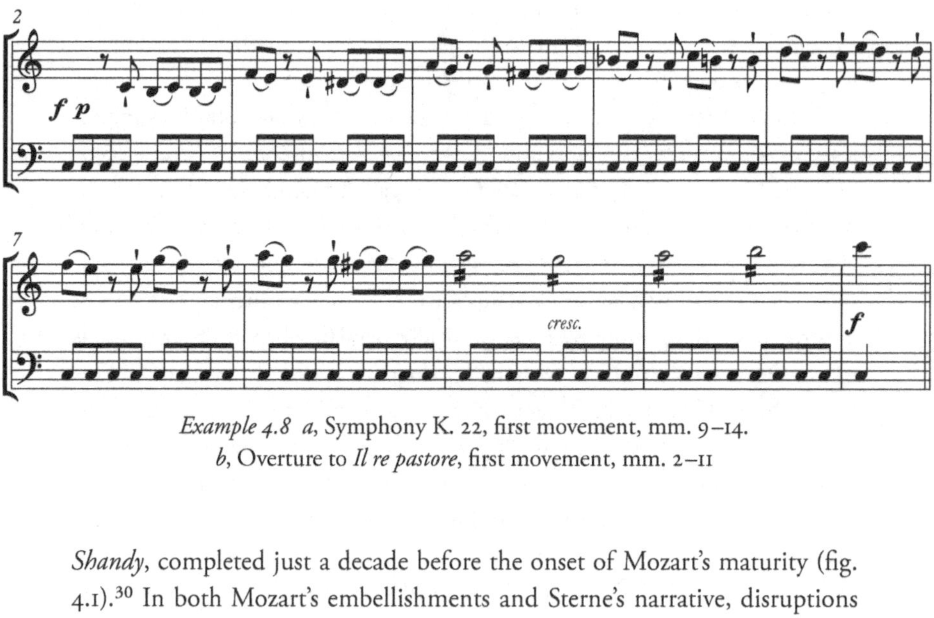

Example 4.8 *a*, Symphony K. 22, first movement, mm. 9–14.
b, Overture to *Il re pastore*, first movement, mm. 2–11

Shandy, completed just a decade before the onset of Mozart's maturity (fig. 4.1).[30] In both Mozart's embellishments and Sterne's narrative, disruptions to the linearity of the surface are elevated to the level of a trope—though in Sterne's case both the content and presentation of the diagram are resolutely comical, whereas the circuitousness of Mozart's embellishments is just as often summoned in the service of expressive lyricism.

This is not to say that Mozart's embellishments never enhance the comedic effect of a passage. They do, as do his melodies more generally. The digressions that beset the ascent in the *Il re pastore* overture harken back to

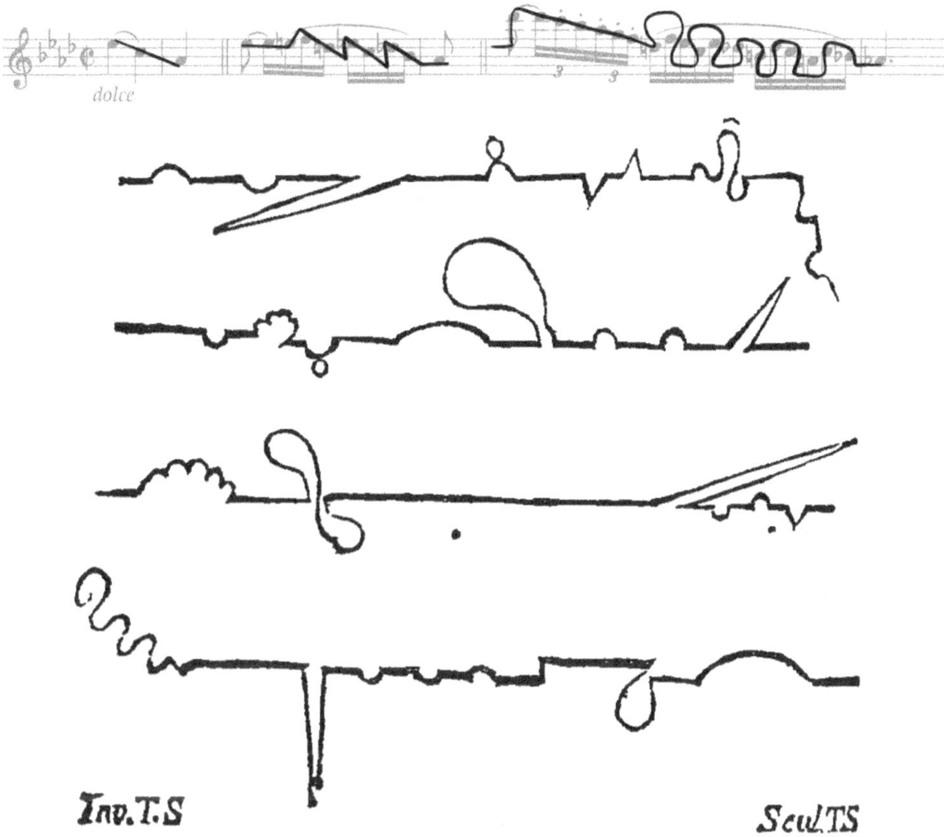

Figure 4.1, Embellishments from K. 481, second movement, alongside the plotline diagram from Laurence Sterne, *The Life and Opinions of Tristram Shandy, Gentleman*, vol. 6 (Becket & DeHondt, 1762), 152

the games of chicken dramatized in some of Mozart's retransitions in which an arrival point, though firmly in sight, proves difficult to reach—an echo of my appraisal of the final embellished upbeat from K. 481 (see ex. 4.3), which flirts with a failure to conform to the original melodic shape before, at the last moment, clamoring so as to preserve the expected alignment. Embellishments also occasionally contribute more overtly to musical humor. We saw in chapter 3 that many of the embellishments from "Ein musikalischer Spass" participate in the serenade's display of incompetence, including the violinist's awkward attempts to bring off a decorative figure better suited to the flute. I also pointed out that the soloist's entrance in the Piano Concerto K. 503 draws in part on embellishment for its comic effect. During the nine-bar oscillation, while the pianist is "killing time" and trying to invent a way out of the simulated memory lapse, Mozart introduces a range of embellishment figures—sixteenth-note divisions, appoggiaturas, and chromatic triplets—all of which are funny precisely because they are incongruous. The pianist, unable to push the music forward in a way befitting such a grand concerto and flubbing the first entrance as a result, idly tinkers with the surface figuration. Of course, the Shandy-esque digression enacted in K. 503 is not only a matter of melodic contour but one rooted in the unfolding of the concerto as a whole. In the reading I have offered, this hesitant and halting solo entrance is itself a digression from the path suggested by the pomp of the ritornello.

In the previous chapter, I invoked Mozart's tendency to "play dumb" or "play chicken." That the same designations apply to his more routine melodic embellishments, even those that are not dramatically marked, suggests that such games constituted a special instance of his more general propensity for play. As I pointed out earlier, Mozart's embellishments are often organized so as to invite recognition through comparison—and, as I can now put it, through counterfactual comparison. The embellishing composer shows off precisely by drawing attention to the difference between plain and elaborated versions of a passage in a way that imbues the embellishments with a sense of contingency. (This also echoes the interpretive fiction of modular contingency I explored in chapter 1.) When constant comparison takes place between multiple versions of a passage, we may hear embellishments not as inevitable features of a musical text but simply as alternative versions of recognizable modules decorated differently in different phrases. This in itself suggests a degree of playfulness. If we take Mozart's embellishments for granted as an aspect of the fixed, aura-laden "work," it is easy to overlook the sense of sheer delight, even surprise, that can accompany the presentation of each elaborate variant.[31] Even in those lyrical contexts in which neither delight nor surprise is the overriding quality of a movement, with the embellishments a delicate smile or a glimpse of sentiment may pierce the veneer of *politesse*.

We may go still further and posit that embellishment is, literally, a playful game for Mozart. Many of his embellishment procedures mirror what the philosopher Bernard Suits has identified as constituent components of the ludic mentality. According to Suits's classic account, gameplay occurs when players introduce a series of constraints that serve as obstacles to the achievement of an arbitrary goal.[32] In a game of chess, each player's goal is to seize the opponent's king. Absent any rules, the most efficient way to accomplish this is simply to nab the piece at the outset and declare victory. Obviously, however, this would not be a game of chess, whose essence lies not in the mere realization of the goal but in its pursuit in light of rules. Players adhere to strictly defined laws governing the movements of each piece, and it is only within these constraints that a game of chess takes place. Suits points out that this definition applies beyond traditional board games. He takes as an example the story of a fictional commuter with two possible paths home: one short and direct (the "efficient" route), the other circuitous (and thus "inefficient"). The commuter might choose a path for any number of reasons: in the case of the short route, to save time; in the case of the long route, perhaps to enjoy the scenery. In this example, the commute is not yet a game—but this changes if we introduce an arbitrary goal along with an external constraint. The goal might be to arrive home early, with the constraint that the commuter must take the less efficient route. Or the goal might be to reach home later, with the constraint that the commuter must take the more efficient route without arriving too quickly. In either scenario, the commute becomes a one-player game.

This theory of games applies directly to Mozart's music.[33] Before turning to embellishments, we can note that the scenario finds an exact counterpart in the account of Mozart's retransitions developed by Leonard Meyer and discussed in the previous chapter. Mozart's retransitions often begin with a circle progression that implies a specific path toward the recapitulation. Although he tends to deviate from the established pattern before reaching the destination, the recapitulation generally arrives just when it would have had the original pattern been maintained. In effect, Mozart sets up an efficient if banal means to reach a predetermined goal at a given time and then deviates in order to explore a more interesting and circuitous route to the same destination—with the added constraint that the detour must take precisely as many bars as the efficient route would have taken.

Embellishments participate in such gameplay on two levels. The first is concrete, as suggested by the content of the figures themselves. Embellishments, like Mozart's retransitions, draw on notions of route, destination, and timeframe—not in their formal or structural implications but in the very nature of their gestural shapes. Because the original, unembellished version of a melody dictates the structural and functional points the embellishments must track, the act of embellishing becomes a ludic challenge to composer or improviser. The music must arrive at a specific melodic destination at a given metrical point but must also introduce deviations along the way, complicating the path from one note to the next. Some of these deviations might take the form of new, chromatic shadings that the player must navigate; but others are more firmly performative, related to the introduction of virtuoso instrumental or vocal techniques that make a phrase not only more complex but more difficult to execute.

The second level involves not the content of the gestures but the practice that gives rise to them. The most efficient way to produce a melody conforming to a particular set of precepts is, of course, to compose it in advance rather than to improvise it and risk failure. That Mozart adopted a highly prescriptive system of notation when preparing drafts for publication suggests that he was fully capable of codifying texts when he so wished. It follows that when he employed skeletal notation he did so by choice—perhaps to save time, but perhaps also for the private, improvisatory challenge such passages would present. It is interesting to recall that Mozart often hid his improvisatory excursions behind the pretense of reading finished compositions, for instance by putting blank pages on the music desk while improvising the keyboard part to the Violin Sonatas K. 379 and K. 454. If this represents a kind of gameplay, it is one Mozart most likely pursued for private pleasure.[34] Even the use of decoy pages would raise the improvisatory stakes, since failures of invention would seem all the more egregious if the performer appeared to be reading from a written score.

Melody, Embellishment, and Autonomy

Throughout this chapter I have repeatedly emphasized the importance of melody in defining the character and substance of a musical phrase. My examination of embellishment has focused attention away from large-scale structure, away from harmonies and basslines, and toward melodic filigree—improvised or not—as the locus of expression, rhetoric, plot, and play. Embellishments help to draw our ears toward these facets of Mozart's music, but the insights they suggest also apply more broadly to an understanding of his melodic writing. Embellishment is, after all, a microcosm of the melodist's art, and as such it represents one instance of more general dispositions at work throughout much of Mozart's music.

An emphasis on melody has already been latent within the explanations I invoked in the first two chapters of this book. Although my focus there was not melodic writing per se but rather bassline gestures and various harmonic protocols, one implication of those discussions is that Mozart treated such gestures as melodic entities even when they occurred in voices usually conceived as accompanimental. It is no accident that schema modules, though used as basslines in more normative contexts, are regularly revoiced so as to appear in Mozart's melodies. Mozart's facility with complex harmonic chromaticism is attributable in part to his propensity for treating individual voices as autonomous melodic lines. Even his contrapuntal abilities most likely arose as a result of the sophistication with which he could manipulate, combine, and layer melodic lines rather than through the mechanical application of harmonic rules. Mozart himself seems to have recognized the importance of melodic technique for all aspects of compositional craft; hence, a glance through the Attwood lesson books shows adjustments to voice leading that suggest an interest in maintaining a linear melodic profile for all layers of a texture. He even accompanies one correction with the scribbled statement that Attwood should focus "more melodic interest in the principal voice." Michael Kelly, who played Don Basilio and Don Curzio in the 1786 premiere of *Figaro*, reminisced that Mozart referred to melody as "the essence of music," comparing "a good melodist to a fine racer, and counterpointists [*sic*] to hack post-horses."[35] Even Mozart's compositional method—notating a melodic line as fully as possible before returning to fill in other voices—speaks to the primacy of melody in his imaginings of musical structure. The surface would crystallize first, and other elements would follow.

The question of how Mozart conceived melody in relation to other musical parameters is no idle curiosity. It is an important explanatory indication of the causal chain that would have led to the shape his compositions ultimately took. The creative process is a series of decisions, each of which influences the range of choices subsequently available—and this is especially true in a style as rule bound as the one within which Mozart worked. Although it is never easy to unravel the details of centuries-old compositional thought, some simple examples can help demonstrate a process that attributes increasing degrees of causal, compositional agency to melody. The first two phrases of Mozart's song "Sehnsucht nach dem Frühlinge," K. 596, each end with a cadence to the tonic. Both cadences are ushered in by a dominant seventh chord; in the first, Mozart places the seventh (B♭) in the melody, whereas in the second he relegates it to the left hand of the accompanying piano part, giving G in the melody. In a strictly harmonic sense, there is little to say about this shift of voicing: Mozart is simply adhering to rudimentary compositional standards. Yet on an expressive level, a logic of melody governs the opening. The parallel phrases begin alike, and this provides a constant against which the two cadences assume different levels of weight. The comparatively tentative closure of the first cadence, whose melody arrives on the weaker chord tone A, is reiterated and affirmed by the more decisive rejoinder, which arrives on the tonic, F. This melodic process was undoubtedly a consideration on Mozart's part, and it serves as an explanation for the two cadences' altered voicing. Whether the seventh appears in the soprano or tenor line is, from the perspective of functional harmony, a triviality. From the perspective of musical rhetoric, however, it is the melodic trajectory that gives direction to the phrase.

The sense of active causation in Mozart's melodic writing is a pervasive feature of his language. As in the Lied, many of Mozart's basslines and inner-voice patterns seem to respond to the melodic shape of a given passage rather than vice versa. In the third movement of the Piano Sonata K. 333, the voicing of a dominant chord (m. 146) is adjusted so as to avoid doubling when the melody races up to a high E♭, and in the Piano Concerto K. 595, the largely static bassline of the opening is continually redirected to accommodate the lyrical melody unfurling phrase by phrase. In neither case is there an intrinsic reason that the accompaniment, beneath a different tune, could not continue in the voicing with which it began each measure. The adjustments are necessitated by melody alone.

The causal chain connecting melody to other parameters also finds manifestations in more abstract elements of compositional structure. Melody's interplay with accompanimental texture, for instance, is not rule based to the same degree as its interplay with harmony, but here, too, Mozart's music often gives the impression of a similar relationship in which all aspects of a phrase respond to its style of melodic expression. Throughout his concertante writing, textural accompaniments undergo rapid changes to reflect the character and affective style of the soloist's lines—so much so that the accompaniments often seem, in the end, to bring every feature of the melodic foreground into high magnification.[36] Elsewhere, accompaniments reflexively mimic the melodic content of a piece, as in the finale of the "Prague" Symphony, when the first violins' three-note upbeat resounds in the lower voices. Harmonic modules, too, which as I noted previously Mozart treats in a distinctly melodic style, are, in their simpler forms, often bent according to the processes played out in the melodies above. Rather than adhering to the strict pacing characteristic of each module's idealized form, Mozart frequently elongates or shortens various steps in the progressions to accommodate melodic gestures whose structural implications override all other concerns; and in some cases, notably in the Piano Concertos K. 456 and K. 482, melodies even "escape" from the confines of the underlying schema modules, pushing forward to the next phrase before the harmonies have been fully rounded off.

The broad implications of melodic causation once again bridge history with interpretation: we begin by asking after the compositional criteria that led Mozart to make certain artistic decisions but soon arrive at the suggestion of an aesthetic stance with which to hear his music. The notion that melodic shapes can dictate the contents of a composition's other parameters is an invitation to approach Mozart with attention to the surface, hearing phrases pour out through ornate, finely sculpted melodic filigree. Once adopted, this stance clarifies details in passages that are less straightforward than those described above. This view, then, like so many others I have proposed here, is a starting point—one that acquires increasing consequence in light of the foregoing discussion of embellishments.

One outgrowth of this focus on melody as the basis for musical expression involves the attribution of "virtual agency." An expanding literature has taken up the question of whether and in what ways we can assign causal power to the elements of musical compositions, including chords, notes, rhythms, key areas, and so forth.[37] Studies that take this approach proceed by anthropomorphizing these and other devices, invoking designations of human character couched in terms of desire and action. Thus, one harmony may *want to* resolve to another, a deceptive cadence may *thwart* a phrase's attempt at closure, or one rhythmic idea may *take hold* of a texture, edging out competing gestures. Recent scholars have begun to apply the same language to entire instrumental parts in pieces for multiple players such that a quartet's second violinist may sneakily undermine a process proposed by the violist, or one concerto soloist may seek to upstage the other in a battle of virtuosity that itself becomes a motivating explanation for a composition's musical events.[38] Although the theorists who explore these manifestations of action and agency take very different objects as the focus of their analyses, ranging from the atomic (individual notes, rhythms, harmonies, or tonalities) to the holistic (topics, individual fictionalized performers), they arrive at a highly consistent style of thought whose ethos aligns with the one I have been defending in this book. All such approaches, despite the different levels of abstraction they engage, become explanatory aids: they do not simply describe musical features in analytic terms but convincingly account for their presence and organization in each composition.

Embellishments, too, take their place among the entities to which we can ascribe agential power and which can help to explain other elements of Mozart's music. Embellishment figures vie for inclusion in musical phrases—a tendency at work in Mozart's output as early as the accompanied Violin Sonata

Example 4.9 String Quartet K. 465, first movement, mm. 49–52

K. 8, composed at age seven. In the first movement, Mozart decorates a cadence in B♭ with a circling gesture. Within two measures the gesture has taken over the musical argument, becoming the primary focus in both the keyboard and violin parts. This sonata predates the onset of Mozart's maturity by some fifteen years, yet identical processes continue in his later compositions. The same occurs, for instance, in the "Dissonance" Quartet in C, K. 465, when an embellishment introduced in the first violin entrenches itself, carrying the melody forward while also resonating throughout the other parts (ex. 4.9). Elsewhere, Mozart stages similar processes across different movements, as in the "Kegelstatt" Trio, K. 498, when an embellishment briefly suggested by the clarinet in the opening Andante becomes the theme on which the entire rondo-finale is based.[39] An analogy with evolutionary theory suggests itself: "selfish" embellishment gestures, the cellular constituents of Mozart's melodic style, replicate continuously, with successful variants spreading throughout subsequent thematic reprises or even entire compositions.[40]

This propensity of embellishments to replicate and reinstate themselves operates not only in individual compositions but across different phases of Mozart's career. In his earliest period, florid melodic chromaticism appears almost exclusively in embellishment gestures added to repeated passages. However, by the early 1770s, the same chromatic tropes that once defined Mozart's embellishment vocabulary began to feature in his unembellished, first-time phrases as well. In this light, the many melodies from his mature period that consist entirely of stock figuration take on new significance: they are accretions of melodic fragments that, years earlier, existed in his language only as embellishments but that later were subsumed into the compositional background of his style. The first solo from the Piano Concerto K. 482, discussed in the previous chapter, is not simply built from generic stock figures; it is fashioned specifically out of embellishments, here abstracted from their decorative function and strung together without even the pretense of an underlying melody to adorn. The lyrical theme from the second movement of the Piano Trio in B♭ K. 502, too, is composed entirely of melodic cells that, twenty years earlier, existed in Mozart's vocabulary only as high-flown additions to repeated themes. Embellishments in this view are worlds removed from the prettifying graces referred to in contemporary treatises. Rather, they are musical agents that can disrupt established melodies, instigate new melodies, and propagate themselves throughout a composer's vocabulary. When framed thus, as devices that move not only "horizontally" through a composition but "vertically" down the decades of a musician's career, embellishments take on a deeper significance even than the expressive functions explored earlier in this chapter. They become participants in the overarching development of a composer's style—and, too, in the evolution of stylistic convention more broadly.

It is possible that the very act of embellishing, whether as an improvisatory practice or through premeditated composition, itself accelerates the rate at which change accumulates in a style. Many features of Mozart's embellishments would, shortly after his death, come to define the musical vernacular in the first part of the nineteenth century, a period of increased reliance on chromaticism, rhythmic ambiguity, extended and syntactically weakened cadential functions, and circuitous, "endless melodies."[41] For Mozart it was precisely the markedness of these features—their potential to cut across the grain of simpler themes and facilitate listeners' recognition of some gestures *as* embellishments—that clinched their expressive allure and made them suitable sheaths for his most rhetorically charged melodic fascinations. It is therefore striking that, within decades of his death, the same features had been so thoroughly absorbed by a new generation of musicians. Indeed, the same may apply to Mozart's own stylistic evolution. Considering the brevity of his career, it is remarkable that his musical language developed as quickly as it did. That he achieved a "late" style at all, particularly one so daring and progressive, suggests that some catalyst must have prompted him toward ever more complex, experimental writing. Embellishments, through their chromaticism and dissonance, may have served just such a role. They allowed Mozart to test the boundaries of the galant vernacular he inherited, introducing into his vocabulary expressive techniques that dominate his later output.

To continue the evolutionary analogy, embellishments are, in essence, mutations—in specific melodies, in the melodic vocabulary more broadly, and in the musical style at its broadest level. They accelerate change by providing a wider range of modules, transformations, and sonorities for use in future compositional decision-making. As in biology, such mutations are the engines of evolution.[42]

For evolution to occur, however, mutation is not the only prerequisite. Equally crucial is an environment in which the replicating variants and their successors can sustain a stable existence.[43] The diachronic flourishing of embellishments in Mozart's music may therefore owe as much to the nature of his stylistic language as a whole as it does to the local functions of the embellishment gestures themselves. One striking feature of Mozart's earliest compositions is their general resistance to the insertion of further decorations. His early melodies often give the impression of being run-on phrases with little or no modular repetition or differentiation, and as a result, present few opportunities to insert progressive variation. This changes with maturity, however, and his music soon becomes increasingly amenable to embellishment. Such a shift may be ascribed to any number of causes. One possibility is that, if embellishments are replicators, their own tendency to proliferate might itself have wrought fundamental changes in the nature of his melodies, opening up possibilities for the inclusion of further decoration. Another possibility is that he consciously adjusted this aspect of his melodic style for professional, performative reasons. To write music so as to invite and facilitate the insertion of embellishments would have allowed him to satisfy his improvisatory and pianistic urges all while showing off his prowess as a melodist. If this is the case, the directions in which musical style and culture developed during and directly following Mozart's lifetime were, in a real sense, outgrowths of the productive interaction between composition and performance.

VARIATION 5

Mozart the Dramatist

To focus on embellishment in Mozart—to approach his compositions under the critical mindset I described in the previous chapter—is to experience his aesthetic as one of restlessness and clutter. Melodic shapes mutate when they repeat, motivic cells interrupt each other, vying for aural attention and for inclusion in subsequent phrases, and through it all the composer-performer flaunts his powers of creative invention. Yet for all their liveliness, Mozart's compositions do not ultimately give the impression of incoherence. On the contrary, following an initial wave of contemporaries who struggled to parse his musical complexities,[1] listeners over the centuries have often detected in Mozart a simplicity bordering on guilelessness, such that, despite the moment-to-moment bustle of his language, each piece of music seems to evanesce into a cogent, even inexorable, whole. I argued in chapter 1 that some such assessments reflect the prevailing cultural ideologies at a given time and place. Listeners predisposed to seek graceful innocence in this repertoire often hear little else. Yet even within the playful, performative interpretation I defend in this book, it is difficult not to find in Mozart's music an overarching cohesion that emerges in spite of the many subversive elements of his craft.

This cohesion is, at times, achieved through straightforward technical means. We have already seen that any musical disorder arising as a by-product of the improvisatory mindset was, for Mozart, counterbalanced by a reliance on techniques associated with variation. These would give each composition a tightly bound motivic unity. The Piano Sonata K. 332 has become a mainstay for topic theorists because the first movement leads us through a giddy variety of rhetorical states, from courtly minuets and learned counterpoint to *Sturm und Drang* and symphonic fanfares. Yet although such juxtapositions might easily degenerate into haphazardness, Mozart maintains a sense of purpose by leveraging the unifying "thread" of melodic arpeggiation.[2] Whether in the broad ascents that begin the piece (winging their way up more than an octave in three bars), the disjoint figuration of the counterpoint in measures 5–9, the more frantic arpeggiation of the minor-key excursion in measures 23–36, or, ultimately, the grand, symphonic gestures that end the exposition, arpeggios serve as a stabilizing presence. We have seen that embellishments, too, serve a similar purpose, binding the structural background of successive phrases while pushing the music ever forward.

Even these modes of unity that would come to be associated with "organicism" in later centuries, however, fall short of the rhetorical, expressive unity evinced by much of Mozart's music. His compositions hang together not only in their technical makeup but in the sense of perspectival continuity that they often suggest. Mozart does not simply move through a series of topical affects or variation states; nor do the many finely grained decorative gestures that adorn his melodic surfaces give way to meaningless clutter. Instead, his music caries a strong implication of internal causation, a sense that, despite a multiplicity of affect and gesture, the musical landscape is observed through a single lens—a sustained implication of subjectivity whose nature and technical underpinnings are the focus of this chapter.

The mention of perspective and subjectivity suggests an analogy with opera. Many of the descriptions we may be tempted to apply metaphorically to Mozart's instrumental output find concrete manifestation in his stage works. Operas present plots, and thus draw together disparate musical numbers and phrases in the service of a unified, dramatic whole. They also contain fictional characters, who in the hands of a skilled composer come to exude a coherence and psychological depth that expand as a narrative arc develops. These terms apply most precisely to opera, yet they also capture something of the quality of Mozart's instrumental music, both in its construction and in the subjectivities toward which it often points.

One risk of drawing comparisons between Mozart's operatic and instrumental music is that, as is true of all analogies, perceived similarities may easily mask fundamental differences. These differences must be openly acknowledged. In light of this book's focus, the most pressing is that Mozart's operas do not exemplify the interconnectedness of composition and performance to the same degree as his keyboard music, nor does Mozart's performance background carry the same relevance for opera as it does for instrumental genres. Although he was familiar with vocal techniques and may even have taken lessons with the celebrated castrato Giovanni Manzuoli while both musicians visited London in 1764–65, Mozart himself was known to have sung in public only until his early teens. Thereafter, his performance efforts turned more fully toward the piano and violin. For the bulk of his career, Mozart would have engaged with the craft of singing primarily through association with other performers—those for whom he "tailored" arias, and even members of his immediate family, most notably his sister-in-law Aloysia Lange (née Weber) and his wife Constanze. That Mozart maintained a thorough understanding of the voice is clear from his sophisticated treatment of operatic roles and, more concretely, from a set of vocal exercises he wrote for Constanze in the lead-up to her appearance as soloist in his C-minor Mass.[3] Even so, we should not be hasty in assuming that the types of performative thought and experience that helped Mozart compose his instrumental music also applied to the operas, a realm in which a hefty imaginative effort would have had to serve as a proxy for the tactile immediacy of his keyboard or string writing.

There is, however, a close alignment of artistic vision that draws together Mozart's operatic and instrumental techniques. The subjectivity and sense of character suggested by all of his compositions, vocal and instrumental alike, may be fruitfully conceived as outgrowths of the processes I have been examining in this book's previous chapters. My arguments rest partly on the many stylistic overlaps between Mozart's operatic and instrumental music, particularly the piano concertos. Mozart himself probably conceived of elements of operatic and concertante music as continuous, since both involve a tightly controlled, dialogic relationship between soloist and orchestra.[4] In addition, the compositional devices available to him when crafting opera arias were identical to those he used in instrumental music. In the letter quoted at length in chapter 1, in which Mozart describes the conception of two arias from *Die Entführung aus dem Serail*, his framing of musical drama makes reference primarily to those most basic elements of music, rhythm and harmony. "Just when you think [Osmin's aria] is over," he states, an unexpected fast passage "in a completely different meter and different key" will "make a tremendous effect." He goes on: "I've not chosen a key foreign to F (the key of the aria) but one related to it, but not the one closest to it, D minor, but the more remote A minor." Such calculations might have helped him to produce music in any form or genre. Although the letter aims to portray the psychological makeup of an operatic character, Mozart makes no distinction to speak of between the dramatic exigencies of plot and the ideals he pursued as a composer of instrumental music.

At times, these points of intersection illuminate elements of Mozart's instrumental music. As I have already mentioned, his concertos draw significantly from operatic conventions. The practice of beginning piano concerto solos with new material not heard in the opening ritornello (which helped solve the balance problem I discussed in chap. 2) probably occurred to him through his familiarity with a similar move used in many opera seria arias. This device, the *fermata sospesa*, retained its currency in his dramatic and sacred vocal music even as it became a standard procedure for instrumental contexts.[5] The same can be said of Mozart's formal strategies. His early piano concerto first movements follow similar conventions to those on display in arias from *Lucio Silla* and *Il re pastore*, which allow for significant back-and-forth between modules allocated to the soloist and those played by the orchestra.[6]

As Mozart's style matured and his adherence to generic conventions loosened, the expressive overlaps between operatic and instrumental writing, too, shifted focus. Mozart placed increasing emphasis on the rhetoric of topics. No longer did he rely primarily on formal slots and alternations of solo and tutti segments, but instead he brought dialogue and shifting characters even into individual musical phrases and instrumental lines. Yet this development was also reciprocal. Although operas are often thought to have contributed to the associative language of tropes that imbue instrumental music with semiotic significance, the technical interchange moved in the other direction too. Allanbrook's classic *Rhythmic Gesture in Mozart* makes the case that social conventions of instrumental music, particularly those involving dance rhythms, provided a ready-made vocabulary from which operatic composers could draw. On the level of structure as well, Mozart's mature operas make frequent references to instrumental forms. In the duet "Se a caso madama" from *Le nozze di Figaro*, the melodic and harmonic plan suggests an exposition plus development section of a sonata-form movement—yet no satisfying recapitulation takes place. The duet ends on a point of formal and harmonic unease that propels the entire operatic plot forward and whose dramatic effect derives almost solely from conventions associated with nontexted music. Later in *Figaro*, the act 3 sextet harnesses another variant of sonata form in which Susanna's entrance coincides with the initial move to the dominant, her misconceived anger with a turbulent development-like section, and the revelation of Marcellina as Figaro's mother—the long-awaited rapprochement—

with the recapitulation.[7] In these cases, operatic communication is effected through semiotic, rhetorical, and formal conventions associated with instrumental writing.

Even notions of plot and drama, which seem to fall neatly within the world of opera, have underpinned my discussions of Mozart's instrumental music. Much of what I have said about the simulated failures of Mozart's improvisatory style makes explicit reference to dramatic narrative. I have argued that pseudo-improvisations seek to establish a theatrical scenario, enacted by a performer who, shrouded in a fictionalized incompetence, attempts to impress on listeners an implied story of risk and recovery. Here as well, instrumental music shares something of operatic planning; the difference between the two is simply that in the former the characters and scenarios are not defined explicitly by a libretto but implied by the content of the textless score.

Musical Characters, Coherence, and the Persistence of Viewpoint

In any of its manifestations, whether in a concerto or an opera, the evocation of character lies at the heart of Mozart's synthesis of composition and performance. Character serves, at times, as a metaphor for the dramatic processes that unfold through much of his music—for instance, for the antics that occur during the simulated memory lapse in the first solo from the Piano Concerto K. 503, whose effect relies on the audience's perception of a fictionalized composer-pianist. Elsewhere, the designation of character takes other shapes. The sustaining cohesion that binds together so many of Mozart's instrumental compositions is, we shall see, a manifestation of the same imaginative processes that gave rise to the psychologically rich operatic roles he composed during the last decade of his career. Considering the many points of interchange between the metaphorical "characters" we encounter in Mozart's instrumental music and their operatic relatives, it is worth temporarily suspending any sense that one type of character is more fully deserving of the designation than the others and instead investigating the musical and technical relationships from which they arise.

One way to frame the concept of character is with reference to the human identity of the performer who brings each musical part to life. This straightforward type of character building was, in Mozart's time, a staple of both operatic and instrumental composition. Because it is usually certain that only one performer will sing each role during an operatic performance, much of the composer's effort at characterization is offloaded onto the personal identities of the cast members.[8] Each time Zerlina walks on stage, she will be seen as herself whether or not Mozart has succeeded in imbuing her with musical consistency. The same is true for some instrumental genres, particularly those performed by a single player per part. Goethe's famous description of string quartets as conversations among four equal partners is essentially a projection of this simple notion of character, since it frames the dialogue in terms of the instruments and their players irrespective of internal features of particular compositions.[9] An accompanimental line that sustains a pedal tone, as the viola does repeatedly in the first movement of the Piano Quartet K. 493, is just as much a participant in the conversation (albeit an obstinate or curmudgeonly one, or even a wallflower) as the voices that engage in more active, imitative exchange.[10] This interpretive stance is equally relevant to solo lines in concertos, as well as to exposed passages in symphonic wind parts (which, being played by individual wind players rather than by entire string sections, occasionally attain a degree of soloistic autonomy). When, in the Concert Rondo for Horn K. 412, Mozart gives humorous annotations narrating the struggles of the soloist in executing some passages, he calls up the same ideal of characterization. In this case, the performer—here, Mozart's friend, the aging Joseph Leutgeb—enacts the role of an ailing soloist by virtue of his actual human identity. The same is largely true of dialogues among instrumental lines in other concertos. In the slow movement of the Piano Concerto K. 488, the pianist and wind players engage in a rapturous series of textural variations, freely exchanging motifs, melodies, and accompanimental passages. The pastoral concord such passages suggest arises in large part from the implication that the pianist, flautist, and clarinetist, represented as much by their human identities as by their instrumental lines, come together in joyful interplay.

These examples consider character as a by-product of the individual performers who play or sing certain parts and for whom the musical composition becomes an exercise in Mozartian portraiture, enacting dialogues and social dramas. However, we might also frame the concept of character in abstract terms. Theories of musical expression that align characters with performers often do so *despite* the wide range of expressive states through which each part moves over the course of composition—and these expressive states are themselves entangled with the evocation of character. In this view, identity has little to do with performers and much to do with the music's rhetorical makeup. The study of topic theory in instrumental music takes this concept of character as its starting point, and in some cases so thoroughly reverses the equation of performer and expression that the task of the performer is to submit entirely to the expressive dictates of each phrase, effectively becoming a conduit through which a range of implied characters will be projected to the audience.[11] Although topic theory as a discipline of study is a modern-day pursuit, it finds historical precedence in a number of seventeenth- and eighteenth-century ideals, including contemporary accounts vesting affective, human qualities in rhetorical figures, melodic structures, tonalities, and rhythmic gestures.[12] However, the individual associations of rhythms or key areas with emotional states, for all their vividness, do not give the complete picture of how musical character arises. Characters are best depicted neither in isolated moments in a composition nor by its constituent elements taken individually; instead, the fullest implications of character thrive on sustained, narrative development that provides the fuel for the depiction of fictionalized thoughts, ideas, and experiences. Although Mozart's *Entführung* letter focuses on localized gestures such as modulations and tempo changes, he also implies, from his very approach in describing the scene, that Osmin's character transcends these building blocks, deriving psychological complexity mainly from their deft combination. Arrayed in succession, the metrical and tonal ploy begins to suggest a being whose conscious experience carries over across a series of mental states. Framed in this way, character emerges longitudinally over a stretch of music rather than within individual phrases. This is even more true for characters as richly painted as Susanna and Donna Elvira, whose psychological depths arise at the level of each opera as a whole in part because each character's musical style shifts from one number to another.

This view of character poses a problem for instrumental music, however. We have seen repeatedly that in instrumental compositions Mozart often generates rhetorical interest through series of local contrasts. (Recall the flirtatious exchange implied by the soloist's line in the Violin Concerto K. 219.) In this way, he harnesses the flexibility afforded by the lack of a fixed text while also allowing the performers to show off their expressive virtuosity. Yet such passages often pursue local contrasts at the cost of evoking longer-range subjectivity. To the extent that Mozart uses local techniques to deepen characterization in his operas, the text, plot, and casting provide a sense of sustained subjectivity not guaranteed amid the kaleidoscopic multivalence of expressive states he often favors in his instrumental output.

Mozart counterbalances the segmentation that arises through the use of short-term expressive modules in a number of ways. One of these—comparatively rare in his output, yet enchanting when it occurs—is through effects related to instrumentation, in which local, modular differences are manipulated so as to highlight longer-term continuity. In the last movement of the Piano Concerto K. 453, the melody beginning in measure 65 is shared among the three principal wind parts. The tune begins as an oboe solo, is taken over by the flute one bar later (when played well, this has a magical quality), and is then transferred to the bassoon before all three instruments join together to end the phrase.[13] The melody seems to stretch itself across musical time precisely because it synthesizes the changes of color introduced on the more segmented level of individual measures. The three instruments merge to create something whose coherence transcends the contribution of any one player. And in this coherence a sustained viewpoint begins to arise. It is by virtue of this overarching perspectival vantage point, in which we listeners regard the phrase as a unified whole, that we even attend to the alchemical color shift from oboe to flute, since in a more individuated context the timbral change might signal dialogue rather than continuity.

Such orchestral effects are potent in part because Mozart does not overuse them. More often, he evokes perspectival coherence through the more familiar structural techniques involving, in particular, carefully handled repetition. It is generally through the subtle reiteration of certain marked, musical elements that a deeper sense of cohesion may arise in a given piece. At times Mozart manipulates these repetitions so as to give an impression of forward movement not unlike what we find in the wind writing of K. 453. In the opening phrases of the Piano Quartet in E♭, K. 493, nearly every module begins with an echo of the gesture that closed the preceding module, with the result that the music seems to follow a careful process whereby each cell grows from what came immediately before (ex. 5.1*a*).[14] In the first movement of the Piano Sonata K. 332, he follows the same strategy, but at the level of the phrase. Every melody, with the solitary exception of the opening four-bar unit, repeats directly after its initial presentation (ex. 5.1*b*).[15] As I remarked in the previous chapter, Mozart varies most of these repetitions through the introduction of embellishments; however, he also introduces phrasal extensions, and the music seems as a result to stretch beyond the two- or four-bar slots of the initial, more compact statements. He invites us to experience the movement's building blocks as spilling over their boundaries and carrying through into a sustained perspectival whole.

Elsewhere, a sense of cohesion arises through the use of devices that are not themselves marked but which, repeated persistently, become defining "premises" of a composition. In the first movement of the Piano Concerto K. 414, Mozart uses sustained pedal notes in either the bass or treble voices in virtually every phrase. Although pedals are hardly notable occurrences in Mozart's out-

Example 5.1 *a*, Piano Quartet K. 493, first movement, mm. 5–13. *b*, Piano Sonata K. 332, first movement, mm. 5–22

put as a whole, the K. 414 pedals are unusual for being deployed so insistently. Mozart did not necessarily expect listeners to notice this feature of the concerto's design, yet the strategy is effective, giving rise to a consistent background against which the various melodies are played out. Nor are the foregrounded melodic elements entirely separable from the concerto's aural background. Selecting the pedal as a structural feature of K. 414 would have determined what types of phrases Mozart could include. It is most likely for this reason that the concerto is so diatonic, tuneful, and comparatively straightforward, woven from harmonies that oscillate between familiar chordal pillars without forging through the chromatic thickets found in his other compositions of the early 1780s.

In other cases the features that unify Mozart's writings are not located in melody, rhythm, or harmony but in sonority and timbre. In the unfinished Minuet K. 355, one of his strangest and most daringly chromatic keyboard pieces, the insistent use of augmented sonorities is the primary source of continuity across a haphazard set of themes and motifs. Mozart does not summon these augmented triads as functional harmonies. He generates them solely through voice leading and the manipulation of more basic techniques such as suspensions. Yet they nonetheless feature as a binding presence throughout this short, troubled work. Music theorist Howard Boatwright has speculated that Mozart's entire *raison* for composing this minuet was to explore this one sonic effect:

> It is not difficult to explain out of existence this first augmented chord. . . . But to so dismiss this harmony is to lose sight of the significant fact that Mozart has given it deliberate prominence. Merely to demonstrate that its function is really that of a V^6 shows that Mozart was working within the bounds of functional harmony, but it does not even touch the more interesting question of why he utilized the freedom within that system to thrust this particular sonority at the listener. . . . The number of augmented chords in this little piece, as well as their prominence, can only suggest that Mozart simply wanted those sounds, and that he was so much a master of the harmonic system of his time that he could bend it to his subjective musical desires.[16]

We can extend this issue of sonority to include the persistent use of certain timbres to create a more prolonged sense of character in music that might otherwise lack structural unity. Returning to opera, in the ritornello that opens the first duet in *Le nozze di Figaro*, Mozart uses orchestration, among other metrical and melodic tools, to differentiate Figaro and Susanna even before either character has begun to sing, setting Figaro's angular melodies in the violins and Susanna's more lilting tunes in the winds. He deepens this association of orchestral color with individual characters as the opera progresses; thus, Susanna's solo numbers in acts 2 and 4, and her duet with the Countess in act 3, place such emphasis on the interplay of wind parts that the timbre of these instruments becomes a marker of the luminous pastoral joys and intimacies of which Susanna is so ardent a champion.[17] Mozart associates her not with individual instruments but with the gentle zephyrs evoked by the wind section as a whole.

Accompaniment and Character

The devices I have discussed so far are concerned with musical parameters other than melody. Specifically, many of these examples point toward the accompanimental background, an element of the music that, though less overtly rhetorical than melody, contributes significantly to the expressive scope of each phrase. This expressive force arises in part through the consistency of perspective suggested by many facets of Mozart's accompaniments, which help bind together the events that occur in the melodic foreground and suggest, as a result, the sustained viewpoint necessary for the evocation of character. But accompaniment also provides rhetorical impetus on a more local scale by helping to define the expressive states through which each phrase passes—and expressive variation on this level, too, is a necessary component of characterization. In Mozart's solo piano sonatas, accompaniments help to establish, for instance, the implied alternation between "solo" and "tutti" passages in movements meant to imitate concertante writing (including the finales of the Piano Sonatas K. 330 and K. 333), and in his operas they crystallize the expressive stance embodied in the melody, as when, in the *Entführung* letter, he describes the orchestral effects that suggest Belmonte's sighs and beating heart.

We can shine a clarifying light on this facet of Mozart's craft by examining music for which he composed *only* the accompaniment—in particular, the early pastiche keyboard concertos, which he created between ages eleven and sixteen by converting other composers' solo sonatas into concertos for piano and orchestra. Mozart generally left the original melodic lines unaltered in his adapted solo passages; thus, a comparison between the original versions and Mozart's settings demonstrates something of the mindset with which he assembled his accompaniments. Especially revealing in this respect are the three Concertos K. 107, written between late 1770 and 1772 and based on sonatas by Johann Christian Bach, a musician whom Mozart respected and whose compositions frequently served him as models for imitation and allusion.[18]

Bach's Sonata in D major op. 5, no. 2 opens as a symphonic fanfare, with full-voiced chords repeated across the keyboard's range (ex. 5.2). In Bach's original, this gesture is followed by a more ambiguous statement: a melody whose slurs suggest lyricism yet whose left hand remains boisterous, much like the energetic bass writing in the third bar of Mozart's own D-major Sonata K. 311. Mozart's arrangement initially, in the opening ritornello, interprets the gesture in the same expressive vein as the previous measure, as implied by the repeated notes in the bass and the sixteenth notes in the second violins. However, in the parallel solo passage, Mozart's setting sharply differentiates this gesture from the opening fanfare. When the soloist first enters, the fanfare sounds alongside a scaled-down version of the original accompanimental writing. Two bars later, this changes. The lyricism latent in Bach's theme is now revealed more

(a)

(b)

Example 5.2 *a*, J. C. Bach, Piano Sonata op. 5, no. 2, first movement, mm. 1–6. *b*, mm. 19–22. *c*, Mozart, Piano Concerto K. 107/i, first movement, mm. 1–4. *d*, mm. 17–20. *e*, mm. 29–32

fully, with slurs and tied notes softening the expressive profile. In this case, Mozart effects the shift entirely through accompanimental writing. The melody is left unaltered in both Mozart's ritornello setting and his solo setting.

This example considers musical expression and character in purely abstract terms, detached from the personal identities of the musicians for whom the piece was conceived. Nonetheless, even here, considerations of persona and performer are still present. One implication of Mozart's arrangement lies in the different treatments of soloist and orchestra, with the former displaying a greater variety of expression than the latter. It is no accident that Mozart treats the theme monolithically in the ritornello, smoothing out Bach's hinted expressive shift, but foregrounds the change during the soloist's rendition. The same relationship comes into greater relief in Mozart's setting of the second theme. In Bach's original, the second theme presents a beguiling combination of playfulness and lyricism. The balance is ambiguous at first; initially, we

(c)

(d)

(e)

hear a neutral bass gesture and a light Lombard rhythm in the melody. Yet soon lyricism takes on a greater presence, with sighing descents and heartfelt subdominant shading. Bach's skeletal left-hand writing leaves the performer's expressive scope unencumbered, since the right hand is free to manipulate tone and timing without regard for alignment of the voices. Mozart's setting preserves this freedom, and this passage during the soloist's exposition is the first in his arrangement of the concerto to dispense entirely with orchestral accompaniment. Mozart's ritornello version, by contrast, places strict bounds on the expressive agency of the orchestral players. He smooths the dotted rhythm (playful in the soloist's hands) into two neutral eighth notes; and the violin writing in parallel octaves forces the players to avoid any hint of rubato. Here the concept of character begins to operate on multiple levels simultaneously. The soloist and orchestra continue to follow their conventional, performative roles as dictated by the genre even as the "music itself" suggests elements of abstract, expressive characterization.

Composer-Performer as Character

The affective flexibility accorded the solo line in concertante works such as K. 107 is partly a practical matter. Considerations of performance, particularly of rehearsal logistics, would almost certainly have featured in Mozart's planning, since the customary lack of rehearsal time (a subject of frequent complaint in contemporary sources) would mean that expressive agency could not safely be granted to the underprepared orchestral players. Yet the issue of soloistic flexibility also indicates a broader aesthetic of character in this music: one entangled with the persona of the composer-performer. Mozart allows for a greater degree of expressive freedom in the solo line because it is through the solo line that he himself would show off his performative prowess. The skills he wished to display were involved as much with the acting up of expressive flexibility as with pianistic virtuosity or compositional inventiveness.

We have already encountered Mozart's propensity for showing off through his pianism, his improvisations (real or feigned), and his embellishments. Although I initially treated each of these in relative isolation, we now might understand all such attempts as arising from a general interest in the depiction of musical character. Like the fictional characters who populate Mozart's operas, the composer, too, is a fully-fledged musical persona, complete with psychological traits, intentions, and beliefs. On some level this is true for all composers and all compositions. The way a piece of music unfolds—its moment-by-moment pacing, the degree of rhetorical coherence with which each phrase gives way to the next, the affects implied throughout, and even the relationship to convention—is often best explained with reference to the fictionalized mind and desires of a composer's virtual proxy, who reveals itself through the wielding of internal, musical devices.[19] Yet although this is generally the case, the persona is foregrounded and sculpted more deliberately in some repertoires than in others. That Mozart's music may constitute one such body of work is a central theme of this book, where my interpretations and analyses often rely on reference to higher-order mental states. The pacing of Mozart's retransitions violates no harmonic rules or formal conventions, so an account stated purely in terms of notes and chords will amount to little more than an affirmation of basic competency. It is only by invoking concepts such as surprise, expectation, playfulness, or even brazenness—concepts, in other words, rooted in narrative and psychology—that we come to possess a potential explanation for *why* his retransitions (or his embellishments, or his melodic contours more generally) took the shapes they did. Nor must we make these explanations fully explicit in order for them to sway our own interpretive experiences. Listeners may be aware on some level that a playful trick is in the offing even if they lack the vocabulary to describe how the process works. Mozart's music is shot through with the implication of such higher-order control: a composerly presence with sophisticated beliefs, intentions, desires, and, most of all, an inveterate playfulness that borders on the subversive. Because this persona is bound up with considerations of display and flair, it brings performance and performativity into the closest alignment with compositional technique.

Although it is possible to chronicle the antics of this virtual composer-performer in any number of ways, the investigation most relevant here involves the question of how such a musical character arises over large stretches of music, rather than through the local effects with which the previous chapters have been concerned. Local effects are certainly relevant to the construction of the composer-performer's persona; however, they do not provide a complete picture of the constituent techniques for the same reason that examining individual phrases within an aria is necessary but not sufficient for understanding the complexities of a given character's thoughts or the drama that emerges across an opera as a whole.

Nonetheless, much of what I discuss in the following pages synthesizes the local qualities I described in previous chapters, particularly Mozart's propensities for showing off, playing dumb, and flouting expectation. Indeed, much of the longer-range sense of persona vested in his music arises through the scaled-up use of these local features. Gestures that seem to make a show of compositional or inventive virtuosity are often used repeatedly, and with increasing intensity, as a movement unfolds. In some cases, this involves the long-term realization of patterns implicit in the technical devices employed throughout a movement. In the Symphony in A major K. 201, Mozart treats all the important themes from the exposition with multivoice canonic imitation.[20] These local canons occur so frequently as to constitute a fixation. In theme after theme, as the strategy becomes increasingly predictable, Mozart dares his listeners to anticipate how and where each new point of imitation will occur—a challenge he ramps up as the music unfolds. At the end of the Allegro, he presents a miniature apotheosis, taking this premise to the limit. He revisits the opening theme but treats it in a closely spaced, four-part stretto in which compositional and performative personae merge (ex. 5.3). On the one hand, Mozart follows the strict structural logic already established in the movement; on the other, the way he does so suggests, in hindsight, that he has spent the entire symphony up to this point playing dumb by failing to realize the theme's full contrapuntal affordances until the last possible moment. In K. 201 the crowning flash of ingenuity seems all the more spontaneous in light of the haphazard treatment it receives, with voices overlapping in a single octave and counterpoint obscured by a flurry of tremolo in the second violins. The persona on display is at once defined by the slow, careful accretion of character in the movement and the summative outburst in the final bars.

Variants of this approach feature in later compositions and generally become more daring as Mozart's technique ripens. In the first movement of the Piano Sonata K. 533, he effects a surprise digression into the parallel minor in the recapitulation. A half-bar cell from the principal theme becomes the subject of a repeating sequence that seems an improvisatory digression gone wrong (mm. 154–66). As the putative improviser gains momentum, the passage loses all connection to either the original theme or the overriding tonal plan, circling back to the intended harmonic destination only after a rambling and haphazard jaunt that touches B♭ minor. A similar process occurs in measures 59–71 in the second movement of the same sonata, when Mozart subjects an innocuous if slightly chromatic gesture to incessant sequential repetition, at each stage becoming more dissonant, more strained, and less connected to the affective world of the movement. The persona displayed here is, in part, that of a composer-performer who plays dumb by getting lost in the tangle, failing to keep the formal plan on track, and even, in the

Example 5.3 Symphony K. 201, first movement, mm. 189–94

slow movement's excruciatingly chromatic development section, shattering functions that define the musical language. But the persona is also that of a tireless obsessive who latches on to a motivic idea and begins a dangerous game of chicken, pushing each sequential step further than can be reasonably expected, never quite knowing when to stop. As in K. 201, such moments derive meaning both from the local techniques on display and also from the sustained brazenness, perhaps even recklessness, the passages suggest.

All of these musical characters, from the fictional entities in Mozart's operas to the compositional persona within so much of his other music, arise out of a carefully maintained balance of continuity and incongruity, the two features necessary for the depiction of psychological depth. It is often owing to the use of contrasting or conflicting elements, whether musical, textual, or dramatic, that characters can take on those ambivalences that make them seem most human. The momentary doubts that flash occasionally across

Susanna's mien, the Countess's conflicted love for her husband, the confusion of Zerlina as she contemplates a tryst with Don Giovanni, and the more poignant self-doubt that besets Fiordiligi all arise through internal tensions in which disparate elements evanesce into these characters' personalities and music. At the same time, we have also seen that the evocation of character depends on continuity that stretches across larger swathes of music such that local contrasts themselves become marked and significant points of development that help secure these figures' identities. Such considerations do not differ fundamentally whether applied to the fictional entities who populate Mozart's operas or the compositional voice I have ascribed to his language as a whole. This voice, too, is often most keenly sensed when its outlook takes on a level of ambivalence: during passages where Mozart seems to smile through tears, as in the many slow movements that float effortlessly between light and dark moods, or in more disruptive jests in which polite, learned counterpoint loses its poise and tempts disaster. His music seems always to sustain an uneasy tension between two expressive worlds. The depth of his fictionalized characters arises from this emphasis on ambivalence; it is rooted straightforwardly in the modular contrasts inherent to his style. Yet it reaches beyond, realistically encapsulating the vicissitudes of human emotional life.

From Character to Drama

Perhaps this is why Mozart's instrumental music consistently emphasizes surprise. Surprise is, strictly speaking, a feature of plot. It arises through the same careful balance of continuity and disruption that helps Mozart achieve a sense of expressive ambivalence—though, when brought into the service of surprise, the relevant techniques are used more playfully. On a local level, surprise suggests a clashing of gears, unexpected contrasts, and unresolved tensions of either expressive topic or functional technique. At the same time, the very concept of surprise (as well as related ideas including expectation, anticipation, and contrast) is meaningful only against the background of overarching coherence. Surprise depends on the belief that each gesture should have some bearing on what follows and that a sustained viewpoint is present to carry the music through one instant and the next. It is in light of this broader perspective that the constitutive modules of a phrase, set in contrast to each other, can become either jokingly arch or more thoroughly subversive.

Such overlaps suggest one of the ways in which instrumental music takes on the sense of drama found in opera. Those who object to the use of *dra-*

matic as a description of instrumental music generally argue that, in Mozart's stage works, the true dramas are the deeply psychological processes each character undergoes rather than the mere twists of plot.[21] To some extent, they are correct. However, the confluence of techniques that feature in Mozart's character development and in the surprises and jests of his instrumental compositions suggest an alternative way to frame the issue. By drawing from a unified aesthetic ideal and consistent mode of technical application, Mozart's instrumental music shares with his operas a sense of character in which the progressive unfolding of each piece can suggest psychological dynamics very much like those at work in the operas. Even more, by pursuing these techniques using an aesthetic of surprise and unrest, Mozart builds on the inherent linearity of music. He shows that, even without the scaffold of a libretto, he can establish a narrative, repeatedly disrupt it, and in this way create within wordless music an arc in which "plot" becomes a concrete explanation rather than a strained analogy. Music, used thus, can suggest the growth and development he depicts in the minds of operatic characters and in the dramatic worlds those characters inhabit.

Mozart's symphonic writing lends itself well to a dramatic, surprise-oriented reading, for the symphony was a genre in which public display was a prime consideration and in which Mozart's recourse to subversion is particularly transparent. Perhaps the most celebrated instance of symphonic drama in Mozart's output occurs in the "Paris" Symphony, K. 297. His own description of the premiere, quoted at greater length in chapter 1, captures his efforts to engage listeners through subversive play: "Because I heard that here all final allegros, like opening ones, begin with all the instruments playing together and often in unison, so I began mine with 2 violins only, playing piano for 8 whole bars—followed at once by a forte—the listeners, as I expected, went "shhhh" at the piano—then came the forte—and as soon as they heard it, they started to clap." In fact Mozart understates the comic complexity of the last movement. The theme plays out three times: twice at the opening, and once during the recapitulation. At first, the quiet opening is hardly its most subversive element. Far more disorienting are the syncopations in the first violins, which, particularly alongside the scurrying second-violin accompaniment, can make the entire metrical structure difficult to parse on an initial hearing. Listeners may easily misinterpret the violins' syncopes as strong, rhythmic impulses. The quietness, though not a primary point of confusion, would have contributed, since there would be no strong downbeat by which the audience could establish an intuitive sense of the bar lines. Although measures 7–8 offer listeners a brief chance to align their perceptions with the actual meter, at a fast clip this respite from the preceding ambiguity would hardly offset the jolting arrival of *forte* in measure 9. That the *forte* gesture occupies a three- rather than four-bar outburst does not help: the uneven phrasal structures keep listeners guessing. Amid all this, it is only the familiar harmonies that ensure intelligibility. Surface decorum belies a deep-set disorder.

Perhaps the one feature of this opening that sits neatly alongside contemporary convention is the eight-bar length of the first phrase, whose well-proportioned structure even first-time listeners may have sensed despite the disorienting syncopations. Following the *forte* fanfare, the repeat of the quiet phrase in measure 12 would probably have seemed even more straightforward, given the fanfare's neat elucidation of meter and tempo. Mozart's joke is not finished, however. Having built an expectation of a well-behaved eight-bar *piano*, Mozart tacks on a small extension, delaying the onset of the *forte* by two measures whose continued quietness would be all the more surprising in contrast to the blast a listener might expect. Perhaps the thrill contemporary audiences experienced, and the cause of the wild applause Mozart reports, was due to the quick succession in which various expectations are aroused and then confounded. Each twist of the plot has hardly landed before another hilarious turn follows.

The remainder of the exposition, boisterous and lively, is full of humorous incongruities—for instance, a passing B♭ in measure 28 that insinuates itself into an otherwise standard half cadence on A. But the surprise that responds most directly to the opening of the movement occurs in the recapitulation. When the theme returns in measure 159 for its third iteration, an exact repetition of the jokes that accompanied the first is no longer possible. For one thing, jokes lose potency when retold; in addition, by this point the movement's tempo and meter are thoroughly ingrained. The recapitulation, therefore, proceeds with no new surprises, even perhaps occasioning some relief as the eight-bar *piano* phrase repeats without incident, followed by the on-time arrival of the *forte*. Yet having lulled his listeners, Mozart immediately presents the most disruptive trick of all. The three-bar fanfare, a simple descent through the D major scale, does not usher in a return to the quiet theme but lands on a shocking "wrong" note on the downbeat of measure 170: a surprise D♯, animated by a *sforzando* in the strings and a diminished seventh chord in the winds.

This reading of the "Paris" Symphony highlights some general attributes of Mozart's persona, all of which point toward a distaste for simple predictability and a resulting unwillingness to repeat himself verbatim. This suggestion aligns with his aesthetic of embellishment: he cannot help but tinker with melodies, constantly reshaping thematic nuance. But the avoidance of repetition on display in the "Paris" Symphony is still more flamboyant. Although on some level Mozart hoped to please his listeners in crafting symphonic hijinks such as these, the subversions here transcend the mere pursuit of an audience's satisfaction, appearing instead as the outgrowth of an almost maniacal boredom that seeks constantly to undermine listeners' basic musical comfort and familiarity. This tendency on the part of the compositional persona underpins Mozart's output in virtually every genre in which he worked, from the grandest of concertos and symphonies to the lightest of ballroom minuets and contredanses—pieces in which constant shifts of hypermeter, phrase length, and accompanimental patterning make it difficult to know at any given moment what will come next.[22] Even in the variation sets, where repetition (particularly harmonic repetition) is a structural necessity, Mozart often reimagines chords so as to nudge listeners out of complacency, as in the fourth variation from K. 455 when he interprets one of the theme's harmonies first as a dominant seventh chord in G major (its original function in m. 2 of this variation), then as a dominant seventh of C major (V^4_3/IV, m. 6), then as a dominant of E minor (V^6/vi, m. 14), and finally as a dominant seventh of D major (V^6_5/V, m. 22).[23] Whereas I previously argued that Mozart's affinity with variation may have arisen through the acquisition and application of compositional technique in its most rudimentary form, I am now suggesting that he pursued it as a means to achieve a distinct, and distinctly unsettling, expressive end. These local instances of modular substitution or harmonic recasting are, in his hands, agents of musical manipulation by which he foils listeners' attempts to track how a piece, or even individual thematic recurrences, will unfold.

Similar antics beset the majority of his symphonic output, including pieces dating from early in his career. The first movement of the Symphony in D K. 84, shows the young composer experimenting with many of the ideals that would feature in his more mature music. (Although the authorship of this symphony's second and third movements is doubtful, the first movement is generally agreed to be by Mozart.[24]) As in the "Paris" Symphony, much of the unrest in K. 84 arises through the use of modules placed in close but incongruous succession. The grand fanfares of the opening two measures, with their rocketing ascent, broadly spread chords, and propulsive bass, make a strange antecedent to the flippant, syncopated, thinly orchestrated consequent that follows. Elsewhere, the symphony's subversions are less surprising and more straightforwardly humorous. Beginning in measure 17, the first violins incessantly repeat a joking figure, misusing a coup d'archet gesture normally reserved for grander unisons, yet they do so in a way that generates little musical interest and lapses into a rollicking downward arpeggio, as if to comically overcompensate for the lack of melodic invention. Other jests in this movement are formal. Mozart builds expectations for a lyrical theme in measure 28 but confounds this expectation when the glib first violin entrance one bar later extends the lighter affect of what came before. This formal ploy repeats: the arrival of a *forte* in measure 36 seems to usher in the closing theme of a short exposition—yet rather than following the implied course and proceeding to the development, Mozart goes on in measure 42 to present the lyrical theme that might have been expected earlier. Along with it comes the requisite textural shift, with long slurs, emphasis on the subdominant, and a lush accompaniment. When the closing theme finally arrives in measure 50, the end of the exposition proceeds as planned, though not without the occasional insertion of surprise *piano* tremolos between the louder orchestral blasts.

In other symphonies in Mozart's oeuvre, playfulness and surprise are byproducts of the theatricality, drama, and thrills suggested by the simulated improvisations I discussed in chapter 3. I have already argued for Mozart's ability to "play dumb" in my discussions of his pseudo-improvisations, his embellishments, and even some aspects of the composer-performer persona I mentioned earlier in this chapter. Perhaps its most entertaining symphonic manifestation comes in the first movement of the "Haffner" Serenade, K. 250, composed in Salzburg in 1776 and one of the grandest compositions from this phase of his career. If the Symphony K. 84 was the early work of a budding humorist, the "Haffner" Serenade shows Mozart's ability to handle the more sophisticated dramas that would soon become his norm (ex. 5.4).

Mozart introduces the principal theme in measure 36, at the start of the exposition. The opening gesture repeats a total of eight times: twice at the outset, twice again when the exposition repeats, twice in the recapitulation, and twice in the coda. This music exudes a sense of stability. It is played in unison by the full orchestra; it carries a quasi-cadential flavor in its emphatic assertion of the tonic; and its symmetry—its alternation of scalar motion and leaps, its emphasis on major sixths, its balance of ascents and descents—makes it irresistibly memorable. The solidity suggested by both the theme's internal features and its frequent restatements mirrors the pomp of the movement as a whole. Although the piece is by no means routine, neither is it actively disruptive. There are hints of affective play, for instance when a figure in measure 92 seems to suggest a broad, closing gesture but instead, three measures later, evaporates into light comedy. Yet, aside from isolated moments of levity, the work suffers no breach of decorum. Indeed, so serious is much of its outlook that the development section seems to prefigure the stormy, turbulent style Mozart would explore in his mature concertos and that would later become standard procedure for Beethoven's developments.[25]

The ostentatious display of stability is, it turns out, the protracted setup for a gag in the coda. As the recapitulation ends, surprises and inconsistencies begin to pile up. The first breach occurs directly after the cadence that should, by all formal rights, end the recapitulation and the movement as well. Instead, just as the music seems to wind down, a quiet motor of eighth notes begins in the second violins. A perceptive listener might experience a flash of suspense: the gesture recalls Mozart's simulated improvisations, for the second violins initiate this accompaniment with seemingly little forethought as to what melody might sound above it or what will follow it. The recapitulation has brought into play all available themes, and it is not clear what remains to be heard. The suspense is partly resolved when the winds present a figure that appeared in the movement's grand introduction, and which suggests that the current section is a coda, rounding things off symmetrically. However, the figures as given here are halting and quiet, with interpolated bars of silence. The winds' response to the second violins' challenge seems tentative. Measure 265 brings a return of the familiar principal theme, heard here for the reassuring seventh and eighth time. Yet familiarity now betrays the audience. The first two bars of the restatement are uneventful; but beginning in measure 268 the theme loses its way. Perhaps the composerly persona is shaking his fist, dismayed by the coda's faltering start; or perhaps he wishes to exceed the scope and energy of the previous iterations of the theme but has not yet considered how to do so. In any case, a fragment of the theme initiates a sequence that spirals higher and higher for nearly two bars before giving up and plummeting—splat!—onto an unexpected G#. Silence follows: the composer, reeling, wonders how to recover the thread. The following bar shows one attempt, but the hopeful (if entirely unprepared) dominant chord defaults into a deceptive cadence. There follows another bar of silent exasperation. Finally, marshaling the brute force of an authentic cadence, the music recovers, and we hear the closing fanfare. Yet even now, despite renewed grandeur, the arrival on the final chord remains strangely halfhearted. The tonic, prolonged for four bars, ends on an uncertain metrical foot, and we wait two

(a)

(b)

Example 5.4 "Haffner" Serenade K. 250, first movement. *a*, mm. 36–40. *b*, mm. 259–84

more empty bars for the final coup d'archet—all resulting in a seven-bar phrase that leaves us primed for a "real" final stroke that never comes.[26] The calculated haphazardness of this passage is particularly transparent: the entire coda teems with silences of various lengths, uneven phrase structures, and inconclusive cadences. As in the pseudo-improvisations discussed in chapter 3, the passage dramatizes a lapse of invention. A new formal section brings the promise of new material, but Mozart forces the audience to wait while his fictionalized proxy fumbles in the dark, ultimately throwing up its hands in a mix of frustration and despair.

We have come some distance from the aesthetics of improvisation discussed in chapter 3 and are now in a position to appreciate the deeper relevance of passages such as these. In the symphonic music I have discussed until now, Mozart's compositional persona crystallizes a particular type of musical subjectivity: one arising directly from the surprises and pratfalls toward which I have been gesturing. The shattering of expectations does not only depend on an implicit belief that musical continuity should bind each phrase to the next; in this music's very strangeness it places still greater emphasis on the sustained sense of character and continuity that courses through all such passages. It is precisely these dramatized lapses that help to establish and maintain the continuity over the course of each movement as a whole. Through the series of surprises throughout the "Paris" Symphony and K. 84, and through the events of the coda in the "Haffner" first movement, we become aware of an overarching presence that repeatedly makes itself subtly—or in some cases, less subtly—known and which therefore guides perception of each composition at the broadest level. Becoming aware of this presence and focusing on it as an interpretive touchstone, we, too, may begin to observe the unfolding of musical events from the single, continuous perspective of the implied composer-performer, watching through his eyes and listening through his ears as he demonstrates, through the unexpected turns of phrase, a wellspring of narrative creativity. If this perspectival subjectivity draws at times from the more technical elements of character building discussed above—harmonic devices, sonorities, and accompanimental textures that suggest expressive and rhetorical continuity—it also transcends them by infusing a plot-like linearity that leads carefully from one eventful phrase to the next.

Listening, Viewpoint, and Subjectivity in Opera

It is the nature of Mozart's persona to play chicken by taking any technique to the edge of, and at times just beyond, its reasonable point of conclusion. Thus, the sense of character and drama in his symphonic music is only the beginning of his constructions of subjectivity. If he can represent subjectivity at arm's length, he can also evoke it, not only imbuing the music with a sense of a sustained perspective but turning the very nature of perspectival listening into an object of dramatic conjuring. For Mozart to have conceived of such perspectival listening would have been a trivial matter indeed, an imaginative skill he would necessarily have honed when crafting his persona-laden music, which depends as much on a fictionalized, abstract conception of his listeners as it does on the depiction of a fictionalized composer. For it is against the imagined beliefs and desires of these listeners that Mozart would have needed to weigh his compositional and performative decisions.

Nowhere is this more apparent than in the operas, which derive their psychological potency in part from the way they bring characters' perspectives and subjectivities into the audience's sphere of perception. Throughout the operas, only a small minority of scenes suggest an impartial, external viewpoint—and such scenes generally occur near the ends of the act finales, in which the individual characters' musical material (though not always their beliefs and desires) is subsumed into a unified, satisfying musical whole. More often, however, Mozart's operas lead listeners through a thicket of subjectivities. *Le nozze di Figaro* begins while the audience watches unambiguously through Figaro's eyes. Even as Susanna sings her first phrases, enjoining Figaro's attention, his counting proceeds and his melody persists. But by the end of the number, our gaze has adjusted: we have learned to take in the world from Susanna's perspective as well as through her melodies, and Mozart accordingly abandons the counting tune Figaro sang during the first portion of the duet. This process—a shift from Figaro's perceptions to those of his betrothed—is played out in parallel in the first two numbers, both of which dramatize Susanna's subtle but decisive abilities to assert her view of reality and steer a musical number away from the trajectory that seemed likely at its start. Similar progressions occur in *Don Giovanni*, for instance during the seduction duet "Là ci darem la mano." Zerlina's imitation of Giovanni's melody is no mere nod to convention but a dramatized indication that, despite her professed ambivalence, she takes his offer seriously. As Zerlina repeats the opening melody, Mozart invites us to regard Giovanni's proposal exactly as she does, carefully considering its melodic content even while avoiding outright acceptance.

These scenes depict a straightforward type of musical subjectivity. They use familiar devices such as melodic imitation to dramatize conversation and persuasion. Yet elsewhere, the same processes assume greater complexity, particularly when Mozart seems to direct the attention not only of his characters but of the orchestra and audience as well. In the opening of the act 1 quartet from *Don Giovanni*, Donna Elvira begs Donna Anna and Don Ottavio to believe her claims as to Don Giovanni's treachery. Elvira's entrance moves through a series of expressive gestures. She begins, as is her default up until this point, in a state of comically overwrought anger. She swoops in during the preceding recitative and, in her eagerness, preempts the orchestra's downbeat by half a bar. However, rage immediately gives way to forbearance. She holds her first note as though calming herself. She adjusts her manner to suit the station of her interlocutors. The angularity of her melody suggests a lingering, tightly controlled unrest—yet even this melts into a lyrical plea as she embarks on a scalar ascent whose sincerity is reinforced both by the subdominant shadings and the warm halo of winds. Her phrase, in the end, is eloquent rather than desperate. The dotted rhythm of her closing gesture hints at the firm resolve with which her melody began, yet it is held now in a more delicate poise, emphasizing the percussive consonants of the word *tradir* while nonetheless effecting a smooth cadence.

This closing gesture is the locus of communicative interest.[27] Instead of segmenting the phrases in the exposition of this number so as to cap off Elvira's statement and clear musical space for Anna and Ottavio's response, Mozart lingers on the cadence, repeating it first in the violins, then in the clarinet, and finally in the flute. These gentle echoes continue even as Anna and Ottavio begin their response, subsumed entirely within the effect produced by Elvira's words. Anna and Ottavio do not simply adopt Elvira's melody, though they do that as well, repeating and embellishing the second half of her phrase. Even more, they inhabit her viewpoint and her sonority. In this passage, Mozart dramatizes the mechanics of listening, attention, and belief, as Anna and Ottavio take in Elvira's message. And as the entire fictional world turns to focus on Elvira, so do we. Mozart brings the orchestra and audience, as much as Anna and Ottavio, into Elvira's mental space when her cadential tag hangs in the air. His handling of this passage has a cinematic quality: he directs attention using the sonic equivalent of a close-up, guiding both the musical and moral perspective through which we take in the remainder of the scene.

By the time Mozart composed *Così fan tutte* in 1789, he had become still more adept at manipulating the dramatic nuances of attention and perspective, and this is the most likely explanation for the sense of deeply pained irony that permeates the opera. The plot of *Così* takes as its focus the vicissitudes of deception—deception of one's lovers, of one's friends, and even of oneself. Mozart's emphasis on subjectivity seems to emerge from this preoccupation, becoming so pervasive that the opera unfolds with little sense of an external frame of reference. In *Figaro*, the various march topics scattered throughout provide one stabilizing force against which Mozart brings the more personal, amorous viewpoints of Cherubino, Susanna, and the Countess into greater relief; in *Don Giovanni* it is the supernatural *ombra* music heard at the beginning and end of the opera that calibrates our perspective. In *Così*, by contrast, virtually every number emerges within the skewed, interior space inhabited by individual characters. This is least surprising in the solo arias, which were, for Mozart, always conceived as vehicles for the elaboration of a character's psychology—though even here, *Così* represents an extreme case, since Fiordiligi is the only character in Mozart's output who sings two high-flown *seria* arias that both dramatize such thoroughgoing and harrowing self-deception.[28] Yet it is more remarkable in his treatment of the ensembles, which seem unmoored from the objectivity of the external, overarching plot, instead focusing on the individual characters' misconceptions and lies.

Mozart shapes and reshapes musical subjectivity throughout *Così*, but his manipulations are perhaps clearest in the extended departure scene in act 1.[29] Even at this relatively early phase of operatic plotting, deception has entered into Ferrando and Guglielmo's relationship with their lovers. The scene is organized around a sham farewell staged by Don Alfonso to make the ladies believe that the two men are leaving for battle. At the opening of the first quintet, the music is halting and stilted, as though the men, unused to lies, cannot quite bring themselves to act out the deception more thoroughly. Yet as the fabrication progresses, they ease into their roles, and the music becomes increasingly exquisite. This "irony of beauty," whereby the lyricism associated in his other operas with intimacy and revelation is heard most plainly during moments of deception, reaches its peak in the next quintet, "Di scrivermi ogni giorno." Here, the lovers' affirmations take on a hymnlike quality that seems more in keeping with Mozart's sacred vocal style than his operatic writing. This beauty suggests the men's success in deceiving their sweethearts as well as the innocent and faithful belief on the part of the sisters, for whom these professions of love will soon take on darker shades. Throughout, Mozart once again plays film director, his orchestration and voicing cutting between the lovers and Don Alfonso, architect of the scenario, whose wry text "I'll choke if I don't laugh" and simple bassline provide an incongruous foundation for the lush chorale in the upper parts—one on which our ears focus when the chorale texture clears: a brief but pointed reminder that such extraordinary beauty rests on the simplest, and flimsiest, of foundations. Even Alfonso, for all his ironic remove, seems temporarily taken in by the theatrics he has created and joins the sisters in lyrical three-part counterpoint during the trio that closes the scene—until, here as well, Alfonso fractures the apparent sincerity of the moment with the droll outburst, "I'm not a bad actor!"

Composer-Performer as Actor

The sophistication of these and other scenes suggests that Mozart, too, was not a bad actor. The disparate techniques that made up his compositional and performative arsenals all find a unifying logic in his approach to, and interest in, the musical dramas played out within his operas. This is as true for his instrumental music as it is for his stage works proper. His ability to anticipate listeners' beliefs and desires when crafting a symphony does not differ in essence from the more concrete depictions of individual operatic characters' viewpoints; and although the reading I proposed for the first movement of the "Haffner" Serenade is only one of many possible interpretations, any explanatory account of the piece must sooner or later make reference to the mental states implied by the music, attributing them to *some* entity—whether the imagined audience, the implied compositional persona, or the music itself. All of the compositions I discuss in this chapter, and indeed in this book, share an emphasis on the projection of elaborately crafted personae, and we must ultimately invoke language associated with opera in order to capture the theatrical effectiveness of any of this music.

But to invoke Mozart's dramatic imagination does not in itself explain either the nature or the workings of that imagination. Any operatic composer possesses a dramatic imagination, and the same applies to Mozart as instrumental composer, to artists working in different dramatic media, and indeed to most other humans as well. Which attributes and mechanisms, then, should we ascribe to Mozart's dramatic imagination in particular, and by extension can we use to explain the workings of his musical language?

One answer lies in the types of viewpoints Mozart's imagination seems to have been predisposed to assume. Mozart seems often to have written with the attitude of an imagined dramaturge. As we have seen, his perspectival flexibility often arises by depicting the active attention of characters on stage: Zerlina, when she considers Giovanni's promises of love and riches; Anna and Ottavio, when they heed Elvira's warnings; and Susanna, who starts as a spectator to Figaro's machinations but always draws him into her musical world rather than allowing him to bury her identity beneath his hammed-up flair. Elsewhere, Mozart's depictions take the more concrete form of implied stage actions, as if while planning each scene he imagined himself into the role of the characters and envisaged the types of physical motions that would suit their personalities. Such gestures include the menacing ascending scalar fragments heard in the opening bars of the act 1 trio from *Le nozze di Figaro*, which accompany the Count as he bears down on Basilio, and in Dorabella and Guglielmo's love duet in act 2 of *Così*, the "heartbeat" played in the orchestra that offers a flirtatious way for the two characters to make tentative but suggestive physical contact, feeling for each other's pulses and experiencing the belated consummation of desire. Even when Mozart's music does not provide specific hints at characteristic actions, it may respond to, or clarify, an element of the dramatic situation and physical motions required in the course of performance. The long closing ritornello in Zerlina's act 2 aria allows her to exit slowly, impeded by her attempt to help trundle an injured Masetto off the stage.

A still deeper attribute of Mozart's dramatic imagination is neutrality. Mozart does not judge the characters he composes; he inhabits their inner worlds and projects what he finds there. That he took seriously the necessity of imagining oneself into another's mindset as an integral component of performative musicianship is suggested by instructions he occasionally made to his collaborators. Sending his soon-to-be sister-in-law Aloysia the concert aria K. 272, he advised, "put yourself seriously into Andromeda's state and situation!— [. . .] imagine that you really are that person herself."[30] Mozart seems to have followed his own advice. Unlike the many operatic composers who view their creations from an authoritative perspective as moral as it is aesthetic, Mozart adopts no comparable strictures of normativity. This applies even to characters who might receive rather harsher treatment at other artists' hands. The Count, Don Giovanni, all three men in *Così*, and the Queen of the Night are living entities in Mozart's output, brought to life with music that projects their beliefs rather than the composer's. Mozart does not consign the Count to the minor-key music we might intuitively associate with a predatory figure, though he accurately depicts a menace that befits the Count's station and temper—and yet even this is balanced with humanity and vulnerability, displayed during the Count's fumbling attempt to flirt with Susanna in their act 3 duet. Don Giovanni, too, is censured not by Mozart but by the otherworldly forces that intrude in the opera's second act. Although his actions make him look thoroughly despicable to audience and other characters alike, this judgment does not color his music, which, in its irresistible tunefulness and vigor, continues to reflect Giovanni's own blithe amorality rather than the condemnation of a central, controlling voice. The same applies throughout *Così*. The horn calls that so cruelly taunt Fiordiligi in the embellished reprise of her second-act aria are absent from Dorabella's music not because the moral issues at stake are any less severe but because Dorabella is not freighted with the self-doubts that plague her sister. The horn is, in this sense, an audible projection of Fiordiligi's own conscience as she grapples with her divided passions—a conscience that, significantly, makes itself heard through the type of detailed embellishments that so often imply the autonomy of individual musical voices. Here, as in his other dramatic works, Mozart is willing to imagine himself into his characters' minds and hearts. He avoids depicting the rightness or wrongness of their actions, focusing only on the psychological mechanisms that give rise to them.

Mozart's commitment to neutrality in the face of moral complexity is most pointed at those moments when he depicts characters who lie to each other or, more poignantly, who lie to themselves. We have already seen that an "irony of beauty" attends the farewell scene in *Così*, when Ferrando, Guglielmo, and Don Alfonso first actualize their elaborate ruse. Mozart's music for the scene is effective because it dramatizes both the fervent energy with which the men spin their deception as well as the innocence with which the sisters believe what they are told. The musical beauty seems ironic because it so intently gives voice to each character's inner world no matter how clearly an external observer recognizes the proceeding as an abasement of the sisters. Although few other passages are so heavily laden with irony, similar processes come into play throughout his other operas. Even within the relatively straightforward musical world of *Figaro*, Susanna lies to the Count at the beginning of act 3 with an unsettling ease. As she modulates sweetly into C major and delivers her effortless, false assurance, it is difficult not to wonder whether she is perhaps less innocent than we had previously believed.[31] Lying can also take the form of self-deception, as in *Don Giovanni*, when Zerlina professes indecision in the face of Giovanni's advances but nonetheless imitates his melody, as if, just beyond the reach of conscious awareness, she has already yielded, and all that remains is for her to justify her desires. Such a moment says much about the imaginative nuance with which Mozart approached his compositions. Da Ponte's poetry speaks only of doubt; it is in the music that we find a foregone decision as yet unacknowledged even by the character herself. In the gap between these two views of Zerlina, we glimpse the extent to which Mozart, in developing the scene, managed to view the world through her eyes.

For Mozart, then, the dramatic imagination is geared toward ventriloquism rather than externalized depiction. The achievement of his operatic technique is to have found the means to conjure these psychological nuances using the musical tools at his disposal. In many cases, such tools are similar to those used throughout his instrumental compositions. His willingness to depart radically from convention meant that musical style itself became a rich source of reference and that psychological states could be depicted through subversion of familiar norms. In act 3 of *Figaro*, Mozart skews the relative lengths of antecedents and consequents to dramatize the Count's tongue-tied infatuation. The Count requires eight bars to articulate a halting plea for Susanna's affection, during which his stammers unravel into limp monosyllables. Susanna's response, assured and masterful, occupies a brisk three bars. A more "competent" composer might have brought the dialogue off in two balanced four-bar phrases (just as a less brilliant librettist might have relegated the entire exchange to a recitative), whereas Mozart bends metrical conventions to accommodate each character's inner life. Similar considerations shape tonal structures too. The culminating duet between Ferrando and Fiordiligi in act 2 of *Così* follows a complex harmonic plan that tracks the shifting balance of both characters' unacknowledged desires. The first seventy-five measures touch on a plethora of distinct key areas, with Ferrando pursuing Fiordiligi as she continuously modulates to escape the tonal pull of his melodies. At the moment that Fiordiligi finally admits the reality of her passion, she returns with Ferrando to A major, the key of his act 1 aria and the key in which the duet began. The remainder of the number, though nearly equal in length to the first half, continues in A major without so much as hinting at another key. The flurry of harmonic activity in the first half and the stasis in the second are best explained in terms of these characters' psychological states: their fear and tension at first and, later, their desire to bask in a newly realized love.

Equally crucial in developing Mozart's technical capacities in this regard would have been the many variation principles that he honed as a composer of instrumental music and whose use in opera would allow him to deepen characters' psychological development by drawing cross-references between musical numbers. These internal allusions often reveal a mental or emotional state to which even the character in question has no conscious access. Some such references are comparatively simple, as in *Figaro* when the pastoral arpeggiation of Susanna's act 4 love aria simultaneously recalls the motif that closes the opera's first duet and prefigures the reconciliation tune she shares with her husband in the act 4 finale.[32] Others, meanwhile, are more biting. In the Countess's introductory soliloquy in act 2 of *Figaro*, an unwitting reference to a charged G♭ from Cherubino's act 1 aria suggests a muted erotic connection between the two characters.[33] It also serves as a reminder, through its pained chromaticism, that loss of love—the waning of that force epitomized by the opera's "Cherubin d'amore" (as Basilio dubs him in the earlier trio)—is itself the cause of the Countess's grief. Nor is it accidental that the allusion arrives on a chromatically altered note, marked both musically and psychologically as a departure from the objective frame of reference of the aria's marchlike ritornello. We watch as the musical vantage moves inward—first, when the

Countess eschews the martial in her solo entrance, and now, when she more forcefully shrugs off the noblewoman's habit and asserts a depth of feeling that defies normative phrasal and formal convention.[34] The chromatic pall that gives depth to the Countess does so for the same reasons that convention-defying chromatic techniques used in improvised fantasias were thought to capture the inner minds of performers. In both cases, the escape from convention seems to open a space for the assertion of a musical expression that was intensely personal.[35] Such chromaticism breathes life into so many of the lovelorn women in Mozart's operas, from Konstanze to Pamina.

Even in the absence of chromaticism, cross-referencing serves its purpose in the evocation of musical subjectivity. In *Così*, indeed, this structural strategy becomes the primary mode in which characters' inner lives are revealed and, as such, is so thoroughly woven throughout the opera that to play it up with additional chromatic emphasis would be a shade contrived. Instead, the pervasive cross-referencing is carried out as a matter of routine such that virtually every important melody presented during the second act is derived from a tune heard earlier in the opera.[36] As was the case with the Countess vis-à-vis Cherubino, these references are, in the minds of their characters, unknown. In the culminating duet between Ferrando and Fiordiligi, described above, the opening measure refers to a parallel figure that begins Ferrando's act 1 aria—a scene to which Fiordiligi was not privy. This reference is no mere stroke of structural cleverness but a deep-set statement of dramatic irony. The duet begins with Fiordiligi alone on stage, cloaked in both Ferrando's traveling gown and his characteristic key of A major, and the variation-like reference suggests how deeply her own sense of identity is bound to his. She does not mean to adopt Ferrando's key and melody while claiming to repudiate his love, yet it is precisely because the allusion is unknowing that it seems all the more sincere—and this is in large measure what imbues her character with such richness. (In Rosen's words, for Mozart, "the mere rendering of sentiment was not dramatic enough; Orestes must be shown to go mad *without his being aware of it*, Fiordiligi must desire to yield while trying to resist, Cherubino fall in love without knowing what it is that he feels."[37]) Neither, of course, do the men in *Così* realize that, upon their staged "return" from make-believe war, the tune they sing in histrionic anger is borrowed from the act 2 duet in which the two sisters first agree to dally with the new suitors. Here as well, the pathos of the scene derives from this reference, with the men cruelly forced to intone music associated with the moment of betrayal and the women forced to listen as, beneath the level of awareness, they are reminded of their part in the day's proceedings. For composer and audience, such references constitute a running commentary on the contents of each character's mind while also giving the opera an overarching sense of cohesion, binding its mosaic of viewpoints into a unified whole.

When Mozart successfully channels the needs of his characters, it is through an imaginative awareness of how they might feel or react as well as a willingness to translate that awareness into music. It is in this respect that we can consider Mozart a virtual stage actor who plied his craft by inhabiting other minds and projecting their intentions and beliefs without imposing on them his own moralizing gaze. Although this is an achievement of his operatic technique, it applies equally to his corpus as a whole. The neutrality I ascribed to Mozart's treatment of operatic characters is also a unifying feature of his piano concertos, string quartets, and other instrumental compositions. The topics and affective gestures that populate his instrumental corpus are, like those of his operas, detached from any sense of normative bias. This freedom from morality's gaze may be the defining feature of Mozart's musical presence, one enabled by the performative playacting he pursued for the entirety of his career.

One indication of the lack of normative, moral control in Mozart's nontexted music is the broad range of colors and expressive states associated with individual key areas. Minor tonalities are, for Mozart, not inherently bad places—a point which stands in contrast to conventions that arose in the 1760s and which would find an apogee at the beginning of the nineteenth century in Beethoven's C-minor style. The association of minor modes with discomfort and strain was, for Mozart's contemporaries, firmly rooted in mores of the day. Haydn's "Farewell" Symphony provides one concrete manifestation of this view: throughout, major tonalities feature as objects of aspiration, with each successive movement trying (and, until the fourth movement, failing) to come to rest in a related major key.[38] For Mozart, no such associations tarnish minor modes, which teem with just as many affects and characters as their major counterparts. In the Symphony in G minor K. 550, the arrival of G major in the trio section of the third movement is not the long-awaited teleological climax listeners may feel at the parallel moment in Beethoven's Fifth; it simply represents a brief visit into a key whose expressive affordances need not differ fundamentally from those already at play.[39] It is telling that the slow movement of the same symphony, despite being harbored in E♭ major, far outstrips the fast movements in strained dissonance and unsettling affects. Indeed, the relative neutrality of tonality in Mozart explains a broader facet of his language as it compared to those of composers working during and immediately after his lifetime. Whereas many of his contemporaries and successors used complex key signatures as a primary means of evoking ethereal sound worlds, Mozart rarely composed pieces whose principal tonalities had more than three sharps or flats; yet within those strict confines his audacious modulations and daringly juxtaposed affects are all the more potent in their expressive reach.

Perhaps this is why, of Mozart's large-scale minor-key compositions, only a handful finish with a move to the parallel major. The Piano Concerto in D minor, K. 466, and the String Quintet in G minor, K. 516, are two of the best-known examples—yet even here, if the works were revised so as to remain fully in the minor until the end, it is difficult to imagine that the lasting musical impression would be any less satisfying than what is offered by the actual versions, with their major-key finales. The case of K. 466 is particularly vivid, whose last movement suggests a jumble of playful and elegant characters, some set in major keys and some in minor. The music moves so freely among them that it is doubtful whether the D-minor setting exerts any sustained pull on expression, rhetoric, or experience.

Equally noteworthy is the comparative freedom with which Mozart floats between major and minor modes. In the opening ritornello of the stormy Piano Concerto K. 491, he softens an otherwise turbulent introduction in C minor with hints of E♭ and A♭ major, interpolations that, formally speaking, need not occur within the initial statement of the concerto's musical ideas. Within moments of the soloist's entrance, Mozart consummates the move to E♭. Even so, he maintains flexibility. He has modulated to the major mode, but he continues to glance back at the minor, shading even the most serene of melodies with inflected B♮s that hint at the darker world from which the movement emerged.

Similar examples of modal shape-shifting appear throughout his music. One of the most beguiling demonstrations of expressive flexibility occurs in the slow movement of the Sinfonia Concertante for Violin and Viola, K. 364. Set in C minor, the movement initially strikes a tragic tone: we hear violins in octaves, a throbbing accompaniment, and rich inner-voice writing reminiscent of operatic arias. This image lasts through the violin soloist's entrance, yet when the viola begins, the music veers away. The viola replaces the violin's B♮ with a B♭, steering effortlessly into E♭ major. As in K. 491, even with E♭ firmly established, the soloists wistfully linger on sonorities that were associated moments earlier with the minor, passing through the gravitational fields of F minor, G minor, and even A♭ minor without fully modulating. There is a palpable ambivalence: melodic shadings either draw a veil over the warmth of E♭ major or show a ray of light that momentarily pierces the minor-key darkness.

Mozart's tonal flexibility, here as before, as well as the related moral neutrality he adopts in his operas, is a natural outgrowth of the pianistic and improvisational strategies described in chapters 2 and 3. Modal shifts were a sine qua non of the variationist's tool kit, and Mozart's familiarity with the related techniques, as well as a restlessness that seeks constant change, would have given him both a desire for suppleness with harmonic shadings and the technical acumen to realize the expressive ideal. More importantly, an overarching emphasis on ambivalence depends on the modular underpinnings of Mozart's style, which facilitated his long-practiced art of juxtaposing contrasting elements in close succession. Modularity contributes to the ambiguities discussed in this chapter, whether those of operatic characters or instrumental melodies, for it is through the use of discreetly segmented material that Mozart maximizes local contrasts of any type, all the while coaxing from them a coherent whole. Modularity is, at root, a technical feature of Mozart's style, yet it is also a mindset suggestive of an interpretive stance, one that allowed Mozart to portray the quicksilver emotional shifts experienced by operatic characters and to imbue his instrumental output with an equally marked aesthetic multivalence. Neutrality, too, necessarily features in these technical achievements. Just as Don Giovanni's melodies are not burdened with the weight of Mozart's moral gaze, so, too, are the darker passages from his instrumental compositions free to hint at, digress into, and assimilate modules of any affective flavor. It is through the synthesis of these technical tools and artistic priorities that Mozart's music becomes a theater of imaginative possibility.

CODA

Performing Mozart

Da capo: An Embellished Reprise

On paper, a musical score is an intricate but lifeless pattern of dots. But listen to the sounds that pattern encodes, or hear them in your mind's ear, and you enter an imaginary world teeming with motion. Individual notes disappear into the flow of melodies; rhythms incline toward each other as if gently magnetized; and chords take on a gravitational attraction to any harmonies that cross their tonal orbit. Such aural alchemy is magical in itself; but the musical experience goes further. Within this world, we sometimes sense the organizing presence of a human mind, a consciousness whose perceived emotional states and overarching worldview bind a musical work into a coherent whole. In this book I have explored the nature of one such presence: that of the virtuoso composer-performer embedded in Mozart's music. I hope to have shown how the persona is constructed, how it functions, and perhaps most of all, what it means to approach Mozart's output with this playful, theatrical image in mind. Surveying the landscape through which my arguments have passed, the biographical details enumerated in chapter 1 seem worlds away from the densely cluttered operatic stage onto which we tumbled in chapter 5. Yet both, and the many points in between, are connected by a thread drawing together Mozart's life, career, working habits, and aesthetic aspirations as a virtuoso performer.

Where does my investigation end? In some sense, it need never end. The survey I have undertaken could continue, moving through ever more examples of dramatic gestures in Mozart's music and suggesting further interpretive nuances with which to understand them. Alternatively, the investigation might go on to pursue the same lines of inquiry in the music of Mozart's contemporaries. In this case the study would end in dissolution: it would turn its focus back onto the culture in which Mozart worked, replanting him within that milieu whose affordances helped shape his development. Or perhaps the study could culminate in a broader examination of other composer-performers from across the centuries. How do different creative minds use (or avoid, as the case may be) expressive modules, embellishments, or Mozartian effects of surprise or ambiguity? In which other compositional voices does operatic amorality flourish? The critical tools I have used in these pages might fruitfully apply to any such matters or others besides.

Instead, my study closes where it began—in the world of performance, grounded in the activities of musicians past and present and alive to the points at which the exigencies of making music intersect with the more analytic modes of engagement I have adopted. Although I have avoided dwelling on the practicalities of modern-day Mozart performance, issues surrounding the performance of his music have, in their way, been a focus throughout, not only because I have examined the performative impulse that drove Mozart's career but because I have pushed the reader to imagine how various compositions might set the stage for particular types of phrasing and display. I have tried to examine Mozart's music by testing it through the application of conjectured interpretive stances, all with the aim of rehearing it under new critical ideals. Thus, while my subject has ostensibly been a mode of listening, the answers I have developed also apply to the question of how we might play or sing Mozart so as to bring such ideals to the fore. My purpose in this brief coda, then, will be to engage the concept of performance, reconsider its relationship to the analyses, interpretations, and historical discussions I have already carried out, and ultimately offer some concrete advice to those musicians who wish to highlight the theatrical elements of Mozart's style.

The relationship between analysis and performance—or, more broadly, between thinking about music and playing it—has been a subject of active critical investigation for at least a century. Such eminent figures as Donald Francis Tovey and Heinrich Schenker have weighed in on the topic, as have numerous recent voices.[1] The consensus is that the two activities can and should inform one another, although, since dominance is generally accorded to one craft, there are few calls for true reciprocity. Tovey's famous injunction that performers "should understand what they play" is a worthy ideal, yet at no point does he admonish theorists to test their ideas by performing the music they analyze.[2] When theorists and musicologists give persuasive arguments as to the ways that structural or historical matters might influence performers' phrasing, they imply that knowledge generated through research somehow takes precedence over players' personal intuitions, a "page-to-stage" model that has come under criticism from eminent scholars such as Nicholas Cook.[3] Conversely, some philosophers of music hold that all sonic imaginings constitute performances of a kind—not in the sense I have suggested above, applied to specific interpretations of music by one composer, but more thoroughly, because even theorists given to the most arcane speculations cannot help but "perform" (and draw on their experiences of others' performances) whenever they hear their way through a phrase.[4] It is difficult if not impossible, after all, to conceptualize music without intuitively layering it with at least a tempo and timbre—and the moment one does so (the argument runs) a type of performance has necessarily taken place in the mind's ear. This model suggests that analysis is in its way subservient to performance and, once again, not vice versa.

Despite disagreeing as to the causal weight accorded each activity, these two straightforward accounts share a consistent scheme for the interaction of performance and analysis. In both views, one of the activities bears directly on the other. Scholars and performers may differ in their visions of the ideal balance such interactions should strike, yet the prevailing theories generally hold either that what one thinks about music should influence how one plays it or, conversely, that how one plays and hears music should influence what one thinks about it (fig. 6.1*a*).

This model holds intuitive appeal, but it breaks down under scrutiny. How, for instance, do musical ideas transfer from scholarship to performance? Theorists may identify a feature of a composition—a deceptive cadence, a moment of metrical instability, a minuet topic—but as any performer knows, such observations vastly underdetermine the decisions that take place when actually playing a given passage. Is *this* deceptive cadence to be lingered over or bounded through? Is it best expressed through the manipulation of time or a change of tone quality, or perhaps with a playful glance toward the audience, or indeed with all three? What bow stroke or pedaling best suits a metrically unstable passage, and why? The question of how any musical detail can be instantiated in performance raises further questions that the analytic statement glosses. The identification of a minuet topic prompts an open-ended series of possibilities. Does *this* minuet subvert convention in its rhythmic structure?[5] Is it incidental or self-consciously diegetic? Even in Mozart's simplest minuets—the last movement of the Piano Concerto K. 246 comes to mind—subversive dissonances occasionally push against the metrical hierarchy. How should a pianist realize these? To identify the topic is to set, rather than settle, an interpretive challenge. The very fact that creativity is needed in order to translate analytic observations into performance is a reminder that the one act is not an unmediated reflection of the other. The same is true if we reverse the equation. Interpretations developed through performance often carry nuances so subtle as to elude even the most insightful of verbal descriptions. A performed interpretation may spur theorists to rethink foundational intuitions about the expressive thrust of the music, but it will not delimit further discoveries produced in the course of close reading.

In this book, I have presumed a different relationship between performance and analysis, one that is less immediate than what the familiar model suggests. In my view, performance and analysis do not interact directly but issue jointly from the more general explanations I described in chapter 1 (fig. 6.1*b*). As I have argued, interpretive decisions are always based on broad, explanatory ideas, implicit or explicit, about the workings of a musical style or the nature of a composer's craft. Thus, the question I take up in this coda is not how the discussions presented throughout the book might apply to performance: it is, more precisely, how the interpretive mindset that spurred those discussions in the first place might also give rise to new approaches among those who play Mozart's music.

Although I have repeatedly stated that my outlook is not primarily that of a historian, I have nonetheless taken some contextualizing assumptions for granted, concerning the known facts of Mozart's life as well as the cultural history of the late eighteenth century. Broadly speaking, this orientation suggests an affinity with the ideals of the historical performance movement. Although it is by no means obligatory that all listeners or performers commit to the use of period instruments, even when playing on modern instruments certain interpretive questions are best settled through an awareness of past practices. Basic points of notation or style are good candidates for historical investigation since the answers such inquiries may yield—for instance, concerning the execution of grace notes, the phrasing of slurs, the elucidation of metrical hierarchies, and so forth—will inform performance on instruments of any vintage. In other cases, using period instruments does help to clarify and deepen the mindset explored in these pages.[6] Most telling is the case of the fortepiano, whose action, sound, and responsiveness evolved in lockstep with Mozart's keyboard idiom. As Malcolm Bilson has provocatively argued,

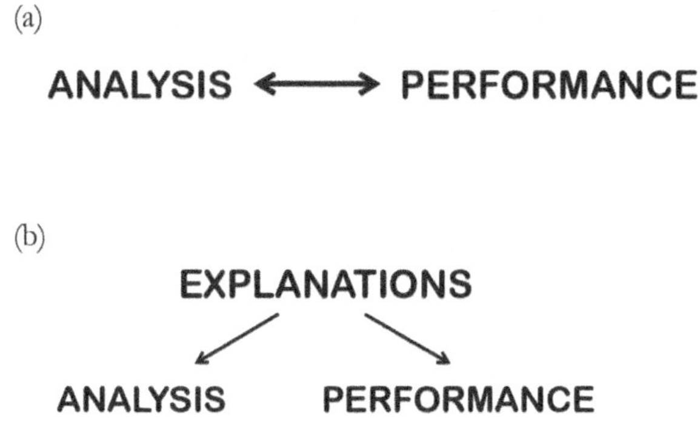

Figure 6.1 a, The conventional view of analysis and performance. *b*, The explanatory view

certain expressive gestures (most notably those pervasive, tapering slurs) are simply impossible to render on a modern piano, with its slowly blooming tone, but are easy to bring off with the fast-decaying sound of a period piano.[7] This suggests an alignment between a performer's expressive decision-making and the types of instruments that performer elects to play. Mozart's music derives its meaning in part from quicksilver affective shifts and daring modular juxtapositions, and the fortepiano's responsiveness, percussiveness, and relative lack of sustain make it the ideal vehicle with which to emphasize a fundamental characteristic of the style—one that may prove elusive on its modern counterpart. Even the fortepiano's quietness is an asset, since players can summon enormous physical intensity without running the risk of overwhelming either the instrument or the music. This is one reason that the athleticism on display in Mozart's mature variations and concertos is easier to convey on a period piano than on its larger descendants, in whose presence players often adopt a polite, glassy sound for fear of overplaying.

At the same time, choice of instrument dictates only so much. Most crucial is a performer's interpretive attitude, which does more than the sound or size of instruments to shape an audience's experience. Approaching Mozart as I have proposed—with attention to playfulness and theatricality—itself opens possibilities for expressive music making. Particularly relevant is the simulation of improvisation (that recurring theme in the preceding chapters), whereby a performer can pretend to execute a series of compositional choices, playing up moments of implied risk as though musical details had not been settled in advance. Like so much else in this book, the style of interpretation I will describe here depends on a theory of the composer-performer relationship—though whereas I previously argued that Mozart composed by imagining himself into the role of performers, I am now suggesting that it is performers who must imagine themselves into the role of the composer, locating instances at which the unfolding music affords an opportunity to sham real-time decision-making.[8] Such decision-making is, of course, illusory: listeners know on some basic level that Mozart set notes on the page two and a half centuries ago. But no matter. Even a familiar composition can be infused with wit and unexpected improvisatory energy by a performer who, like the composer, is willing to play dumb.

To illustrate this, consider the first movement of the Piano Sonata in D K. 311 (ex. 6.1), whose development, retransition, and recapitulation already served as models of simulated improvisatory difficulty. How might ideas from earlier in the book apply to an actual performance so as to heighten the sense of drama and volatility so essential in Mozart's style?

Performance begins with the problem of silence—specifically, of how to transition from the silence that precedes the music into the music itself.[9] When attempting to evoke improvisation, the first decision available for theatrical manipulation concerns the degree of forethought a performer wishes to suggest. How soon should the simulation of struggle set in? In K. 311, the answer is: almost immediately. The Allegro begins with a full-voiced chord redolent of the symphonic style, a gesture similar to the one that begins Mozart's earlier, less improvisatory Sonata K. 284. But whereas in K. 284 the symphonic topic continues through the grand gestures that follow, in K. 311 the bombastic first chord goes nowhere, leading to a series of abortive attempts to get the piece underway. First, Mozart hints briefly at melodic grace; then he summons a more propulsive accompaniment. Both fail, and we come to rest on an inconclusive cadential gesture, its rhetorical thrust undermined by the cheeky, chromatic appoggiatura. This three-bar (rather than four-bar) idea repeats verbatim before the pianist manages to move the exposition forward. The performer can emphasize such difficulties through physical byplay and careful phrasing. The beginning of the sonata should shatter the preceding silence as frenetically as possible—the player dashes to the keyboard and frantically sounds the opening chord, in all its unearned confidence, perhaps even before being properly seated. In the silence that follows, the lack of planning becomes evident to performer and audience. The pianist splutters, searching for the next gesture. To suggest real-time thought, the pianist should slightly elongate the rest, as if in genuine doubt as to what comes next. When the pianist finally ventures the short ascending gesture, this, too, is frantic, and

Example 6.1 Piano Sonata K. 311, first movement, mm. 1–16

can be played more quickly than the tempo of the movement proper. Another elongated rest follows (are the pianist's hands actually thrown up in frustration?) after which the broadly spaced accompaniment, labored, lends the third bar an air of absurdity. The pianist becomes a clown and starts to bait the listeners, an effect best achieved with a more deliberate tempo, in which the accompaniment can be made to seem clumsier. The same stance holds even when the metrical flow is established in the following phrase, with the sixteenth-note interjections in the left hand noisily and rudely interrupting the playful trills in the right. The end of the first theme, and its series of full chords, should be as cacophonous as possible.

The beginning of the development section provides another opportunity to simulate improvisatory thought. As noted in chapter 3, the development emerges out of the exposition's closing gesture, a device Mozart uses in other contexts as well to suggest an improviser who latches on to the most recent idea and begins to expand it. Here, the move from exposition to development can be effected as if the elaborative potential of the closing gesture has already occurred to the pianist, who moves swiftly through the cadence, eager to begin the next section. However, the downbeat of measure 41 brings shock for listeners and pianist alike. This dissonance is one of the harsher sonorities in the movement, and its juxtaposition with a strain of polite appoggiaturas is subversively incongruous. Perhaps the affect shifts yet again in the following measure, when the descending gesture echoes playfully in the bass. Here, the use of a period instrument enhances the reading, since bass notes sound decidedly more comical on a fortepiano than on a modern grand.

Further obstacles appear in measure 56, after the fantasia portion of the development has closed. It should not be difficult for a competent improviser to move from B minor to D major, a straightforward modulation by eighteenth-century standards. Here, however, the attempted modulation comes too late; the performer has already exhausted the improvisatory potential of the foregoing material and is left without an obvious means to initiate a retransition. Thus, the resort to brute force. Two block chords (perhaps requiring expansion with very short cadenzas) frustratedly push the music through to D—but either through a wrong note or a misguided attempt at artfulness, the modulation fails. D becomes dominant of G, and a new section begins. The performer can once again seem flustered, slowing the entrance of the subsequent theme and playing up the apparent uncertainty as to what follows. As the familiarity of the G-major melody becomes clear, the performance gathers confidence, accelerating. Yet this confidence is unearned, and the player lapses into pure repetition rather than development, presenting both phrases exactly as they appeared in the exposition. The end of the melody brings another moment of potential indecision, but it does not last. The performer finds the exit and, beginning in 66, begins to pile stock figuration above familiar chord progressions. Momentum and speed continue to build—the tempo should increase steadily—but overconfidence again betrays when the stock figures take on a life of their own and cause the player to bypass the recapitulation. Instead, the retransition, when finally wrestled to a close, ends with the same thick chords which, in the exposition, heralded the move to the dominant. Although the chords are just as clamorous here, they must also be tinged with a degree of resignation following the overlooked recapitulation—a gaffe so serious that it even falls within our fictionalized improviser's conscious awareness. A slight pause, perhaps a very subtle diminuendo, is in order before the pianist, now stoic, enters into the second theme and accepts the formal casualty that has occurred. Perhaps the sudden turn to minor, a surprise not presaged in the exposition, is meant to suggest faux pathos.

Playfulness and surprise are central to the remainder of the movement as the pianist becomes increasingly reckless. The familiar third theme (91–98) is played initially in a high treble octave and then repeated lower, as if in a quieter restatement—but this is interrupted by an unexpected *forte* and an expansion of the passage's range. The performer should pounce, exaggerating the dynamic shift and capitalizing on the contrast between what is expected and what is heard. As the passage ends, the brief hint of symphonic voicing prepares the best trick of all: a last-ditch attempt to atone for the missed recapitulation just when the movement seems ready to wind down. The elision of these two melodies means that the flash of insight occurs just after the broadly spaced chord that harkens to the opening bar; this can be suggested with yet another slightly lengthened pause before launching into the ascending sixteenth-note motif. The pianist, pleased, adds celebratory embellishments to the stock closing gesture that follows. This should be played with abandon, rushing forward through the passagework. Still, one final shock is in store: a deceptive cadence in the closing phrase whose effect is heightened if *not* delivered with a sensitive softening of the tempo, but rather charged through in the same brazen manner as the movement's opening chord. The final cadence, with its gracious appoggiatura, indicates a sheepish smile at the audience: decorum has at last been restored.

This narrated performance incorporates a number of ideas presented earlier, including the dramatization of improvisatory risk, the rhetorical potency of embellishments, and suggestions of persona and character. A single underlying principle unites all these ideas when applying them to performance: the performer's task, in this mode of interpretation, is to act out the implied ease or difficulty of the musical decision-making at each point in the sonata. The first prerequisite for creating such an interpretation, then, is an awareness of convention so that routine elements of the sonata can be differentiated from hijinks. This, in turn, requires a sensitivity to modular discontinuities, since these often serve as points at which the performer may wish to play up apparent compositional difficulties. When a pattern grows into a sequence, it can proceed with little simulated effort; but when patterns are disrupted or problematized, musical thought becomes labored.

Although performers can summon many expressive devices to bring off these effects, it is through the manipulation of tempo and timing that the theatrical fiction of improvisation becomes clearest. This is as true in K. 311 as it is in the improvisatory music discussed in chapter 3. The opening solo of the Piano Concerto K. 503, which simulates both a memory lapse and a momentary failure to improvise successfully, merits a similar push and pull of tempo, subtly slowing as the soloist feigns consternation and speeding up as possible solutions arise. These manipulations of time are equally effective in passages that dramatize successful rather than failed improvisations. When a solo episode in the first movement of the Piano Concerto K. 414 launches out of the orchestra's transitional motif, the performer should exude energetic confidence by adopting a slightly quicker pace. Nor are such rhythmic manipulations limited in their usefulness to explicitly "improvisatory" contexts. Mozart's music abounds with moments of compositional suspense—transitions calculated to leave the audience guessing at what will follow and that therefore invite the simulation of musical thought. In the first movement of the Piano Concerto K. 482, the onset of the lyrical second theme presents just such a transition. The previous phrase closes on the dominant of B♭, and although the implied destination is clear, the timing is not. At the beginning of measure 149, the pianist might slow the tempo, continuing to decelerate through the downbeat of the next bar. An elongated rest will build tension, after which the short burst of sixteenth notes, played abruptly in a faster tempo, lightens the mood. The following rest provides another shift of affective pose, after which the gentler character of the remaining descent ushers in the new melody. Likewise, a moment of compositional suspense toward the end of the first movement of K. 414 follows the same rhythmic style, with question-mark rests and short bursts of sixteenth-note activity that would benefit from push and pull of performative time (mm. 257–64). Because these passages occur while the orchestra is silent, the soloist can speed and slow more freely than is normally possible.

Equally crucial for expressive performance is the projection not only of improvisatory playacting but of musical character. The notion that the performer inhabits a fictional character has featured more or less explicitly in the past three chapters and indeed underpins the improvisatory pratfalls I described in K. 311, which are premised on the notion that the identity projected throughout is that of a composer-performer rather than, as is actually the case, a pianist playing a prefabricated text. The unfolding sonata dramatizes a series of events that beset the attempted act of improvisation, and these events cohere only if the performer represents a sustained character. However, many of the expressive turns in Mozart's instrumental music locate character on a more finely grained level. Stances often shift from phrase to phrase or even within phrases, and the performer must then inhabit a series of poses combined in close succession. We have seen examples of this in the dialogic exchanges discussed in chapter 5. In some cases, the evocation of character depends on accompaniment. In the concertante finales of the Piano Sonatas K. 330 and K. 333, Mozart suggests the alternation of "soloist" and "orchestra" solely through the manipulation of left-hand writing. The melodic lines repeat virtually unaltered while Mozart adjusts the texture, range, and density of the underlying figuration to suggest either a lone soloist or the bustling energy of a full orchestra. In such movements, awareness of the two character-like entities determines not only the possibility for embellishment (extensive in the "solo" passages, minimal in the "tuttis") but a range of other nuances—the rhythmic freedom and playfulness that can be applied in the soloist's iteration of each theme as contrasted with the strictness of the orchestral versions, and the weight with which the "orchestral" left hands must sound.

Other accompanimental shifts interact with the melodies they support, facilitating a more nuanced manipulation of character in the upper voices. In the Adagio from the Piano Concerto K. 488, a subsidiary melody begins with a brisk, arpeggiated accompaniment in the soloist's left hand. Although the right hand doubles the winds and is thus free to depart significantly from the written melody (which indeed is what occurs in the extravagant embellishments composed by Mozart's pupil Barbara Ployer),[10] the left hand's pulse nonetheless defines the metrical feel and forward momentum of the passage. When the pulse ceases and the left hand, joined by the strings, plays a single chord on the downbeat of measure 41, the pianist may gently suspend time in the right hand. Perhaps the ascending sixth in the melody implies a sudden, yearning sigh as the pianist strains against the darkness of F♯ minor, soon to return as the movement's prevailing tonic; or perhaps it mimics the portamento swooping of an operatic soprano. Either way, whether we hear a thoroughgoing change of character or simply a brief textural reprieve, the expressive possibilities for the right hand arise through the cessation of the accompanimental motor in the left. In the following bar, another shift occurs, introducing in the piano solo a three-part texture. A new mode of expression seems to present itself here: the right hand is absorbed into a brief but strict cadence in the manner of a stately minuet.

Similar considerations apply in Mozart's chamber music. In the opening phrase of the Oboe Quartet, K. 370, the music passes through three distinct character states and, although the effect derives in large part from the accompanimental writing, all of the performers come together to enact the drama. The first bar presents a fanfare-like upbeat in the oboe and a broad, arpeggiated tonic triad in the cello. In the second half of the bar, this fanfare evaporates into a courtly dance with a rising series of turns in the solo line and a polite, eighth-note accompaniment in the violin and viola. Immediately thereafter, the accompaniment becomes more soulful. Although the remainder of the oboe line is neutral with regard to pulse, time feel, and expressive profile, at the transition from measure 2 to 3 the violin and viola leave behind their lighthearted staccatos and adopt a serious, chromatic pose firmly entrenched in a *alla breve* of arias sung by the Countess or Donna Anna. This phrase, like the excerpt from K. 488 discussed above, derives potency largely from its rhythmic underlay, which in both cases moves freely between smaller and larger divisions of the beat. In the Oboe Quartet, this trajectory slows the passage of time by exchanging brisk quarter notes for languorous half notes. In K. 488, by contrast, the accompaniment accelerates. Mozart initially gives the phrase with two large pulses per bar but ultimately shifts metrical weight to the eighth note. In both compositions, the textural changes, differing levels of chromaticism, and interplay of voices all help to suggest the multiplicity of characters performers might attempt to display.

Expressive shifts such as these are easiest to imagine and execute in the context of solo sonatas, chamber music, and concertos, which offer individual players a high degree of autonomy. But in Mozart's symphonies, too, musical characters are often present, and projecting them is one task of ensemble performance. In the last movement of the Symphony in B♭ K. 319, Mozart presents what first appears to be a lyrical second theme, beginning in measure 82. Against a light, staccato accompaniment, the melody initially sighs down though an F-major arpeggio, whose two-note slurs seem of a piece with the much-loved Andante from the Piano Concerto K. 467. Immediately following this antecedent, he interjects a joking, almost flippant consequent: a simple descending scale whose grace notes and rests tug against the preceding segment's earnestness (mm. 87–90). This lighter gesture is followed by a regaining of the lyrical (91–98), though not a return to the original arpeggios. Slurs in the accompaniment replace the light staccatos, and empty downbeats suggest breathless silences. In the melody, the violins now play in octaves, a timbre Mozart described in the *Entführung* letter as representative of Belmonte's tenderness and passion. The immediacy of these effects in performance depends on the musicians' willingness to highlight the textural, timbral, and affective contrasts as quickly and vividly as possible.

Although my discussion so far has invoked surprise, character, and drama, I have for the most part avoided reference to opera in these narrated instrumental interpretations. The reason is, in part, that instrumental compositions are textless affairs. Their effects must come across through strictly musical means—though, in the context of live performance, the available devices also include body language and stage deportment. My hesitation to invoke opera also stems from the precarious and sometimes strained analogies between texted and nontexted music, which I discussed in chapter 5. Nonetheless, when it comes to practical questions, opera has much to reveal about expressive instrumental performance.

Most straightforwardly, opera can clarify issues in the performance of instrumental music when players are aware of melodic figures that cross between the two domains, especially when these figures occur repeatedly with highly consistent text settings in the operas. The gesture Donna Anna introduces at the start of her first duet in *Don Giovanni* is taken up later by Elvira in the act 1 finale and reappears again in the Queen of the Night's famous act 2 aria in *Die Zauberflöte*. In all three, the text entreats wrath and vengeance. It is striking, then, that the figure resonates exactly with the opening melody in the Piano Concerto in D minor, K. 466. Other features in the first phrase of K. 466 offer little assistance in identifying the movement's expressive outlook, which at this early stage may seem subdued, *misterioso*, or portentous. Yet the operatic reference suggests a reading characterized less by mystery and more by tightly coiled rage. The syncopations should be sharp and angular, with local dynamics that belie the overarching quietness, right until the music explodes into a *forte* much as in the beginning of the Queen of the Night's aria.

The comparison between K. 466 and the Queen of the Night is solidified by other elements as well: the orchestration with its pairs of trumpets, the tremolos in the strings, and the Neapolitan harmonies that feature prominently in both concerto and aria.

Indeed, among Mozart's mature operas, *Die Zauberflöte* proves a particularly rich source of thematic interchange with instrumental music. Some of these are linked to key area: Pamina's act 2 aria crystallizes many motifs from Mozart's other compositions in G minor (including specific overlaps with the String Quintet K. 516 and the Symphony K. 550), as does Tamino's act 1 aria for Mozart's music in E♭ major (including the slow movement of K. 550).[11] Although other operas also participate in similar exchanges, they generally suggest looser comparisons, best discovered not by seeking precise overlaps but rather through a search for instrumental phrases that encode a more diffuse affinity with individual characters. Of course, some degree of caution is needed when taking this approach: there is a long tradition, stretching back to the early nineteenth century, whereby interpreters would tack texts onto instrumental lines, and these often reveal more about those who draw the comparisons than they do about the music.[12] Even so, when handled judiciously, such overlaps are revealing. A piece that lends itself well to this treatment is the finale of the Violin Sonata in B♭, K. 454. I have already pointed out ways in which this movement might be considered a dramatic dialogue in the miniature, with each performer engaged in competitive struggles, including the flamboyant battle of virtuosity in the final phrases. Equally striking are the gestures within the movement that prefigure operatic melodies. The sighing eighth notes in the movement's various episodes share both sound and shape with Elvira's plaints in "Mi tradì," just as the repeated eighth notes in a subsidiary theme point to Papageno's music (ex. 6.2). Such comparisons are fascinating in their own right as we mark the consistency of Mozart's style, but they are also crucial for developing an expressive mode of performance. As before, many performative nuances follow from these judgments. By pecking their way through the Papageno-like passage or lavishing Elvira's phrase with rubato, players can imbue the sonata with significant dramatic flexibility.

Having practiced this art of cross-referencing between Mozart's operas and instrumental music, it becomes clear that we may draw the same types of intertextual allusions among instrumental compositions without invoking opera. Many of Mozart's most vivid performative gestures occur when one family of instruments imitates another, as in the topical "horn calls" played by the violas at the outset of the String Quintet in E♭, K. 614. These are identical

Example 6.2 Violin Sonata K. 454, third movement, mm. 58–70

to the types of music played by actual horns in compositions by Mozart and his contemporaries, yet in K. 614 they derive much of their theatrical effect, paradoxically, from the fact that they are *not* played by horns.[13] Because they are given in a viola part, they represent exactly the kind of ventriloquism rendered in so much of Mozart's music, enclosed in quotation marks and treated as character-like stances to be assumed rather than as simple timbral identities taken for granted. The same applies to passages across his piano writing, from the "wind band" in the finale of the Sonata in A minor, K. 310, to the piquant "oboe and horn" interjections in the slow movement of the Sonata K. 311 and the first movement of the Sonata K. 332. Still more instructive are references in the violin sonatas. In K. 454 (whose finale brought Elvira and Papageno together), the first movement draws melodic, harmonic, and textural devices from the "Gran Partita" for winds, K. 361. Both pieces open with nearly identical material: full chords, stately dotted rhythms, descending melodies, and interjections from "solo" instruments; they even share specific melodic overlaps, when the violin's tune and the piano's accompanimental rhythm played after the opening statement in the sonata draws from the third movement of the serenade. In an earlier violin sonata, K. 302 in E♭, such references take on broader orchestral colors as they follow a series of timbral states suggestive of the opening of the Piano Concerto K. 482, with a *tutti* fanfare followed by interjections from individual orchestral sections. In the sonata, the mere presence of a violin playing the opening arpeggio alongside the pianist lends the solo passage a mellower air, as though it were delivered in the muted voices of clarinets, horns, and bassoons. As before, each of these observations carries specific interpretive clues for modern-day performers. Violists imitating horns, pianists imitating wind ensembles, and violinists imitating oboes—such directives hint at virtually every element of expressive performance, from the minutiae of touch, pedaling, and even choice of fingering, to abstract considerations of sound, articulation, and persona.

Written words are a poor substitute for the nuances of musical performance, and it is perhaps fitting to end this exploration with a reminder that the readings I offer are not interpretive prescriptions. They are merely speculations as to how a set of broad ideals might manifest themselves when applied to particular passages in Mozart's output. All of my suggestions resonate with the explanatory mindset I have pursued throughout this book, whether by dramatizing the implications of composerly choice or by aiming to show the music as an unfolding, theatrical process rather than a fixed entity, glassy and perfect but held at a safe distance. They reveal within Mozart's text the maximum number of characters and expressive states; and, through a heightened sensitivity to topical and modular shifts, they seek to conjure the playacting, both humorous and heartfelt, of a composer-performer whose restless spirit and expansive imagination become irresistibly palpable.

I argued at the outset that my explanatory approach—the "theory of Mozart" underpinning both my analyses and these imagined performances—

aspires to be comprehensive. I have sought to connect the many facets of his music and career and to celebrate the full range of styles, genres, and voices in which he wrote. In large part the breadth of this interpretation rests on the bedrock of a fundamentally comic outlook that can feign tears and play at earnestness, eschewing the rigid pathos of the tragic. Yet the view at which I have aimed also encompasses the historical origins of Mozart's music, not just its content. It seeks, behind his many activities, a core of playfulness, technical mastery, and imaginative facility—and ultimately strives to hear these traits within the music.

In making the case for a comprehensive view of Mozart's craft, I do not want to suggest that my explanations are in any sense final. Our understanding of Mozart's style will continue to evolve, pushed forward by the ever-shifting intellectual and cultural trends within which interpretations arise. In the nineteenth century, it would have seemed bizarre to claim that Mozart might someday be understood as an impish jokester, just as some listeners in the early twentieth century would most likely have scoffed at the suggestion that the tactile and aural characteristics of eighteenth-century pianos influenced his compositional structures. Yet from our present-day vantage, it is the older theories that seem dusty, relying on outmoded ideas about the divine font of creative genius. The explanations outlined in this book, too, will come to seem out of date. This is a point of hopefulness, for it means that they will have been replaced with a more compelling, more beautiful, and perhaps still more fundamental vision of this captivating and beguiling repertoire. New interpretations will be discovered and with them new ways for us to hear, play, and understand Mozart's music.

ACKNOWLEDGMENTS

I grew up in a musical household, and it is to my family that I owe my first thanks. Mozart has been a presence in my world for as long as I can remember: I listened to his sonatas through the walls when my parents practiced the piano; as children, my brother and I enjoyed singing duets from *Don Giovanni*; and my formative chamber-music experiences centered around homemade arrangements of his symphonies and operas. Every member of this environment helped shape my relationship with this art, but I am especially indebted to my mother, Ruth Komanoff Underwood, whose extraordinary musicianship has been a lifelong inspiration. Although her own career unfolded in the world of rock 'n' roll, it was she who first sparked my love of Mozart and she who has nurtured that developing enthusiasm ever since. Malachai, my brother, has challenged me over the decades, spurring my growth as a thinker and performer. This book could not have been written without the lifelong benefit of their company.

Equally crucial was the guidance I received as a student at Cornell University, where I encountered Malcolm Bilson, Annette Richards, James Webster, David Yearsley, and Neal Zaslaw. These musicians contributed greatly to my understanding of Mozart as well as to my practices as a performer, and all five are present throughout these pages. So too are three Mozartians I have admired from afar: Wye J. Allanbrook, whose view of the comic, mimetic element of Mozart's music permeates my analyses; Robert Levin, whose conception of Mozart's improvisatory volatility staked out the territory I explore at greater length here; and Roman Ivanovitch, whose writings on variation catalyzed my interpretive outlook. I also wish to thank my teachers Pavlo Beznosiuk and Elizabeth Wallfisch, who showed me repeatedly that theatrical, energetic readings of Mozart's violin music can also be sublimely elegant. I am beholden, too, to the collaborators, ensembles, and opera companies in North America and Europe with whom I have performed Mozart's music over the decades, who were willing to indulge my unorthodox interpretive proclivities in rehearsal and performance. Owing to their generosity, as well as their tolerance for improvisatory risk-taking, my career has been a laboratory in which I developed and tested the theories outlined here.

While writing this book I have benefited from the feedback and support of a wide range of mentors, colleagues, and friends. My thanks go to John Butt, my PhD advisor, who read sections of chapters 1, 2, and 4, and whose advice, provocations, and criticism over the years have been invaluable. The earliest written incarnations of the ideas in this book were shaped by input from David Code, John Irving, and David McGuinness. My approach to explanation and conjecture was honed through illuminating discussions with David Deutsch (who read excerpts from chapter 1), Clifford Siskin, and Lulie Tanett. More recently, Dean Sutcliffe and Ellen Lockhart offered incisive readings of large portions of chapter 4, strengthening my arguments and prose. David Hyun-Su Kim encouraged me, discussing many of the ideas in these pages and weighing in on matters of piano fingering. Without the support of Tom Beghin and David Yearsley, this book might not have been published. Rachel Friedman bolstered me through the process of writing and revision. Sharlene He read the Theme and portions of chapter 3, repeatedly and generously discussing the framing, argument, and narrative. Most of all, I am grateful to those who made time in their busy schedules to read complete drafts of the manuscript and give expert feedback: Edward Klorman, Elizaveta Miller, Clifford Siskin, Jeffrey Swinkin, David Yearsley, and my two anonymous peer reviewers. The book has benefited from their remarkable insights both on the global level and on matters of detail. Needless to say, all remaining flaws are my own.

McGill University's Schulich School of Music is a unique and stimulating intellectual home, and I wish to thank the many local colleagues who have engaged with this work. William Caplin and Jon Wild joined me on a series of walks in Montreal during which our discussions strengthened elements of chapters 1 and 3. My life at McGill would be immeasurably poorer without the deep friendship and musical camaraderie of Tracy Smith Bessette, Elinor Frey, Hank Knox, Sara Laimon, Violaine Melançon, and Mika Putterman, all of whom have seen me through the best and worst of times. I owe an especially large debt to Edward Klorman, a most generous colleague, brilliant scholar, sensitive critic, and steadfast friend. He remained cheerfully willing to discuss this project over the past three years even as I plied him with what must have seemed an endless series of questions both musical and literary. I am grateful for the insights he pushed me to develop. In addition, I would like to thank four of McGill's graduate students: Gracie Carney, who rendered the Shandy-esque squiggles in figure 4.1; Maryse Legault, who advised me on matters of historical clarinet technique discussed in chapter 2; Shanti Nachtergaele, who assisted with the index; and Hester Bell Jordan, who assisted with the musical examples.

Marta Tonegutti, the incomparable music editor at the University of Chicago Press, has been a generous and thoughtful guardian of this project, offering exceptional editorial support, repeated close readings, and criticism that was at once exacting and encouraging. I am grateful for her enthusiasm for the manuscript, and for her expertise in shepherding it through the process of publication. Her assistant Kristin Rawlings provided guidance on an impressive range of matters. I am grateful also to Adriana Smith and Meredith Nini of the University of Chicago Press; to Steve LaRue for his careful copyediting; and to Kate Brubeck, Clare Counihan, and Carolyn Savarese, who provided input along the way. I would also like to thank Cambridge University Press for allowing me to reuse, in chapter 4, revised versions of material that originally appeared in *Eighteenth-Century Music* and the *Cambridge Opera Journal*.

Finally, during the initial stages of work on this project I was immensely privileged to share a home with the brilliant art historian Ruth Ezra. Ruthie's keen eye and acute mind—as well as her literary sensibilities, aesthetic perceptiveness, virtuosic interpretive talents, and profound humanity—have been an unflagging source of scholarly inspiration and personal joy. Long before I began to write this book, I benefited enormously from discussing the underlying ideas with her, and later, when the project was underway, from showing her drafts of some portions of the manuscript. During this time, I was also fortunate to watch her work, learning from her example and insights as she discussed art and ideas with friends, colleagues, and students. She, more than anyone, has taught me what it means to attend to the powers of a great work of art and to attempt to convey those powers in writing. I dedicate this book to her, with deepest gratitude, admiration, and love.

NOTES

Variation 1

1. I use *performance* and *performativity* to describe Mozart's activities as a performing musician (his public appearances as a pianist or violinist, or as a conductor of operatic productions) as well as the skills he practiced (his piano technique, the physical and intellectual habits that allowed him to improvise, and so forth). I am not invoking resonances these terms have accumulated in other disciplines, such as Butlerian notions of gender performativity.

2. Even so, we should not overstate the confluence of composition and performance. As Adeline Mueller explains in *Mozart and the Mediation of Childhood* (Chicago: University of Chicago Press, 2021), 14–31, during Mozart's lifetime the two skills were understood and trained differently from each other, and his particular acquisition of talent in both is therefore not merely a matter of general cultural practice.

3. The distinction between performance and professional composition in the eighteenth century is a recurring theme in Stephen Rose, *Musical Authorship from Schütz to Bach* (Cambridge: Cambridge University Press, 2019).

4. Palestrina and Corelli serve as examples in the nuanced examination of the composer-performer relationship in John Butt, *Playing with History* (Cambridge: Cambridge University Press, 2002), 118–20. Butt goes on to explore tensions between the compositions and performances of twentieth-century figures including Bartók, Messiaen, and Stravinsky.

5. Cf. Beethoven's Piano Concerto op. 15, first movement, measure 172. The highest melodic note should be f♯‴, one half step higher than the highest key on his pianos, so Beethoven notates the "incorrect" F♮ rather than reshaping the passage. The difficulty of Beethoven's music, and the many unsuccessful performances given during the composer's lifetime, have been the subject of much study, mostly concerning the middle and late periods. However, William Kinderman surmises that Beethoven's propensity for writing overly difficult music stretched back to the first phase of his career, exemplified by the 1790 *Cantata on the Death of Joseph II*. See William Kinderman, *Beethoven*, 2nd ed. (New York: Oxford University Press, 2009), 24.

6. On the challenges of freelance life in Vienna, see Jessica Waldoff, "Mozart and Finances," in *Mozart in Context*, ed. Simon P. Keefe (Cambridge: Cambridge University Press, 2019), 171–72. On the contemporary musical marketplace and the stylistic ferment it facilitated, see the account of Mozart and Haydn (written from the perspective of economic history) in Tyler Cowen, *In Praise of Commercial Culture* (Cambridge, MA: Harvard University Press, 1998), 137–40.

7. Mozart, letter to his father, Mannheim, 28 February 1778, *MBA*, 2:304. Mueller (*Mozart and the Mediation of Childhood*, 84) observes that Mozart adopted this goal as early as age eleven when crafting *Apollo et Hyacinthus* for specific singers. For a useful overview of Mozart's letters organized by topic, see Robert L. Marshall, *Mozart Speaks: Views on Music, Musicians, and the World* (New York: Schirmer Books, 1991).

8. Michael Lorenz, "'Mademoiselle Jeunehomme.' Zur Lösung eines Mozart-Rätsels," in *Mozart. Experiment Aufklärung im Wien des Ausgehenden 18. Jahrhunderts*, ed. Herbert Lachmayer (Vienna: Hatje Cantz, 2006), 423–29.

9. Letter to his father, Mannheim, 6 December 1777, *MBA*, 2:170–71.

10. The human comportment enacted in contemporary chamber music has been the subject of recent studies, including Edward Klorman, *Mozart's Music of Friends: Social Interplay in the Chamber Works* (Cambridge: Cambridge University Press, 2016), and W. Dean Sutcliffe, *Instrumental Music in an Age of Sociability: Haydn, Mozart and Friends* (Cambridge: Cambridge University Press, 2020). On the family relations in K. 242 and K. 299, see Mueller, *Mozart and the Mediation of Childhood*, chap. 5.

11. Letter to his father, Vienna, 23 March 1782, *MBA*, 3:199, emphasis in original.

12. This concern is expressed with reference to music publishing more generally in a letter to his father, Vienna, 20 February 1784, *MBA*, 3:301–2.

13. Letter to his father, Mannheim, 4 November 1777, *MBA*, 2:101.

14. This point and its broader ramifications are explored most thoroughly in Simon P. Keefe, "'We Hardly Knew What We Should Pay Attention to First': Mozart the Performer-Composer at Work on the Viennese Piano Concertos," *Journal of the Royal Musical Association* 134, no. 2 (2009), 185–242, and, more recently, *Mozart in Vienna: The Final Decade* (Cambridge: Cambridge University Press, 2017).

15. Letter to his father, Paris, 3 July 1778, *MBA*, 2:388–89.

16. Letter to his father, Vienna, 26 September 1781, *MBA*, 3:162–63. The effects Mozart describes are all the more comically incongruous in light of the aria's text, which catalogs the absurd litany of punishments Osmin advocates for his victims—beheading, hanging, impaling on red-hot stakes.

17. Such revisions are detailed in Keefe, "'We Hardly Knew What We Should Pay Attention to First.'" For an expanded treatment of timbral and balance issues, see his *Mozart in Vienna*, 82ff, 218.

18. On the various versions of the embellishments in K. 457, see Eugene K. Wolf, "The Rediscovered Autograph of Mozart's Fantasy and Sonata in C Minor, K. 475/457," *Journal of Musicology* 10, no. 1 (1992), 3–47, and chapter 4 of this book.

19. Popular legend holds that the insertion of "Dalla sua pace" was necessitated by Morella's inability to sing "Il mio tesoro." Though this may be correct, the details are unclear, and Dexter Edge has even proposed that Mozart wrote "Dalla sua pace" before cutting the original aria; see Dexter Edge, "Mozart's Viennese Copyists" (PhD diss., University of South-

ern California, 2001), 1801–3. Even so, given conventions for tenor roles, Mozart may have expected Ottavio to sing only one aria; see Stefan Rohringer, "Don Ottavio and the History of the Tenor Voice," in *Dramma Giocoso: Four Contemporary Perspectives on the Mozart/Da Ponte Operas* (Leuven: Leuven University Press, 2012), 50. For a study of Mozart's operatic revisions before his work with Da Ponte, see Keefe, *Mozart in Vienna*, 100–107, which updates and amends Ulrich Konrad's research.

20. On Ottavio's musical resemblance to the Countess, see Wye J. Allanbrook, *Rhythmic Gesture in Mozart:* Le nozze di Figaro *and* Don Giovanni (Chicago: University of Chicago Press, 1983), 230–32.

21. Maria Anna Mozart, letter to her husband, Paris, 5 April 1778, *MBA*, 2:330.

22. Letter to his father, Vienna, 1 August 1781, *MBA*, 3:144. Both letters, and Mozart's need for a keyboard more generally, are discussed in Neal Zaslaw, "Mozart as a Working Stiff," in *On Mozart*, ed. James M. Morris (Cambridge: Cambridge University Press; Washington, DC: Woodrow Wilson Center Press, 1994), 102–12.

23. For a brief discussion of Haydn's relationship to improvisation, see James Webster, "The Rhetoric of Improvisation in Haydn's Keyboard Music," in *Haydn and the Performance of Rhetoric*, ed. Tom Beghin and Sander M. Goldberg (Chicago: University of Chicago Press, 2007), 174.

24. Quoted in Franz Niemetschek, *Lebensbeschreibung des K.K. Kapelmeisters Wolfgang Amadeus Mozart, aus Originalquellen* (Prague, 1808), 62–63. Constanze altered her story when speaking with Vincent and Mary Novello in the 1820s, claiming that Mozart composed entirely in his head; but it is generally agreed that the earlier reminiscence is more likely to be accurate.

25. Letter to his father, Salzburg, 20 July 1782, *MBA*, 3:212.

26. Christoph Wolff, "The Challenge of Blank Paper: Mozart the Composer," in *On Mozart*, ed. James M. Morris (Cambridge: Cambridge University Press; Washington, DC: Woodrow Wilson Center Press, 1994), 113–29. Wolff revisits the topic and expands his critical approach to these "torsos" in *Mozart at the Gateway to His Fortune: Serving the Emperor, 1788–1791* (New York: W. W. Norton, 2012).

27. Contemporary training in composition and improvisation was symbiotic. For a description of the overlapping techniques as practiced and taught by Georg Joseph Vogler, a musician with whom Mozart repeatedly crossed paths, see Dana Gooley, *Fantasies of Improvisation: Free Playing in Nineteenth-Century Music* (New York: Oxford University Press, 2018), 25–37.

28. This model for the relationship between improvisation and planning in artistic creation is not limited to music. See, for instance, R. Keith Sawyer's account of Picasso's free-form, improvisational paintings as artistic experiments aimed at the discovery of new ideas. R. Keith Sawyer, "Improvisation and the Creative Process: Dewey, Collingwood, and the Aesthetics of Spontaneity," *Journal of Aesthetics and Art Criticism* 58, no. 2 (2000), 149–50.

29. Recollection of Jan Nepomuk Štepánek, quoted in Georg Nikolaus Nissen, *Biographie W.A. Mozarts* (Leipzig, 1828), 517, and translated by Katalin Komlós in "'Ich praeludirte und spielte Variazionen': Mozart the Fortepianist," in *Perspectives on Mozart Performance*, ed. R. Larry Todd and Peter Williams (Cambridge: Cambridge University Press, 1991), 34–35. Another similar account can be found in Niemetschek; see Keefe, "'We Hardly Knew What We Should Pay Attention to First,'" 186–88.

30. These and other similar contemporary accounts are collected in Keefe, *Mozart in Vienna*, 8–9, italics and capitalization in original.

31. On K. 379, see the letter to his father, Vienna, 8 April 1781, *MBA*, 3:103–4. On K. 454, as well as the more general connection to Mozart's penchant for risk-taking and "sailing close to the wind," see Roger Moseley, *Keys to Play: Music as a Ludic Medium from Apollo to Nintendo* (Oakland: University of California Press, 2016), 203.

32. On the origins of Mozart's variation sets in improvised performances. see Komlós, "'Ich praeludirte und spielte Variazionen,'" 40. The compositional performativity of these sets (and many other compositions) is treated throughout Roman Ivanovitch, "Mozart and the Environment of Variation" (PhD diss., Yale University, 2004).

33. That simple musical gestures can, though variation, be spun into more complex forms is a recurring theme in historical and modern theoretical texts. Friedrich Erhard Niedt's *Musikalische Handleitung*, for instance, demonstrates how to write a chorale and then use it as the basis of a prelude and a series of dances so that all movements are, in effect, variations of the others. This anticipates Heinrich Schenker's concept of the *Auskomponierung eines Klanges* and receives further mention in chapters 2, 3, and 5. On its applications to Mozart analysis and performance, see Carl Schachter, "20th-Century Analysis and Mozart Performance," *Early Music* 19, no. 4 (1991): 620–28. The same method of improvisation through variation was ascribed to both Haydn and, at greater length, Beethoven, who, according to eyewitnesses, improvised by single-mindedly developing individual motives—a description applicable to his compositional aesthetic as well. For an analysis of a Haydn piano trio movement that explicitly treats the sonata form as an expansion of a theme through variation procedures, see Charles Rosen, *The Classical Style: Haydn, Mozart, Beethoven*, enl. ed. (New York: W. W. Norton, 1997), 83–88.

34. Ivanovitch, "Mozart and the Environment of Variation," 14.

35. Mozart's postscript to a letter from Anna Maria Mozart to her husband, Paris, 14 May 1778, *MBA*, 2:356–57.

36. This point is made throughout the literature on partimento, particularly by Robert Gjerdingen, in *Music in the Galant Style* (New York: Oxford University Press, 2007). A "reductionist" account of musical form, compatible with this view of modules, is given in Yoel Greenberg, *How Sonata Forms: A Bottom-Up Approach to Musical Form* (New York: Oxford University Press, 2022).

37. The term *module* is used throughout the literature, including by Michael Callahan, Ellwood Derr, Derek Remeš, Neal Zaslaw, and others. For a recent discussion and overview of analytic sources relevant to eighteenth-century German lands, see Derek Remeš, "Some (Dis)Assembly Required: Modularity in the Keyboard Improvisation Pedagogy of Jacob Adlung and Johann Vallade," *Music Theory Online* 26, no. 1 (2020).

38. Mozart's stylistic imitation of C. P. E. Bach, J. C. Bach, and Hüllmandel is the subject of detailed discussion in John Irving, *Mozart's Piano Sonatas: Contexts, Sources, Style* (Cambridge: Cambridge University Press, 1997).

39. Compare the horn call in the opening of the String Quintet K. 614; the symphonic fanfare that ends the exposition of the Piano Sonata K. 332/i; and the accompanied recitative in the Violin Concerto K. 216/i/147–51. The term *topic* was introduced to music analysis by Leonard Ratner, in *Classic Music: Expression, Form, and Style* (New York: Schirmer Books, 1980). For a comprehensive account of topics from the perspectives of musicology, theory,

and performance, see Danuta Mirka's extensive introduction in her edited *Oxford Handbook of Topic Theory* (New York: Oxford University Press, 2014). See also the philosophical and analytic account of topics in Sutcliffe, *Instrumental Music in an Age of Sociability*, 230–45.

40. Particularly the Neapolitan traditions examined by (for instance) Gjerdingen in *Music in the Galant Style* and Nicholas Baragwanath throughout *The Solfeggio Tradition* (New York: Oxford University Press, 2020).

41. Leonard B. Meyer, *Style and Music: Theory, History, and Ideology* (Chicago: University of Chicago Press, 1989), 3.

42. On the conventions of the Romanesca and Prinner, see Gjerdingen, *Music in the Galant Style*, chaps. 2 and 3 respectively.

43. Gjerdingen, *Music in the Galant Style*, 61–63.

44. Although I focus on Mozart's idiosyncratic use of the Fonte, his breaches of convention with other figures, such as the Prinner and Quiescenza, have been a subject of study, for instance, in Gilad Rabinovitch, "Reimagining Historical Improvisation: An Analysis of Robert Levin's Fantasy on Themes by W.A. Mozart, October 29, 2012," *Music Theory Online* 26, no. 2 (2020): para. 1.1.2–1.1.6.

45. Vasili Byros, "Towards an 'Archaeology' of Hearing: Schemata and Eighteenth-Century Consciousness," *Musica Humana* 1 (2009): 252–54, notes that the opening of K. 465 traces a Fonte while also embedding le–sol–fi–sol and Fenaroli/Monte. The Fonte emerges from these other schemata, occurring in measures 1–4 and 5–8.

46. Byros, "Trazom's Wit: Communicative Strategies in a 'Popular' Yet 'Difficult' Sonata," *Eighteenth-Century Music* 10, no. 2 (2013): 213–52.

47. This reading of the left hand's teasing is due to Robert Levin, quoted in Sheila Guymer, "Eloquent Performance: The Pronuntiatio of Topics," in *The Oxford Handbook of Topic Theory*, ed. Danuta Mirka (Oxford: Oxford University Press, 2014), 580–90.

48. Ivanovitch ("Mozart and the Environment of Variation," 4) briefly describes this passage in light of variation principles; however, because the modular break so neatly separates *a* and a_1 from any of the subsequent answering ideas, the movement is less a demonstration of variation than it is of the combinatorial segments that seem to have been detached and reshuffled as the piece unfolds.

49. Kofi Agawu suggests that Mozart's aesthetic may be one of "discontinuity" rather than "continuity" in Kofi Agawu, "Prospects for a Theory-Based Analysis of the Instrumental Music," in *Wolfgang Amadè Mozart: Essays on His Life and His Music*, ed. Stanley Sadie (Oxford: Clarendon Press, 1996), 128–31.

50. For a case study in the reordering of themes, see Karol Berger's perceptive (if contentious) analysis of the first movement of K. 491, in Karol Berger, *Bach's Cycle, Mozart's Arrow: An Essay on the Origins of Musical Modernity* (Berkeley: University of California Press, 2007), chap. 4.

51. Sutcliffe, *Instrumental Music in an Age of Sociability*, 57, observes that many assertive gestures are answered by gracious ripostes. Although such alternations are usually followed by a phrase synthesizing aspects of each, in K. 219 Mozart continues with an extension of the sighing slurs—an illustration of the motivic digressiveness I will explore in chapters 3 and 4.

52. Kofi Agawu, *Music as Discourse* (Oxford: Oxford University Press, 2009), 37.

53. The misuse of schematic functions is given a general overview in Leonard B. Meyer,

Explaining Music (Berkeley: University of California Press, 1973), 212–15, and *Style and Music*, 26–30. On K. 271 in particular, see Rosen, *The Classical Style*, 202.

54. This is a recurring theme in Melanie Lowe, *Pleasure and Meaning in the Classical Symphony* (Bloomington: Indiana University Press, 2007). The intricate social patterning of chamber music by Mozart and others has recently been examined in a spate of brilliant studies including Rebecca Cypess, *Women and Musical Salons in the Enlightenment* (Chicago: University of Chicago Press, 2022); Klorman, *Mozart's Music of Friends*; Moseley, *Keys to Play*; and Sutcliffe, *Instrumental Music in an Age of Sociability*, all of which discuss the communicative strategies that arise when players themselves are the intended audience. The case of piano sonatas is more complex; although many sonatas fall into this category, Mozart also performed some in public recitals, including K. 279—and it is no coincidence that K. 279 features a greater density of modular play than his other sonatas, as discussed in chapter 3. Evidence that Mozart performed K. 279 from memory, anticipating the norms of later piano recitals, comes from a letter of 17 October, 1777, *MBA*, 2:69.

55. Karl Popper developed at length the view that prior theories inform perception, a central tenet of his work in the philosophy of science. Although Popper's writings are currently out of vogue in academic circles, his arguments concerning the priority of fundamental theories are careful and convincing. (As Popper states, an infinite number of theories can be conjectured to explain any set of observations; thus the choice of theory does not follow from the observation, but precedes it.) The relevant arguments appear throughout his writings, notably in *The Logic of Scientific Discovery*, rev. ed. (London: Routledge Classics, 2002); *Objective Knowledge: An Evolutionary Approach*, rev. ed. (Oxford: Clarendon Press, 1979). Ernst Gombrich applied Popper's theories to aesthetics, and Meyer, too, echoed them repeatedly throughout *Explaining Music* and *Style and Music*.

56. That preconceptions structure engagement with individual compositions is familiar from the lineage of musical analysis championed by Leonard Meyer, who held that "our [prior] theories . . . influence how and what we hear." Meyer, *Explaining Music*, 65n22.

57. Hepokoski and Darcy claim that the second theme area has closed by measure 50; see James Hepokoski and Warren Darcy, *Elements of Sonata Theory: Norms, Types, and Deformations in the Late-Eighteenth-Century Sonata* (New York: Oxford University Press, 2006), 159. William Caplin's theory, which assumes a greater loosening of the second theme area, would place the close at the end of measure 58. See William Caplin, *Classical Form: A Theory of Formal Functions for the Instrumental Music of Haydn, Mozart, and Beethoven* (New York: Oxford University Press, 1998), chap. 8, esp. 101ff. Though K. 333 does not feature explicitly in Caplin's discussion, it exhibits every loosening technique he describes.

58. Klorman's analysis of Brahms's Sonata for Piano and Clarinet op. 120, no. 2, locates significant metrical tension in the differing uses of slurs in both instrumental lines. His reading rests on a set of assumptions about the expressive performance of slurs, which in turn shapes the bulk of his approach to analyzing the "multiple agency" of the movement's metrical hierarchies. See Klorman, *Mozart's Music of Friends*, 215–20.

59. Although Hermann Abert's monumental study is not intended as a philosophical work, he intuitively arrives at precisely this conclusion in his criticism of Otto Jahn's idealized view of Mozart. According to Abert, Jahn was too deeply embedded in the Romantic tradition to understand Mozart's works properly: "In short, Jahn's biography of Mozart is not only an example of historiography, it is also a part of the history of its age, reflecting with

peculiar accuracy its ideas and musical sensitivities." See Hermann Abert's *W. A. Mozart*, trans. Stewart Spencer, ed. Cliff Eisen (New Haven, CT: Yale University Press, 2007), xiv–xv. Zaslaw, "Mozart as a Working Stiff."

60. Malcolm Bilson's first commercial Mozart recordings on fortepiano were released in 1977 during a decade bounded by Leonard Ratner's "Ars Combinatoria: Chance and Choice in Eighteenth-Century Music," in *Studies in Eighteenth-Century Music: A Tribute to Karl Geiringer on His Seventieth Birthday*, ed. H. C. Robbins Landon (London: Allen and Unwin, 1970), 343–63, and the book in which he initially proposed his theory of topics, *Classic Music* (1980). The research that formed the basis for Christopher Hogwood's period-instrument cycle of Mozart's symphonies also led to the publication of Zaslaw's study *Mozart's Symphonies: Context, Performance Practice, Reception* (New York: Oxford University Press, 1989).

61. Laurence Dreyfus, "Mozart as Early Music: A Romantic Antidote," *Early Music* 20, no. 2 (1992): 297.

62. "Erhabene, und aus der Tiefe seines Genies geschöpfte Musik." Niemetschek, *Leben*, 28.

63. *Allgemeine musikalische Zeitung* 7, col. 197–98. For a discussion of Mozart reception in light of Romantic literature and philosophy, see Carl Dahlhaus, "Romantische Musikästhetik und Wiener Klassik," in *Klassiche und romantische Musikästhetik* (Laaber: Laaber, 1988), 86–98. On the afterlife of the Requiem in particular, see Simon Keefe, *Mozart's Requiem: Reception, Work, Completion* (Cambridge: Cambridge University Press, 2012).

64. Christina Bashford, "Varieties of Childhood: John Ella and the Construction of a Victorian Mozart," in *Words about Mozart: Essays in Honour of Stanley Sadie*, ed. Dorothea Link and Judith Nagley (Woodbridge: Boydell Press, 2005), 209.

65. Tim Carter, *W. A. Mozart:* Le nozze di Figaro (Cambridge: Cambridge University Press, 1987), 136.

66. On the history of these revisions, see Rudolf Angermüller, "Bemerkungen zu den französischen Bearbeitungen," in Così fan tutte*: Beiträge zur Wirkungsgeschichte von Mozarts Oper*, ed. Susanne Vill (Bayreuth: Muhl'scher Universitätsverlag, 1978), 66–90.

67. Music theorists' increased attention to historical sources is acknowledged and discussed in Greenberg, *How Sonata Forms*, chap. 2.

68. Jessica Waldoff, *Recognition in Mozart's Operas* (New York: Oxford University Press, 2006), 234.

69. Meyer, *Style and Music*, 11–12.

70. Kofi Agawu, *Playing with Signs: A Semiotic Interpretation of Classic Music* (Princeton, NJ: Princeton University Press, 1991), 19–20. For a brief overview of other literature lamenting the same challenge in topic theory, see Lowe, *Pleasure and Meaning*, 26–27.

71. Abert, *W. A, Mozart*, xxi.

72. This argument against modular explanations was rehearsed at length by Joseph Kerman; see his "Critics and the Classics," in *Write All These Down: Essays on Music* (Berkeley: University of California Press, 1998), 61–62. Similar objections were voiced by Abert, quoted above, criticizing Wyzewa and Saint-Fox, as well as by Mozart's contemporaries, such as Koch and Goethe. The complaint was recently renewed by Edmund Goehring, who argues in *Coming to Terms with Our Musical Past: An Essay on Mozart and Modernist Aesthetics* (Rochester, NY: University of Rochester Press, 2018), that modular theories represent a

failing of modernity's view of art. For historiographic accounts of musical reductionism, see Greenberg, *How Sonata Forms*, 1–9 and 50–53.

73. This comparison with jokes as a means to combat reductionism in artistic analysis is due to Roger Scruton, *Art and Imagination: A Study in the Philosophy of Mind* (London: Methuan, 1974), 170.

Variation 2

1. On Salzburg's political and ecclesiastical culture and Mozart's early family life, see Stanley Sadie, *Mozart: The Early Years 1756–1781* (Oxford: Oxford University Press, 2006), 3–14 and 16–32, respectively. The view of Mozart's youthful performing activities I outline here draws from and augments Katalin Komlós, "Mozart the Performer," in *The Cambridge Companion to Mozart*, ed. Simon P. Keefe (Cambridge: Cambridge University Press, 2003), 215–26.

2. Mueller, *Mozart and the Mediation of Childhood*, 79–82.

3. Leopold Mozart, letter to Lorenz Hagenauer, Wasserburg, 11 June 1763, *MBA*, 1:71.

4. Quoted in Otto Erich Deutsch, *Mozart: A Documentary Biography*, trans. Eric Blom, Peter Branscombe, and Jeremy Noble (New York: Simon & Schuster, 1965), 94.

5. Komlós describes Mozart's short career as a singer in Komlós, "Mozart the Performer," 218. He announces his intention to cease professional activities as a violinist in a letter to his father, Paris, 11 September 1778, *MBA*, 2:473.

6. Letter to his father, Mannheim, 7 February 1778, *MBA*, 2:264.

7. It was usual for Mozart to include instrumental obbligato in opera arias, many of which he is thought to have performed himself. The piano obbligato in K. 505 is one example; others originated earlier in his career. On Mozart's possible performance of an obbligato aria in *Il re pastore*, see Daniel Heartz, *Haydn, Mozart and the Viennese School: 1740–1780* (New York: W. W. Norton, 1995), 612.

8. Richard Taruskin makes this point repeatedly throughout *Text and Act: Essays on Music and Performance* (New York: Oxford University Press, 1995).

9. Leopold Mozart, *A Treatise on the Fundamental Principles of Violin Playing*, trans. Editha Knocker (Oxford: Oxford University Press, 1986), 130, 220.

10. For instance, on the nonapplicability of Leopold Mozart's violinistic advice to Wolfgang's music, see Clive Brown, "Leopold Mozart's Violinschule and the Performance of W.A. Mozart's Violin Music," in *Cordes et claviers au temps de Mozart*, ed. Thomas Steiner (Bern: Peter Lang, 2010), 23–24. Although Carl Schachter ("20th-Century Analysis and Mozart Performance," 624–25) does not share Brown's assumption as to the distance between the violin playing of father and son, he, too, doubts that Leopold's advice on the phrasing of slurs applies straightforwardly to Mozart's music.

11. Letter to his father, Vienna, 27 June 1781, *MBA*, 3:135.

12. Letter to his father, Augsburg, 16 October 1777, *MBA*, 2:62.

13. Letter to his father, Mannheim, 4 November 1777, *MBA*, 2:102.

14. Letter to his father, Mannheim, 26 November 1777, *MBA*, 2:146–47.

15. Letter to his father, Mannheim, 7 December 1777, *MBA*, 2:170.

16. Letter to his father, Mannheim, 17 January 1778, *MBA*, 2:228.

17. Letter to his father, Vienna, 7 August 1782, *MBA*, 3:219.

18. Letter to his father, Augsburg, 23–25 October 1777, *MBA*, 2:83. Mozart's view is

consistent with virtually all contemporary writings on tempo flexibility. For an overview, see Sandra P. Rosenblum, *Performance Practices in Classic Piano Music: Their Principles and Applications* (Bloomington: Indiana University Press, 1991), 362–64.

19. Letter to his father, Augsburg, 23–25 October 1777, *MBA*, 2:83.

20. Letter to his father, Vienna, 7 June 1783, *MBA*, 3:272.

21. Quoted in Hans T. David, Arthur Mendel, and Christoph Wolff, eds., *The New Bach Reader* (New York: W. W. Norton, 1999), 433.

22. Carl Philipp Emanuel Bach, *Essay on the True Art of Playing Keyboard Instruments*, trans. William J. Mitchell (New York: W. W. Norton, 1949), 152–53.

23. Letter to his father, Augsburg, 23–25 October 1777, *MBA*, 2:83.

24. Christina Kobb makes this point in "Viennese Piano Technique of the 1820s and Implications for Today's Pianists," *Music & Practice* 4 (2019).

25. On Hummel's training with Mozart, see Mark Kroll, *Johann Nepomuk Hummel: A Musician's Life and World* (Lanham, MD: Scarecrow Press, 2007), 11–32.

26. See Mueller, *Mozart and the Mediation of Childhood*, esp. chaps. 2 and 4, on the industriousness expected of children during Mozart's lifetime.

27. Although many texts have analyzed Mozart's correspondence, a particularly useful account is Ulrich Konrad, "Mozart the Letter Writer and His Language," in *Mozart Studies* 2, ed. Simon P. Keefe (Cambridge: Cambridge University Press, 2015), esp. 13–16. Konrad analyzes evidence concerning the genesis and performance history of the C-minor Mass, K. 427, showing where and how Mozart's writings complicate the historian's task.

28. The editorial assumption that such inconsistencies represent typographical errors generally applies when the inconsistencies are spread out across larger stretches of music—for instance, when phrases at different formal sections or at opposite ends of a movement receive different articulations or slurs. Here, however, the grace notes occupy a single phrase, and therefore seem to reflect deliberate choice.

29. Additional corroboration comes from Ellwood Derr, "*Basso Continuo* in Mozart's Piano Concertos: Dimensions of Compositional Completion and Performance Practice," in *Mozart's Piano Concertos: Text, Context, Interpretation*, ed. Neal Zaslaw (Ann Arbor: University of Michigan Press, 1996), 395. Derr observes that the grace notes at the outset of piano solo passages in the first movements of K. 379 and K. 450 must be played on the beat, and indeed with deliberate emphasis, if they are to be heard as resolving the harmonies that precede them.

30. Rosenblum provides a thorough description of these and other features of pianos during Mozart's lifetime in *Performance Practices*, 31–33, and chap. 2. For a recent reevaluation of the interplay between composers and their pianos, see the creative study by Tom Beghin, *Beethoven's French Piano: A Tale of Ambition and Frustration* (Chicago: University of Chicago Press, 2022).

31. For a study examining this phenomenon in Mozart's string writing, see Esther Cavett-Dunsby, "Mozart's 'Haydn' Quartets: Composing Up and Down without Rules," *Journal of the Royal Musical Association* 113, no. 1 (1988): 57–80.

32. David Rosen extensively discusses this problem in "'Unexpectedness' and 'Inevitability' in Mozart's Piano Concertos," in *Mozart's Piano Concertos: Text, Context, Interpretation*, ed. Neal Zaslaw (Ann Arbor: University of Michigan Press, 1996), 266–74. Daniel Heartz (*Haydn, Mozart and the Viennese School*, 618) surmises that this doubling is meant to reinforce the piano's melody.

33. On the elements contributing to the sense of climax in this passage, see Rosen, "'Unexpectedness' and 'Inevitability,'" 201.

34. Ellwood Derr, "Mozart's Transfer of the Vocal 'Fermata Sospesa' to His Piano-Concerto First Movements," in *Mozart-Jahrbuch 1991*, ed. Rudolf Angermüller et al. (Kassel: Bärenreiter, 1992).

35. For a thorough study of piano-orchestra relations in the mature concertos, including issues of thematic handoff and dialogue, see Simon P. Keefe, *Mozart's Piano Concertos: Dramatic Dialogue in the Age of Enlightenment* (Woodbridge: Boydell Press, 2001), esp. chaps. 3 and 4.

36. On Mozart's departures from contemporary standards in the formal playing out of concerto movements, see the recent corpus study by Omer Maliniak and Yoel Greenberg, "Follow the Solo," in *Music Theory Spectrum* 44, no. 2 (2022): 231–59.

37. Letter to his father, Augsburg, 17 October 1777, *MBA*, 2:68–69.

38. Christoph Wolff, "The Many Faces of Authenticity: Problems of a Critical Edition of Mozart's Piano Concertos," in *Mozart's Piano Concertos: Text, Context, Interpretation*, ed. Neal Zaslaw (Ann Arbor: University of Michigan Press, 1996), 26.

39. Rosenblum, *Performance Practices*, 212, discusses these exercises. They are reprinted as Fingerübungen KV 626^{b}/48 in the appendix to *NMA* IX/27/2. Contemporary treatises generally advocate the same precept.

40. Charles Rosen, "Tradition without Convention: The Impossible Nineteenth-Century Project," in *The Tanner Lectures on Human Values*, ed. Grethe B. Peterson (Salt Lake City: University of Utah Press, 2002), 353–54.

41. For instance, Roman Ivanovitch ("Showing Off: Variation in the Display Episodes of Mozart's Piano Concertos," *Journal of Music Theory* 52, no. 2 [2008]: 193n25) claims that a scale in broken octaves, played by both hands in parallel tenths, occurs in the display passages of concertos in C major and may thus be associated with that tonality in particular. Although he is correct that C-major concertos do receive more flamboyant use of this device, he does not note that it also occurs in K. 459 (F major), K. 466 (D minor), K. 482 (E♭ major).

42. The tactile and cognitive elements of instrumental playing are the subject of Jonathan De Souza's exemplary recent study *Music at Hand: Instruments, Bodies, and Cognition* (New York: Oxford University Press, 2017).

43. Daniel Gottlob Türk, *School of Clavier Playing*, trans. Raymond H. Haggh (Lincoln: University of Nebraska Press, 1982), 182. Haggh translates "Tändelei" as "whim," but Claudia Maurer Zenck proposes "horseplay" as an accurate rendering.

44. On cyclic design in Mozart's chamber music, see Elaine Sisman, "Six of One: The Opus Concept in the Eighteenth Century," in *The Century of Bach and Mozart: Perspectives on Historiography, Composition, Theory, and Performance*, ed. Sean Gallagher and Thomas Forrest Kelly (Cambridge, MA: Harvard Publications in Music, 2008), 95–99. On cyclic design in his public works, see Ellwood Derr, "Some Thoughts on the Design of Mozart's Opus 4, the 'Subscription Concertos' (K. 414, 413, and 415)," in *Mozart's Piano Concertos: Text, Context, Interpretation*, ed. Neal Zaslaw (Ann Arbor: University of Michigan Press, 1996), 187–210. The final three symphonies may constitute such a cycle. Wolff argues that they might, Sisman that they probably do not; see Sisman, *Mozart: The "Jupiter" Symphony* (Cambridge: Cambridge University Press, 1993), 26. Either way, it is noteworthy that motifs such as pairs of ascending or descending half steps recur prominently in all three works.

45. The term *voice exchange*, popularized in twentieth-century music theory by Schenker, appears in Koch's writings in the eighteenth century under the term *Umkehrung der Stimmen*. Koch refers to this technique in precisely this context, as a way to turn a basic phrase into an expanded phrase.

46. On the voice exchanges in Mozart's cadenzas, see William Drabkin, "An Interpretation of Musical Dreams: Towards a Theory of the Mozart Piano Concerto Cadenza," in *Wolfgang Amadè Mozart: Essays on His Life and His Music*, ed. Stanley Sadie (Oxford: Clarendon Press, 1996), 166–67.

47. Mozart's attention to species counterpoint is visible in both the Ployer and Attwood lesson books. In the Ployer lesson book, Mozart makes numerous corrections to part writing (folios 8r and 11r); in the Attwood lesson book, similar adjustments are visible (22, 30, etc.). Robert Gjerdingen, Joel Lester, and David Huron have explored voice leading as a generative compositional device.

48. These revisions are discussed with an eye to compositional ingenuity in Ivanovitch, "Showing Off," 187–88.

49. Alan Tyson, *Mozart: Studies of the Autograph Scores* (Cambridge, MA: Harvard University Press, 1987), 20. See also Irving, *Mozart's Piano Sonatas*, 112.

50. Irving, *Mozart's Piano Sonatas*, 91, estimates 1781 as the date of K. 400, but Tyson suggests that 1782 is more likely; see Alan Tyson, "Proposed New Dates for Many Works and Fragments Written by Mozart from March 1781 to December 1791," in *Mozart Studies*, ed. Cliff Eisen (Oxford: Clarendon Press, 1991), 217.

51. These are reproduced and analyzed in Keefe, "'We Hardly Knew What We Should Pay Attention to First,'" 197–99.

52. Two representative studies include William Kinderman, *The Creative Process in Music from Mozart to Kurtág* (Urbana: University of Illinois Press, 2012), chap. 1; László Somfai, "Mozart's First Thoughts: The Two Versions of the Sonata in D Major, K. 284," *Early Music* 19, no. 4 (1991).

53. Irving, *Mozart's Piano Sonatas*, 51.

54. For one case study in such alterations, see Daniel Leeson's essay on the variation set from the Serenade K. 361, which also survives in a version for flute quartet, K. 285b: Daniel N. Leeson, "A Revisit: Mozart's Serenade for Thirteen Instruments, K. 361 (370a), the 'Gran Partita,'" in *Mozart-Jahrbuch 1997* (Kassel: Bärenreiter, 1997): 181–223.

55. On the implied contest in K. 454, see Moseley, *Keys to Play*, 195. As Klorman has observed, Koch and other contemporary writers described various forms of gameplay, striving, and contests in their analyses; for an overview particularly in light of the dialogic style, see Klorman, *Mozart's Music of Friends*, chap. 2. On the dialogic drama of Mozart's mature concertos, see Keefe, *Mozart's Piano Concertos* and *Mozart's Viennese Instrumental Music: A Study of Stylistic Re-invention* (Woodbridge: Boydell Press, 2007), 185–86. The operatic aesthetic of these concertos is explored in numerous texts, the most elegant of which is Wye J. Allanbrook, "Comic Issues in Mozart's Piano Concertos," in *Mozart's Piano Concertos: Text, Context, Interpretation*, ed. Neal Zaslaw (Ann Arbor: University of Michigan Press, 1996), 75–105.

56. Mozart's clarinet passagework is most awkward in K. 361/vi/var. 3 and 4 (both featuring difficult leaps between B♭ and F♯); K. 581/iv/var. 4; K. 622/i/134–40; and the obbligato arias from *La clemenza di Tito*, which require the player to jump back and forth between the basset and upper registers. For information on the instruments Mozart's collaborators

would have played, see Eric Hoeprich, *The Clarinet* (New Haven, CT: Yale University Press, 2008), 122.

57. I owe these observations to Frances Kelley.

58. On contemporary approaches to upbow staccato and portato, see Robin Stowell, *Violin Technique and Performance Practice in the Late Eighteenth and Early Nineteenth Centuries* (Cambridge: Cambridge University Press, 1990), 176.

59. This reading of the dramatic physicality of Mozart's bowing prescriptions draws from the "cello-and-bow thinking" described in Elisabeth Le Guin, *Boccherini's Body: An Essay in Carnal Musicology* (Berkeley: University of California Press, 2006), 17–33, esp. 31.

60. For a straightforward overview of these improvisatory genres, see Robert Levin, "Instrumental Ornamentation, Improvisation, and Cadenzas," in *Performance Practice: Music after 1600*, ed. Howard Mayer Brown and Stanley Sadie (London: Macmillan, 1990).

61. In addition to the better-known fantasias, this corpus includes Four Preludes K. 284a, which were once assumed to be a single composition, as well as modulating preludes (F–e, KV deest, and K.626a I), which are probably two halves of a single work. Mozart also began, but did not finish, a fantasia for keyboard and violin, K. 396. Levin provides an exhaustive source history in "Mozart's Non-Metrical Keyboard Preludes," in *The Keyboard in Baroque Europe*, ed. Christopher Hogwood (Cambridge: Cambridge University Press, 2003), 198–216.

62. On the origins and source history of this modulating prelude, as well as its procedural overlaps with C. P. E. Bach, see William Kinderman, *Mozart's Piano Music* (Oxford: Oxford University Press, 2006), 84–86, and Levin, "Mozart's Non-Metrical Keyboard Preludes." A significant amount of forensic research has been needed to establish the date. On the one hand, the prelude is written on a paper Mozart used in Salzburg as early as 1776; on the other hand, the manuscript is folded in a way that suggests it was sent by post, which means it was most likely composed after Mozart departed Salzburg in 1777. The two halves of this prelude (from F to E minor and E minor to C) have been printed in the *NMA* as separate compositions.

63. This style of modulation as it appears in other written compositions has been discussed by various theorists; see, for instance, Scott Burnham, *Mozart's Grace* (Princeton, NJ: Princeton University Press, 2012), 122–23 (on K. 453), and Wye J. Allanbrook, "Two Threads through the Labyrinth: Topic and Process in the First Movements of K. 332 and K. 333," in *Convention in Eighteenth- and Nineteenth-Century Music: Essays in Honor of Leonard G. Ratner*, ed. Wye J. Allanbrook, Janet M. Levy, and William P. Mahrt (Stuyvesant, NY: Pendragon, 1992), 144 (on K. 332). On its precedents in historical theoretical sources such as Vogler's "Summa of Harmony," see Gooley, *Fantasies of Improvisation*, 34–36.

64. Bach, *Essay on the True Art*, 438.

65. Hans T. David, "Mozartean Modulations," in *The Creative World of Mozart*, ed. Paul Henry Lang (New York: W. W. Norton, 1991).

66. See also the discussion of scales embedded into the middle-ground melodies in K. 387, K. 311, and K. 377 in Schachter, "20th-Century Analysis and Mozart Performance," 620–23. Allanbrook, too, locates similar ascents and descents in Mozart's melodies; for an example in K. 333, see Allanbrook, "Two Threads through the Labyrinth," 168.

67. Ludwig Holtmeier suggests that the chromaticism of K. 280 even outdoes that of the fantasias, since all four implied voices participate simultaneously in the descent. Ludwig

Holtmeier, "Zur Komplexität Mozarts: Analytischer Versuch über eine Sequenz," *Musik & Ästhetik* 16, no. 4 (2000): 5–23.

68. Robert D. Levin, *Introduction: Klavierkonzert C-Moll, KV 491*, Bärenreiter Facsimile (Kassel: Bärenreiter, 2014), 2–3.

69. Rosen, *The Classical Style*, 270–71.

70. Beethoven's assessment is deduced by Richard Kramer from an oblique statement in his conversation books. See Richard Kramer, *Cherubino's Leap: In Search of the Enlightenment Moment* (Chicago: University of Chicago Press, 2016), 37n4. See also Rosen, *The Classical Style*, 268.

71. For a more complete analysis of this effect, see Burnham's poetic and detailed reading in *Mozart's Grace*, 50–54.

Variation 3

1. The crude qualities often associated with improvisation, in music and beyond, receive a brief overview in Gary Peters, *The Philosophy of Improvisation* (Chicago: University of Chicago Press, 2009), 2, 10–19. On the attributes stereotypically associated with musical improvisation, see Carl Dahlhaus's perceptive essay "Composition and Improvisation," trans. Derrick Puffet and Alfred Clayton, in *Schoenberg and the New Music* (Cambridge: Cambridge University Press, 1990), 265–73. The same preconceptions apply to music in other traditions; in a recent survey, Katya Davisson notes that "musics outside the notated European tradition were often thought of as improvised, [quoting Leo Treitler] 'in the negative sense of something unprepared and unforeseen,'" and she goes on to cite the jazz pianist and scholar Ted Gioia, who stated that "the finished [improvisation] will show moments of rare beauty intermixed with technical mistakes and aimless passages." Katya Davisson, "Improvisation as a Method of Composition: Reconciling the Dichotomy," *British Journal of Aesthetics* 62, no. 3 (2022): 373, 374. Andy Hamilton, too, has synthesized these views into an accounts of the "aesthetics of imperfection," arrayed across a series of publications.

2. Ratner, *Classic Music*, 233.

3. Richard Kramer, "Diderot's *Paradoxe* and C.P.E. Bach's *Empfindung*," in *C.P.E. Bach Studies*, ed. Annette Richards (Cambridge: Cambridge University Press, 2006), 11.

4. Rosen, *The Classical Style*, 79.

5. Gooley, *Fantasies of Improvisation*, 35. Richard Kramer, too, in a recent description of C. P. E. Bach's fantasias, affirms many of the same dichotomies. He writes of "reason and its adversary" head-to-head in this music; of an "improvisatory rush" that must be "reconciled" with "grounded structure." Kramer. *Cherubino's Leap*, 14–15.

6. For a selection of eighteenth-century accounts of the haphazardness of improvisation, see Annette Richards, *The Free Fantasia and the Musical Picturesque* (Cambridge: Cambridge University Press, 2001), 15–20, 34–40. As Richards shows, most descriptions of improvisation, whether in treatises or reviews, frame improvisation exclusively in opposition to notated music and thus perforce emphasize its apparent departures from methods associated with planning and revision. See also the historical survey (based on Lydia Goehr's writings on the "work concept") at the outset of Davisson, "Improvisation as a Method of Composition."

7. Türk, *School of Clavier Playing*, 388; translated in Richards, 39.

8. Gooley, *Fantasies of Improvisation*, 199.

9. Quoted in Deutsch, *Mozart*, 543.

10. Ivanovitch, in "Mozart and the Environment of Variation" (154), gives this example to demonstrate melodic variation techniques.

11. Richards, *Free Fantasia*, 176. The associations between improvisations (particularly of fantasias) and the perception of subjectivity has been taken up recently by Mark Evan Bonds in *The Beethoven Syndrome: Hearing Music as Autobiography* (New York: Oxford University Press, 2020), 58–73.

12. On historical audiences' uncertainty as to the reality of some improvisatory feats, see Gooley, *Fantasies of Improvisation*, 261–62.

13. Maria Anna Mozart, postscript added to Leopold Mozart, letter to his son, Salzburg, 28 September 1777, *MBA*, 2:20. The modulating prelude F–e, discussed in the previous chapter, was intended to fulfill this function for Nannerl. See Robert Levin, "Mozart's Solo Keyboard Music," in *Eighteenth-Century Keyboard Music*, ed. Robert L. Marshall (New York: Routledge, 2003), 309.

14. Leopold Mozart, letter to his son, Salzburg, 13 August 1778, *MBA*, 2:446.

15. Vincent Novello and Mary Novello, *A Mozart Pilgrimage: Being the Travel Diaries of Vincent and Mary Novello in the Year 1829*, ed. Rosemary Hughes (London: Eulenberg Books, 1975), 167–68.

16. Levin's comment comes from an interview with Derek Bailey, broadcast on the BBC Channel 4 in 1992 as part of *On the Edge: Improvisation in Music*. The video of this interview is widely available online.

17. The necessity of risk is a recurring theme in Davisson: "It is crucial to note that risk is fundamental to the aesthetic of improvisation and . . . the errors that creep into such improvisations are part of this aesthetic and not to be shied away from"; "The jazz improviser . . . improvises within the inexorable passing of real time, which brings with it a considerable element of risk, a fundamental component of improvisation." Davisson, "Improvisation as a Method of Composition," 374, 377.

18. If this reference to an aesthetics of music composed in pencil versus ink seems tendentious, consider the perceptive and nuanced study of the composer Michael Finnissy's drafts undertaken in Richard Beaudoin, "The Pen as Camera: Finnissy and Overexposure," *Music Theory Online* 27, no. 3 (2021). For Finnissy, who writes his sketches and autographs in pen, the medium does not delimit aesthetic content. As Finnissy himself has stated, ink even allows for compositional freedom: "I say to people, although they always look puzzled, you can improvise with a pen in your hand." Quoted and discussed in Beaudoin, paragraph 2.6. See also the discussion of the New-Critical debate concerning the extent to which processual issues may remain evident in a finished artwork in Sawyer, "Improvisation and the Creative Process," 152–53.

19. Although Richard Taruskin does not explore the broader ramifications of imperfection as a marker of improvisation, this assumption seems to underpin his writings. In a review of Robert Levin's performance of K. 467, Taruskin states: "Levin . . . commands the intellectual and digital means to improvise his cadenzas. (How can you tell, you say? You can tell because, if written down, the improvisations would have faults of composition by Mozartean standards.)" *Text and Act*, 285. The same implicit assumptions guide Tom Beghin's reading of Haydn's Sonata in E♭, Hob. XVI:49, in which Beghin deems a passage improvisatory because it suggests a stalling for time—that is, a lapse of invention—while the putative

improviser awaits inspiration. See Tom Beghin, *The Virtual Haydn: Paradox of a Twenty-First-Century Keyboardist* (Chicago: University of Chicago Press, 2015), 54–56.

20. Mozart himself comes very near to saying this in the letter criticizing Vogler's piano playing, cited in chapter 2, as an implication of the idea that good sight-reading should give the impression that the person playing the piece puts every detail in place, as if the performer were also the composer—or, perhaps in this scenario, the reenactor of an improvisation from a stage when the piece had not yet become fully fixed, when its continuity was not yet inevitable. Seth Monahan, in his exacting investigation of various modes of musical action and agency, writes of a "fictional composer" and "work persona" that map onto the categories invoked here. See Seth Monahan "Action and Agency Revisited," *Journal of Music Theory* 57, no. 2 (2013): 321–71.

21. See Mueller, *Mozart and the Mediation of Childhood*, 79–82, on his continued involvement with commedia traditions as a composer of operas.

22. Moseley, *Keys to Play*, 142. Nissen, too, remarks on Mozart's continued enthusiasm for dancing (Georg Nikolaus Nissen, *Biographie W.A. Mozarts* [Leipzig, 1828], 692); see Keefe, *Mozart in Vienna*, 553.

23. On K. 279, see Byros, "Trazom's Wit." On K. 522, see Gretchen A. Wheelock, *Haydn's Ingenious Jesting with Art: Contexts of Musical Wit and Humor* (New York: Schirmer Books, 1992).

24. On the association between feigned improvisation and the interruption of patterns, see Oswald Jonas, "Improvisation in Mozarts Klavierwerken," in *Mozart-Jahrbuch 1967* (Salzburg: Internationalen Stiftung Mozarteum, 1968). Jonas's examples include the Violin Sonata K. 378. On improvisational "problem-finding," which Sawyer traces back to the aesthetic theories of Collingwood and Dewey, see Sawyer, "Improvisation and the Creative Process," 153–54.

25. I briefly discuss the misuse of characteristic phrasal gestures in chapter 1. For a historical study, see Wheelock, *Haydn's Ingenious Jesting with Art*, 12–15, 98–110. For a philosophical view of this device and its relation to irony, see Eddy Zemach and Tamara Balter, "The Structure of Irony and How It Functions in Music," in *Philosophers on Music: Experience, Meaning, and Work*, ed. Kathleen Stock (Oxford: Oxford University Press, 2007), 183–84. Concerning the frequency of such modular interactions in Mozart vis-à-vis the music of his contemporaries, see Maliniak and Greenberg, "Follow the Solo." The authors compare the formal schematics of Mozart's Violin Concerto K. 218 with similar works by others, concluding that Mozart's solos are unusual in their thematic connections to ritornellos.

26. Keefe's extended analysis of piano-orchestra relations in the mature concertos begins with an overview of thematic exchange whereby the soloist imitates the orchestra's closing material. He focuses on the Concertos K. 450 and K. 482, sensing in these works a tension between soloist and orchestra as the former veers away from the ritornello material and initiates "confrontational" passages. However, in other cases (including K. 414 as discussed here), no such confrontation takes place, the soloist's line seeming to unfurl more effortlessly from the orchestra's closing. See Keefe, *Mozart's Piano Concertos*, 53–57, and chap. 4.

27. This formal strategy is referred to as "Knüpftechnik" (linkage technique) in the writings of Heinrich Schenker.

28. Alfred Einstein, *Mozart, His Character, His Work*, trans. Arthur Mendel and Nathan Broder (Oxford University Press, 1962), 242. Levin ("Mozart's Solo Keyboard Music," 314)

concurs: "The first of the set, in C major, gives the impression of an improvisation subsequently set down on paper."

29. Heartz, *Haydn, Mozart, and the Viennese School*, 587.

30. Kinderman, *Mozart's Piano Music*, 29.

31. These matters are the subject of an extended analysis in Byros, "Trazom's Wit."

32. It is also striking that, despite being poised to undertake prolific publishing activities at the end of this decade, K. 279 was not printed during his lifetime (even as other sonatas from this cycle were)—another point that may indicate a desire to maintain some of the enigma concerning what was written down and what improvised in K. 279. See Irving, *Mozart's Piano Sonatas*, 53–54. For one reference to Mozart's memorized performances of K. 279, see letter of 17 October 1777, *MBA*, 2:68–69 (see also chap.2, n. 37).

33. Byros invokes Koch's suggestion of absentmindedness represented through the connection of modules or segments that do not properly belong together. Thus, the "overall improvisatory character of [K. 279] was seemingly staged to enact the bungling composer-performer, perhaps in an extemporizing setting." See Byros, "Trazom's Wit," 243–44.

34. Letter to his father, Mannheim, 26 November 1777, *MBA*, 2:148. Translation based on Byros. The German reads "wohlen sie leb. ich gute eine wünsche nacht. sunden sie geschlaf. werdens nächste ich schon schreiber gescheiden;" Punctuation and capitalization *sic*; the letter ends with a semicolon. Similar play occurs in other letters, including a message to his sister written in a scrambled word order and dated 16 January 1773.

35. Hepokoski and Darcy (*Elements of Sonata Theory*, 233–34) draw all of their examples of recapitulatory reording from Mozart's piano sonatas.

36. Julian Rushton, *Mozart* (New York: Oxford University Press, 2006), 66–67.

37. Although other elements of K. 311 suggest a comic synthesis to which this missed recapitulation contributes, this formal move was not unprecedented in Mozart's Mannheim compositions, for instance the Violin Sonata K. 306.

38. On the "Rule of the Octave" as a protocol for keyboard improvisation, see Baragwanath, *The Solfeggio Tradition*, 290–92.

39. The simulation of improvisatory recollection is usually attributed to Beethoven as a trapping of early Romantic aesthetics, as in Charles Rosen's discussion of memory in "An die ferne Geliebte" and the Piano Sonata op. 81a, in *The Romantic Generation* (Cambridge, MA: Harvard University Press, 1998), 170–72, 205. However, the example of K. 282 suggests that Mozart anticipated this practice by some four decades.

40. Wye J. Allanbrook, "Mozart's Tunes and the Comedy of Closure," in *On Mozart*, ed. James M. Morris (Cambridge: Cambridge University Press; Washington, DC: Woodrow Wilson Center Press, 1994), esp. 171–73.

41. For a thorough discussion see Mark Evan Bonds, "Listening to Listeners," in *Communication in Eighteenth-Century Music*, ed. Danuta Mirka and Kofi Agawu (Cambridge: Cambridge University Press, 2008), 34–52.

42. Although Mozart is unlikely to have known Scarlatti's sonatas, the latter is perhaps the figure most associated with this formal archetype, now associated with the "Type 2" Sonata in the terminology of Hepokoski and Darcy.

43. Keefe's brief account of K. 522 provides a useful overview of the ways in which the piece depicts both inept composition and inept performance. See Keefe, *Mozart in Vienna*, 494–95. A more detailed account that furthers the same distinction between composi-

tional and performative errors can be found in Wheelock, *Haydn's Ingenious Jesting with Art*, 6–10.

44. Wheelock, *Haydn's Ingenious Jesting with Art*, 7.

45. On the variation techniques used in this opening ritornello and their import for Mozart analysis more broadly, see Kofi Agawu, "Mozart's Art of Variation: Remarks on the First Movement of K. 503," in *Mozart's Piano Concertos: Text, Context, Interpretation*, ed. Neal Zaslaw (Ann Arbor: University of Michigan Press, 1996), 303–13. See also Ivanovitch, "Mozart and the Environment of Variation," 208ff.

46. Rosen, *The Classical Style*, 196.

47. There may also be a sense of urgency in the soloist's repetitions, analogous to what Klorman (*Mozart's Music of Friends*, 147–48) has described as "treading water" in a passage from the Piano Quartet K. 493. Although Klorman's analysis of K. 493 focuses on an implied stalling for time, the image of "treading water" suggests an element of struggle in the attempt to keep pace.

48. Derr, in "Some Thoughts on the Design of Mozart's Opus 4," 202, gives a similar reading of that earlier C-major concerto, K. 415: "For informed listeners, this entrance "must have been a 'knee-slapper': it is as if the pianist had forgotten what he was about and commenced to play the first solo of the wrong concerto!—and that not very accurately!!" It may be difficult to hear the same effect in K. 503, since the later work has been more thoroughly absorbed into the canon.

49. Gjerdingen (*Music in the Galant Style*, 4) caricatures the propensity to hear musical works as "sonic analogues to a thrill ride, a quest . . . or a melodrama" as a vestige of "Romantic listening" that weighs down a style which, in his view, is more properly associated with courtly decorum. However, as I want to show, the language Gjerdingen lampoons may have its place even in historically inflected readings.

50. On Mozart's use of musical games, see Neal Zaslaw, "Mozart's Modular Minuet Machine," in *Essays in Honor of László Somfai on His 70th Birthday: Studies in the Sources and the Interpretation of Music*, ed. László Vikárius and Vera Lampert (Lanham, MD: Scarecrow Press, 2005), 219–35. On the creation of longer compositions using randomizing elements, see Joel Lester, *Compositional Theory in the Eighteenth Century* (Cambridge, MA: Harvard University Press, 1992), 176–77, 226ff, and Ratner, "Ars Combinatoria."

51. Mueller, *Mozart and the Mediation of Childhood*, 188–89, updating Zaslaw, discusses the games and minuet generators attributed to Mozart.

52. This point is made, and this example given, in Leonard B. Meyer, "Process and Morphology in the Music of Mozart," in *The Spheres of Music* (Chicago: University of Chicago Press, 2000), 132–33.

53. On Mozart's "pedal retransitions" in movements such as this, see Roman Ivanovitch, "Mozart's Art of Retransition," *Music Analysis* 30, no. 1 (2011): 12–15.

54. Although the classical cadence is too multifaceted to be encapsulated by any single rhetorical approach, theorists such as Caplin and Michael Spizter have noted that the same sense of delay characterizes Mozart's approach to other formally significant cadences. Sutcliffe takes the same view in his recent analysis of the first-movement exposition of the String Quartet K. 499, where "the plot seems to be to delay full cadential arrival on the dominant key for as long as possible." See Sutcliffe, *Instrumental Music in an Age of Sociability*, 280–82.

55. Hepokoski and Darcy, *Elements of Sonata Theory*, 201.

56. David Epstein notes that the comparatively sparse harmonic progression is facilitated and bound together by the sustained prominence of E; David Epstein, *Beyond Orpheus: Studies in Musical Structure* (Cambridge, MA: MIT Press, 1979), 186.

57. There are, of course, shades of gray, such that the presence of multiple performers does not in itself exclude the possibility of a fictionalized improviser. For instance, Klorman's analyses of Mozart's chamber music often treat these compositions as unfolding in a process of fictionalized improvisation. However, as Klorman concedes late in *Mozart's Music of Friends* (296), his approach "has the most to offer in passages with polyphonic textures . . . Clearly, it may have less to offer when all parts seem to act in concert."

Variation 4

1. The literature on these local gestures includes writings of Levin, the Badura-Skodas, Katalin Komlós, Andrew Willis, and others. For an overview, see Dorian Bandy, "Thema da capo: Another Look at Mozart's Embellishments," *Eighteenth-Century Music* 19, no. 1 (2022): 38–39.

2. One extended debate took place between Frederick Neumann (given to textual literalism) and Levin (favoring freedom from textual constraints), and plays out across the following writings: Frederick Neumann, *Ornamentation and Improvisation in Mozart* (Princeton, NJ: Princeton University Press, 1986); Robert D. Levin, review of *Ornamentation and Improvisation in Mozart*, by Frederick Neumann, *Journal of the American Musicological Society* 41, no. 2 (1988): 355–68; Frederick Neumann, "Some Problems of Mozart Ornamentation: A Response to Robert Levin," in *New Essays on Performance Practice* (Rochester, NY: University of Rochester Press, 1989), 155–67.

3. This concern is voiced in David Grayson, "Whose Authenticity? Ornaments by Hummel and Cramer for Mozart's Piano Concertos," in *Mozart's Piano Concertos: Text, Context, Interpretation*, ed. Neal Zaslaw (Ann Arbor: University of Michigan Press, 1996), 385. It is echoed in Keefe, *Mozart in Vienna*, 218. The concern is acknowledged but dismissed in Robert D. Levin, "Improvised Embellishments in Mozart's Keyboard Music," *Early Music* 20, no. 2 (1992): 233.

4. On the embellishments in these editions, see Levin, "Improvised Embellishments."

5. Taruskin, *Text and Act*, 56. The notion that composers' expectations are distanced from their actual desires is a familiar thread running through the writings of Charles Rosen, Roger Scruton, and other critics of the historical performance movement. It receives its most thorough philosophical treatment in Peter Kivy, *Authenticities* (Ithaca, NY: Cornell University Press, 1997).

6. I explore the possibility that Mozart intended his embellishments to limit performers' freedom, with reference to his relationship with the soprano Adriana Ferrarese del Bene, in "Mozart's Operatic Embellishments," *Cambridge Opera Journal* 33, no. 1/2 (2021): 17, 20–21.

7. On the discovery and enigma of the Adagio in F major, see Neal Zaslaw, "The Adagio in F Major, K3 Anhang 206a = K6 Anhang A 65," in *Haydn, Mozart, and Beethoven: Studies in the Music of the Classical Period (Essays in Honour of Alan Tyson)*, ed. Sieghard Brandenburg (Oxford: Clarendon Press, 1998).

8. Although K. 284 probably dates as early as 1775, the embellishments were prepared for the first edition, published in 1784. Mozart composed K. 451 in 1784 along with the six-bar

insertion. The Sonata K. 457 is more ambiguous: Mozart composed the sonata between February and October 1784 and, according to Wolf ("Rediscovered Autograph"), probably wrote the slow movement and the embellishments by January/February 1785 at the latest.

9. "The singing style" is, in Sarah Day-O'Connell's words, "arguably the least clear" of all the musical topics enumerated by Ratner. See her chapter "The Singing Style," in *The Oxford Handbook of Topic Theory*, ed. Danuta Mirka (New York: Oxford University Press, 2014), 238.

10. Note that this schema refers to $\hat{5}$–$\hat{4}$–$\hat{3}$ in any key rather than to specific pitches in a fixed-Do system.

11. The importance of the K. 451 embellishments has been defended in particular by Levin, who sees them as a model for similar passages in K. 466, K. 467, K. 537, and K. 595. See Levin, "Instrumental Ornamentation, Improvisation, and Cadenzas," 276. The Badura-Skodas attribute to Levin the claim that all passages with accompanimental textures similar to that of K. 451 should be embellished in the same style; see Eva Badura-Skoda and Paul Badura-Skoda *Interpreting Mozart: The Performance Practice of His Piano Pieces and Other Compositions*, 2nd ed. (New York: Routledge, 2008), 218.

12. On Mozart's prolific publishing activities during this period, see Keefe, *Mozart in Vienna*, 220–22. On Mozart's awareness of his listeners' predilections and the possibility that this awareness would extend to printed music, see Bonds, "Listening to Listeners," 39–40.

13. This notion of recognition and active listening finds a resonance in Gooley's (*Fantasies of Improvisation*, 203) discussion of Liszt's improvisations: "The popularity of the tunes he chose . . . assisted the listener in following Liszt's process of improvisatory reinvention, development, and de-familiarization." The highly engaged form of analytic listening such performative practices would cultivate among audience members is a recurring theme throughout Ivanovich's writings, particularly "Mozart and the Environment of Variation."

14. Quoted and discussed, with an eye to embellishment, in Holly Watkins, *Metaphors of Depth in German Musical Thought* (Cambridge: Cambridge University Press, 2011), 62, 80.

15. A selection of embellishments from Mozart's fragments is reprinted in Bandy, "Thema da capo," 44.

16. The relevant draft pages are shown in facsimile in the *NMA* along with the concertos in question. They are isolated and reprinted in Bandy, "Thema da capo," 44.

17. Irving, *Mozart's Piano Sonatas*, 76–82. See also Wolf, "Rediscovered Autograph," 23–26, 39–46.

18. On the possibility that ornaments can occur at different levels of musical "depth," see Watkins, *Metaphors of Depth*, 84–85.

19. These instances of indirection converge with Leonard Meyer's "gap-fill" theory of melodic structures more generally and suggest the extent to which embellishments reflect features of Mozart's language as a whole. See Leonard Meyer, *Emotion and Meaning in Music* (Chicago: University of Chicago Press, 1956), 134–135.

20. As Meyer (*Emotion and Meaning in Music*, 207) notes, "many ornaments tend to create doubt and uncertainty, however momentary, as to which tone is the structural or substantive one."

21. This also harkens to a melodic structure used more generally by Mozart in which phrases bound together by coherent middle-ground scalar lines receive different motivic

figuration at each step so as to maintain an ideal balance of unity and contrast. One example, from the Violin Sonata K. 377, is discussed in Schachter, "20th-Century Analysis and Mozart Performance," 622–23.

22. This corroborates the notion that Mozart devised melodies with an eye to how he might ultimately develop them, a concept implicit in my brief discussion of drafts above but explored more fully by Irving in *Mozart's Piano Sonatas*, 112. See also Jeffrey Swinkin's study of a similar process played out in later variation sets: Jeffrey Swinkin, "Variation as Thematic Actualisation: The Case of Brahms's Op. 9," *Music Analysis* 31, no. 1 (2012). Although Swinkin places the advent of "thematic actualization" with Beethoven, Mozart's embellishments anticipate the same aesthetic process.

23. Bandy, "Mozart's Operatic Embellishments," 11.

24. For a detailed reading of the horn obbligato in this aria, see Waldoff, *Recognition in Mozart's Operas*, 242–44. Waldoff does not refer to the issue of embellishment, but the significance she ascribes to the horn writing is exaggerated by the presence of the extravagant decorations.

25. This notion of embellishment as an additive, propulsive device is given a brief but perceptive treatment in Abert, *W. A. Mozart*, 893–94.

26. On rhythmic acceleration, see Edward T. Lowinsky, "On Mozart's Rhythm," in *The Creative World of Mozart*, ed. Paul Henry Lang (New York: W. W. Norton, 1991). On the purported significance of cadence strength for the rhetoric of character and large-scale form, see Berger, Chapter 4.

27. On the rhetorical import of melody for both historical and modern-day listeners, as well as for some composers and theorists, see Mark Evan Bonds, *Wordless Rhetoric: Musical Form and the Metaphor of the Oration* (Cambridge, MA: Harvard University Press, 1991), 112–14. The use of melody as a parameter of compositional planning is also explored in recent work on solfeggi. See, for instance, examples given throughout Baragwanath, *The Solfeggio Tradition.*

28. John Spitzer and Neal Zaslaw, *The Birth of the Orchestra: History of an Institution, 1650–1815* (New York: Oxford University Press, 2004), 457.

29. Burnham, *Mozart's Grace*, 20–22.

30. On the musical implications of Sterne's writing, particularly with regard to Haydn's wit, see Mark Evan Bonds, "Haydn, Laurence Sterne, and the Origins of Musical Irony," *Journal of the American Musicological Society* 44, no. 10 (1991): 57–91. Bonds discusses broad aesthetic overlaps, for instance concerning formal elements of Haydn's Symphonies no. 45 and 46, but does not discuss small-scale melodic shapes or the plotline diagram. Richard Kramer (*Cherubino's Leap*, 59) comes closer to my perspective, if only obliquely, when, in a chapter on C. P. E. Bach, he states that "Reading Sterne . . . is to participate in a creative process: to reenact a narrative unfolding in all its improvisatory richness."

31. Peter Pesic, "The Child and the Daemon: Mozart and Deep Play," *19th-Century Music* 25, no. 2/3 (2001/2002): 104.

32. Bernard Suits, *The Grasshopper: Games, Life and Utopia* (Toronto: University of Toronto Press, 1978), 38, 43, 52–54. This account is taken up in more recent philosophical texts, including C. Thi Nguyen, *Games: Agency as Art* (New York: Oxford University Press, 2020), 5ff.

33. For a more extended account of Mozart's relationship with gameplay, see the chapter

on Mozart and Beethoven in Moseley, *Keys to Play*. A further analogy is Hepokoski and Darcy's invocation, in *Elements of Sonata Theory*, of the "sonata game" inevitably played by composers who wrote in sonata forms as they decided which themes to introduce in which order throughout an unfolding composition.

34. Mozart himself claimed, in a letter of April 8, 1781, to have composed K. 379 in one hour, owing to lack of time. However, the inclusion of both sonatas in Moseley's discussion of Mozart and gameplay (*Keys to Play*, 191–93) suggests that these occasions may have involved concerns beyond mere practicality.

35. Quoted in Deutsch, *Mozart*, 531. Kelly's memoirs date from decades after he met Mozart, and some elements may be exaggerated.

36. On a melody from the Clarinet Concerto, K. 622, that "demands" a particular accompanimental style, see Burnham, *Mozart's Grace*, 10.

37. The classic text is Fred Everett Maus, "Music as Drama," *Music Theory Spectrum* 10 (1988): 56–73, which refines and expands work undertaken in Edward T. Cone, *The Composer's Voice* (Berkeley: University of California Press, 1974). For a recent comprehensive study, see Monahan, "Action and Agency Revisited," as well as Robert Hatten, *A Theory of Virtual Agency for Western Art Music* (Bloomington: Indiana University Press, 2018). Sutcliffe nuances the historical elements of theories of agency; see his *Instrumental Music in an Age of Sociability*, 121–25.

38. For a treatment of the topic that vests agency in performers and listeners rather than in "the notes themselves," see Klorman, *Mozart's Music of Friends*. The same stance informs Mueller's analysis of double and triple concertos in *Mozart and the Mediation of Childhood*, chap. 5.

39. On this particular embellishment from K. 498, see Klorman, *Mozart's Music of Friends*, 286.

40. On the applications of neo-Darwinian (gene-level) theory of selection and evolution to music, see Steven Jan's still-unsurpassed *The Memetics of Music: A Neo-Darwinian View of Musical Structure and Culture* (Aldershot: Ashgate, 2007). Greenberg's *How Sonata Forms* represents a recent attempt to account for a single aspect of musical structure—in this case, form—from a bottom-up perspective. Although Greenberg explicitly invokes the language of neo-Darwinian selection and replication in his introduction, his study (unlike Jan's) takes musical analysis, rather than evolution, as its primary focus.

41. Meyer, *Style and Music*, 272–74. On the Romantics' aesthetic of "endless melody," see Margaret Notley, "Late-Nineteenth-Century Chamber Music and the Cult of the Classical Adagio," *19th-Century Music* 23, no. 1 (1999): 33–61. For an analytic case study of the rhetorical and expressive dimensions of embellishment in the early nineteenth century, see Dorian Bandy, "Beethoven's Rhetoric of Embellishment," *19th-Century Music* 46, no. 2 (2022): 125–62.

42. In addition to Jan, see the account of genetic variants and mutations in the classic text on neo-Darwinian theory: Richard Dawkins, *The Selfish Gene*, 40th anniversary ed. (Oxford: Oxford University Press, 2016), 304.

43. For a philosophically incisive discussion of the interplay between replicator and environment, see David Deutsch, *The Fabric of Reality* (New York: Penguin Books, 1997), chap. 8, esp. 170–76 and 179–80. Deutsch emphasizes that a replicator causes its environment to do the copying rather than by copying "itself."

Variation 5

1. For a brief encapsulation of these views, see Ian Woodfield, "Reactions to Mozart in His Lifetime," in *Mozart in Context*, ed. Simon P. Keefe (Cambridge: Cambridge University Press, 2019), 240–42. For a more extended critique of the difficulties presented by Mozart's music, see Bonds, "Listening to Listeners."

2. For an analytic account of the ways in which arpeggiation lends syntactic and structural coherence to K. 332 and other works (including the Clarinet Quintet, K. 581), see Stephen Rumph, "Topical Figurae: The Double Articulation of Topics," in *The Oxford Handbook of Topic Theory*, ed. Danuta Mirka (Oxford: Oxford University Press, 2014), 506–11. The classic account of the "thread" in K. 332, here as before, is Allanbrook, "Two Threads through the Labyrinth."

3. The vocal exercises, collected as K. 393 and labeled "for my dear wife," contain melodic overlaps with material in the C-minor Mass, as though explicitly intended to serve as practice pieces. That Constanze participated in the premiere of the Mass is known from a comment recorded by Nannerl, in *MBA*, 3:290.

4. The classic essay on the relationship between Mozart's concertos and operas remains Allanbrook, "Comic Issues." For a more rigorously historical investigation of the dialogic elements of Mozart's concertos, see Simon P. Keefe, "Dramatic Dialogue in Mozart's Viennese Piano Concertos: A Study of Competition and Cooperation in Three First Movements," *Musical Quarterly* 83, no. 2 (1999): 169–204. For a skeptical view arguing that Mozart's concertos are not dramatic, see James Webster, "Are Mozart's Concertos 'Dramatic'? Concerto Ritornellos versus Aria Introductions in the 1780s," in *Mozart's Piano Concertos: Text, Context, Interpretation*, ed. Neal Zaslaw (Ann Arbor: University of Michigan Press, 1996), 107–37.

5. Derr, "Mozart's Transfer of the Vocal 'Fermata Sospesa.'"

6. Martha Feldman, "Staging the Virtuoso: Ritornello Procedure in Mozart, from Aria to Concerto," in *Mozart's Piano Concertos: Text, Context, Interpretation*, ed. Neal Zaslaw (Ann Arbor: University of Michigan Press, 1996), 149–86.

7. On sonata form in *Figaro*, see Rosen, *The Classical Style*, 290.

8. Nonetheless, as Julian Rushton points out, there were times when Mozart did not learn who would sing each role until relatively late in the process of composing an opera. See Julian Rushton, "'By Their Arias Shall Ye Know Them': Characterization in Aria-Based Opera," in *Dramma Giocoso: Four Contemporary Perspectives on the Mozart/Da Ponte Operas* (Leuven: Leuven University Press, 2012), 14. This explains why, when composing *Figaro*, Mozart moved significant coloratura passages from the Countess to Susanna in the act 2 trio when he learned which role Nancy Storace would sing. On these revisions, see Tyson, *Mozart: Studies of the Autograph Scores*, 304–7.

9. On Goethe and the metaphor of string quartet as conversation, see Klorman, *Mozart's Music of Friends*, chap. 2 and epilogue.

10. Klorman, *Mozart's Music of Friends*, 111–13.

11. For instance, see Tom Beghin, "Recognizing Musical Topics versus Executing Rhetorical Figures," in *The Oxford Handbook of Topic Theory*, ed. Danuta Mirka (Oxford: Oxford University Press, 2014), 564. Beghin, a fortepianist, provides photos of facial expressions he assumes while playing K. 332.

12. Although these historical associations have been explored in a number of texts, the

classic and most comprehensive introduction is Ratner, *Classic Music*. On the association of character with key areas and rhetorical structures in baroque music, see Rita Steblin, *A History of Key Characteristics in the Eighteenth and Early Nineteenth Centuries*, 3rd ed. (Rochester, NY: University of Rochester Press, 1996).

13. On a similar effect in K. 550, see Wolff, *Mozart at the Gateway to His Fortune*, 98.

14. Allanbrook observes that this device, too, features in the first movement of K. 332, when quarter notes slurred over the bar line provide a smooth transition between the horn calls and *Sturm und Drang* passages—a "kind of logic in the midst of illogic," in her words. See "Two Threads through the Labyrinth," 135.

15. The examples from K. 332 and K. 414 in this and the following paragraph are drawn from Epstein, *Beyond Orpheus*, 179–86.

16. Howard Boatwright, "Analysis Symposium," *Journal of Music Theory* 10, no. 1 (1966): 29.

17. Allanbrook's analysis of the opera, in *Rhythmic Gesture in Mozart*, furthers this view of wind writing and the pastoral.

18. On the relevance of texture for the structural rhetoric of concertante movements, see Charles Rosen, *Sonata Forms*, rev. ed. (New York: W. W. Norton, 1988), chapts. 4–5, and, for a brief discussion of Mozart's arrangements, 75–77.

19. The classic account of composer's persona as fictionalized entity is Cone, *The Composer's Voice*. This mirrors the many theoretical approaches, in literary studies, to the fictional narratorial or authorial voice, as discussed in a host of classic texts including Michel Foucault, "What Is An Author?," in *The Foucault Reader*, ed. Paul Rabinow (London: Penguin Books, 1991), and Wayne Booth, *The Rhetoric of Fiction* (Chicago: University of Chicago Press, 1983).

20. Epstein, *Beyond Orpheus*, 186–88.

21. Webster, "Are Mozart's Concertos 'Dramatic'?," 132–33. Webster also argues that drama in Mozart's operas arises as a result of the characters' psychological development; see "The Analysis of Mozart's Arias," in *Mozart Studies*, ed. Cliff Eisen (Oxford: Clarendon Press, 1991), 196–99.

22. Eric McKee, "Ballroom Dances of the Late Eighteenth Century," in *The Oxford Handbook of Topic Theory*, ed. Danuta Mirka (Oxford: Oxford University Press, 2014), 184–87. Even in famously Apollonian compositions such as the finale of the "Jupiter" Symphony, K. 551, Mozart's tendancy toward hijinks and disruption remains present. This finale, described by Alexandre Oulibicheff in 1867 as having a "propensity to relapse into chaos," features a recapitulated passage that Yoel Greenberg narrates as a "horror-movie sequence": "In the midst of the third iteration of the theme, all havoc breaks loose. The violins cross swords in stretto above a distorted version of the theme in the bass, as the sequence descends back down amid rising chromatic screeches in the winds. Then all at once, chaos is banished." See Greenberg, "Precedents for the 'Secondary Development' from Bach to Mozart and Their Implications for Understanding Early Sonata Form," *Bach Perspectives* 14 (2022): 23.

23. Elaine Sisman, *Haydn and the Classical Variation* (Cambridge, MA: Harvard University Press, 1993), 200–201.

24. Zaslaw, *Mozart's Symphonies*, 175.

25. The apogee of this style can be found in the explosive development of K. 491. Similar expressive contrasts, as well as some of the technical devices featured in these passages (in-

cluding tremolos, sudden dynamic shifts, coups d'archet, and the like), occur throughout Beethoven's oeuvre as early as the first-movement development of the Piano Sonata op. 2, no. 2, and continue through his career.

26. Zaslaw (*Mozart's Symphonies*, 302) notes that the trumpet fanfare that appears in some editions during this final grand pause was an afterthought on Mozart's part, added after the composition of the original serenade, when he removed the concertante movements to adapt the piece into a makeshift symphony.

27. Stefan Kunze notes, in connection with this passage, that in Mozart's operas (and in Elvira's phrases in particular) gestures initially associated with textual rhythms often taken on a formal or functional autonomy, resounding through the other parts. See Stefan Kunze, *Mozarts Opern* (Stuttgart: Reclam, 1984), 419–25. Ivanovitch ("Mozart and the Environment of Variation," 233–35), too, sensitively discusses this passage in light of listening and viewpoint.

28. Although it is not often noted that "Per pietà" dramatizes self-deception to the same degree as "Come scoglio," Waldoff perceptively observes that this second aria is explicitly phrased as an appeal to Guglielmo, when in reality Fiordiligi's affections have already shifted to Ferrando. See Jessica Waldoff, *Recognition in Mozart's Operas*, 238–39.

29. Scott Burnham, "Mozart's 'Felix Culpa': *Così fan tutte* and the Irony of Beauty," *Musical Quarterly* 78, no. 1 (1994): 77–98.

30. Letter to Aloysia Weber, 30 July 1778, *MBA*, 2:420.

31. Allanbrook, *Rhythmic Gesture in Mozart*, 139.

32. Discussed in Daniel Heartz, "Susanna's Hat," *Early Music* 19, no. 1 (1991): 585–89.

33. Kramer, *Cherubino's Leap*, 166–70.

34. See the extended analysis of "Porgi amor" (particularly concerning the formal manipulations the second half of the aria) in Webster, "Analysis of Mozart's Arias."

35. On the interiority of fantasias, see Bonds, *The Beethoven Syndrome*, 64. For a case study, complete with detailed analysis of an early nineteenth-century fantasia, see Richards, *Free Fantasia*, 145–49. The same intuitive dichotomy gives rise to Karol Berger's assertion that when playing his concertos, Mozart would have been depicting the character "Mozart" in all passages except the improvised cadenzas, when he would apparently "take off the mask." Berger, *Bach's Cycle, Mozart's Arrow*, 186.

36. For a thorough accounting of cross-references, see chapter 6 of Bruce Alan Brown, *W. A. Mozart:* Così fan tutte (Cambridge: Cambridge University Press, 1995). Daniel Heartz argues that *Così* derives its meaning and psychological import not only from references between the acts, but from references to earlier Mozart operas, stretching back to 1781; see Daniel Heartz, *Mozart's Operas* (Berkeley: University of California Press, 1992), 234–51.

37. Rosen, *The Classical Style*, 43, italics in original.

38. James Webster, *Haydn's "Farewell" Symphony and the Idea of Classical Style: Through-Composition and Cyclic Integration in His Instrumental Music* (Cambridge: Cambridge University Press, 1991).

39. One possible exception is the second movement of the Violin Sonata in E minor, K. 304, whose poignant E-major trio section offers a respite from the bleak E minor of the rest of the movement. Even here, however, tonality itself is not the expressive issue; the topical world of the minor-key first movement is complex and varied. The expressive weight of the trio section arises from its gentle dissonances and its wistful melodic leaps.

Coda

1. The recent literature is vast, but an exemplary compatibilist account is Jeffrey Swinkin, *Performative Analysis: Reimagining Music Theory for Performance* (Rochester, NY: University of Rochester Press, 2016).

2. Donald Francis Tovey, *A Companion to Beethoven's Pianoforte Sonatas* (London: Associated Board of the Royal Schools of Music, 1931), iii.

3. Nicholas Cook, *Beyond the Score: Music as Performance* (New York: Oxford University Press, 2013). For a useful overview of authors who have grappled with the relationship between analysis and performance, see Klorman, *Mozart's Music of Friends*, 290–92.

4. The classic essay is Philip Alperson, "When Composers Have to Be Performers," *Journal of Aesthetics and Art Criticism* 49, no. 4 (1991): 369–73. This view has also been analyzed by Karol Berger, who writes that "Musical understanding . . . is inescapably tied to the one material, sound, in which music is embodied." See Karol Berger, *A Theory of Art* (New York: Oxford University Press, 2000), 40. It is implicitly taken up in the work of scholar-performers such as Tom Beghin, whose hefty intellectual pursuits are often prompted by, and carried out in the service of, performative "embodied" knowledge.

5. Simon Keefe (*Mozart in Vienna*, 60–62) asks this question of the minuet that closes K. 377.

6. The idea that instruments can themselves suggest certain interpretive approaches is contentious and is the subject of Taruskin's fiery polemics throughout *Text and Act*. For an optimistic guide to the interpretive affordances of period pianos, see David Breitman, *Piano-Playing Revisited: What Modern Players Can Learn from Period Instruments* (Rochester, NY: University of Rochester Press, 2021).

7. Bernard D. Sherman, "Restoring Ingredients: Malcolm Bilson on the Fortepiano," in *Inside Early Music: Conversations with Performers* (London: Oxford University Press, 2003), 299–303.

8. In Levin's words, "if modern performers tried to adopt the posture of performer *as composer*, Mozart's music would be played more profoundly, more expressively, and above all more spontaneously." Robert D. Levin, "Mozart's Working Methods in the Keyboard Concertos," in *The Century of Bach and Mozart: Perspectives on Historiography, Composition, Theory, and Performance*, ed. Sean Gallagher and Thomas Forrest Kelly (Cambridge, MA: Harvard Publications in Music, 2008), 406.

9. Edward T. Cone, *Musical Form and Musical Performance* (New York: W. W. Norton, 1968), 12–13, 16.

10. Reproduced in the *Kritischer Bericht* of the *NMA*.

11. On Pamina's music as a culmination of Mozart's G-minor writing, see Steven Jan, "The Evolution of a 'Memeplex' in Late Mozart: Replicated Structures in Pamina's 'Ach ich fühl's,'" *Journal of the Royal Musical Association* 128, no. 1 (2003): 30–70. On the replicating features of Mozart's E♭-major writing and their resonance with Tamino's aria, see Uri B. Rom, "Tonartbezogenes Denken in Mozarts Werken unter besonderer Berücksichtigung des Instrumentalwerks" (PhD diss., Technische Universität Berlin, 2011).

12. See, for instance, Jérôme-Joseph de Momigny's famous vocalized arrangement of Mozart's String Quartet K. 421, discussed in Klorman, *Mozart's Music of Friends*, 58ff. More recently, the Badura-Skodas (*Interpreting Mozart*, 296) have attempted to clarify the metrical phrasing in K. 331 by adding words. They claim that the words clarify aspects of meter that

cannot be settled on purely "philological" grounds; however, as Meyer shows in chapter 2 of *Explaining Music*, the parsing and phrasing of K. 331 is indeed determined by internal features.

13. Kofi Agawu makes this observation, in "Topics and Form in Mozart's String Quintet in E Flat Major, K. 614/I," in *The Oxford Handbook of Topic Theory*, ed. Danuta Mirka (Oxford: Oxford University Press, 2014), 490.

BIBLIOGRAPHY

Abert, Hermann. *W. A. Mozart.* Translated by Stewart Spencer. Edited by Cliff Eisen. New Haven, CT: Yale University Press, 2007. First published in German 1923 by Breitkopf & Härtel (Leipzig).

Agawu, Kofi. "Mozart's Art of Variation: Remarks on the First Movement of K. 503." In *Mozart's Piano Concertos: Text, Context, Interpretation*, edited by Neal Zaslaw, 303–13. Ann Arbor: University of Michigan Press, 1996.

———. *Music as Discourse.* Oxford: Oxford University Press, 2009.

———. *Playing with Signs: A Semiotic Interpretation of Classic Music.* Princeton, NJ: Princeton University Press, 1991.

———. "Prospects for a Theory-Based Analysis of the Instrumental Music." In *Wolfgang Amadè Mozart: Essays on His Life and His Music*, edited by Stanley Sadie, 121–31. Oxford: Clarendon Press, 1996.

———. "Topics and Form in Mozart's String Quintet in E Flat Major, K. 614/I." In *The Oxford Handbook of Topic Theory*, edited by Danuta Mirka, 474–92. Oxford: Oxford University Press, 2014.

Allanbrook, Wye J. "Comic Issues in Mozart's Piano Concertos." In *Mozart's Piano Concertos: Text, Context, Interpretation*, edited by Neal Zaslaw, 75–105. Ann Arbor: University of Michigan Press, 1996.

———. "Mozart's Tunes and the Comedy of Closure." In *On Mozart*, edited by James M. Morris, 169–86. Cambridge: Cambridge University Press; Washington, DC: Woodrow Wilson Center Press, 1994.

———. *Rhythmic Gesture in Mozart:* Le nozze di Figaro *and* Don Giovanni. Chicago: University of Chicago Press, 1983.

———. "Two Threads through the Labyrinth: Topic and Process in the First Movements of K. 332 and K. 333." In *Convention in Eighteenth- and Nineteenth-Century Music: Essays in Honor of Leonard G. Ratner*, edited by Wye J. Allanbrook, Janet M. Levy, and William P. Mahrt, 125–71. Stuyvesant, NY: Pendragon, 1992.

Alperson, Philip. "When Composers Have to Be Performers." *Journal of Aesthetics and Art Criticism* 49, no. 4 (1991): 369–73.

Angermüller, Rudolf. "Bemerkungen zu den französischen Bearbeitungen." In Così fan tutte*: Beiträge zur Wirkungsgeschichte von Mozarts Oper*, edited by Susanne Vill, 66–90. Bayreuth: Muhl'scher Universitätsverlag, 1978.

Bach, Carl Philipp Emanuel. *Essay on the True Art of Playing Keyboard Instruments*. Translated by William J. Mitchell. New York: W. W. Norton, 1949. First published 1753 as *Versuch über die wahre Art das Clavier zu spielen* by Henning (Berlin).

Badura-Skoda, Eva, and Paul Badura-Skoda. *Interpreting Mozart: The Performance Practice of His Piano Pieces and Other Compositions*. 2nd ed. New York: Routledge, 2008.

Bandy, Dorian. "Beethoven's Rhetoric of Embellishment." *19th-Century Music* 46, no. 2 (2022): 125-62.

———. "Mozart's Operatic Embellishments." *Cambridge Opera Journal* 33, no. 1/2 (2021): 1-23.

———. "Thema da capo: Another Look at Mozart's Embellishments." *Eighteenth-Century Music* 19, no. 1 (2022): 37–57.

Baragwanath, Nicholas. *The Solfeggio Tradition*. New York: Oxford University Press, 2020.

Bashford, Christina. "Varieties of Childhood: John Ella and the Construction of a Victorian Mozart." In *Words about Mozart: Essays in Honour of Stanley Sadie*, edited by Dorothea Link and Judith Nagley, 193–210. Woodbridge: Boydell Press, 2005.

Bauer, Wilhelm A., Otto Erich Deutsch, and Joseph Heinz Eibl, eds. *Mozart: Briefe und Aufzeichnungen, Gesamtausgabe* [*MBA*]. 8 vols. Kassel: Bärenreiter, 1962–2005.

Beaudoin, Richard. "The Pen as Camera: Finnissy and Overexposure." *Music Theory Online* 27, no. 3 (2021). https://mtosmt.org/issues/mto.21.27.3/mto.21.27.3.beaudoin.html.

Beghin, Tom. *Beethoven's French Piano: A Tale of Ambition and Frustration*. Chicago: University of Chicago Press, 2022.

———. "Recognizing Musical Topics versus Executing Rhetorical Figures." In *The Oxford Handbook of Topic Theory*, edited by Danuta Mirka, 551–76. Oxford: Oxford University Press, 2014.

———. *The Virtual Haydn: Paradox of a Twenty-First-Century Keyboardist*. Chicago: University of Chicago Press, 2015.

Berger, Karol. *Bach's Cycle, Mozart's Arrow: An Essay on the Origins of Musical Modernity*. Berkeley: University of California Press, 2007.

———. *A Theory of Art*. New York: Oxford University Press, 2000.

Boatwright, Howard. "Analysis Symposium." *Journal of Music Theory* 10, no. 1 (1966): 22–31.

Bonds, Mark Evan. *The Beethoven Syndrome: Hearing Music as Autobiography*. New York: Oxford University Press, 2020.

———. "Haydn, Laurence Sterne, and the Origins of Musical Irony." *Journal of the American Musicological Society* 44, no. 1 (1991): 57–91.

———. "Listening to Listeners." In *Communication in Eighteenth-Century Music*, edited by Danuta Mirka and Kofi Agawu, 34–52. Cambridge: Cambridge University Press, 2008.

———. *Wordless Rhetoric: Musical Form and the Metaphor of the Oration*. Cambridge, MA: Harvard University Press, 1991.

Breitman, David. *Piano-Playing Revisited: What Modern Players Can Learn from Period Instruments*. Rochester, NY: University of Rochester Press, 2021.

Brown, Bruce Alan. *W. A. Mozart:* Così fan tutte. Cambridge: Cambridge University Press, 1995.

Brown, Clive. "Leopold Mozart's Violinschule and the Performance of W.A. Mozart's Violin Music." In *Cordes et claviers au temps de Mozart*, edited by Thomas Steiner, 23–50. Bern: Peter Lang, 2010.

Burnham, Scott. "Mozart's 'Felix Culpa': *Così fan tutte* and the Irony of Beauty." *Musical Quarterly* 78, no. 1 (1994): 77–98.

———. *Mozart's Grace.* Princeton, NJ: Princeton University Press, 2012.

Butt, John. *Playing with History.* Cambridge: Cambridge University Press, 2002.

Byros, Vasili. "Towards an 'Archaeology' of Hearing: Schemata and Eighteenth-Century Consciousness." *Musica Humana* 1 (2009): 235–306.

———. "Trazom's Wit: Communicative Strategies in a 'Popular' yet 'Difficult' Sonata." *Eighteenth-Century Music* 10, no. 2 (2013): 213–52.

Caplin, William. *Classical Form: A Theory of Formal Functions for the Instrumental Music of Haydn, Mozart, and Beethoven.* New York: Oxford University Press, 1998.

Carter, Tim. *W. A. Mozart:* Le nozze di Figaro. Cambridge: Cambridge University Press, 1987.

Cavett-Dunsby, Esther. "Mozart's 'Haydn' Quartets: Composing Up and Down without Rules." *Journal of the Royal Musical Association* 113, no. 1 (1988): 57–80.

Cone, Edward T. *The Composer's Voice.* Berkeley: University of California Press, 1974.

———. *Musical Form and Musical Performance.* New York: W. W. Norton, 1968.

Cook, Nicholas. *Beyond the Score: Music as Performance.* New York: Oxford University Press, 2013.

Cowen, Tyler. *In Praise of Commercial Culture.* Cambridge, MA: Harvard University Press, 1998.

Cypess, Rebecca. *Women and Musical Salons in the Enlightenment.* Chicago: University of Chicago Press, 2022.

Dahlhaus, Carl. "Composition and Improvisation." Translated by Derrick Puffett and Alfred Clayton. In *Schoenberg and the New Music*, 265–73. Cambridge: Cambridge University Press, 1990.

———. "Romantische Musikästhetik und Wiener Klassik." In *Klassiche und romantische Musikästhetik*, 86–98. Laaber: Laaber, 1988.

David, Hans T. "Mozartean Modulations." In *The Creative World of Mozart*, edited by Paul Henry Lang. New York: W. W. Norton, 1991.

David, Hans T., Arthur Mendel, and Christoph Wolff, eds. *The New Bach Reader.* New York: W. W. Norton, 1999.

Davisson, Katya. "Improvisation as a Method of Composition: Reconciling the Dichotomy." *British Journal of Aesthetics* 62, no. 3 (2022): 373–86.

Dawkins, Richard. *The Selfish Gene.* 40th anniversary ed. Oxford: Oxford University Press, 2016.

Day-O'Connell, Sarah. "The Singing Style." In *The Oxford Handbook of Topic Theory*, edited by Danuta Mirka, 238–58. New York: Oxford University Press, 2014.

Derr, Ellwood. "*Basso Continuo* in Mozart's Piano Concertos: Dimensions of Compositional Completion and Performance Practice." In *Mozart's Piano Concertos: Text, Context, Interpretation*, edited by Neal Zaslaw, 393–410. Ann Arbor: University of Michigan Press, 1996.

———. "Mozart's Transfer of the Vocal 'Fermata Sospesa' to His Piano-Concerto First Movements." In *Mozart-Jahrbuch 1991*, edited by Rudolf Angermüller, Dietrich Berke, Ulrike Hofmann, and Wolfgang Rehm, 155–63. Kassel: Bärenreiter, 1992.

———. "Some Thoughts on the Design of Mozart's Opus 4, the 'Subscription Concertos' (K. 414, 413, and 415)." In *Mozart's Piano Concertos: Text, Context, Interpretation*, edited by Neal Zaslaw, 187–210. Ann Arbor: University of Michigan Press, 1996.

De Souza, Jonathan. *Music at Hand: Instruments, Bodies, and Cognition.* New York: Oxford University Press, 2017.

Deutsch, David. *The Fabric of Reality*. New York: Penguin Books, 1997.

Deutsch, Otto Erich. *Mozart: A Documentary Biography*. Translated by Eric Blom, Peter Branscombe and Jeremy Noble. New York: Simon & Schuster, 1965.

Drabkin, William. "An Interpretation of Musical Dreams: Towards a Theory of the Mozart Piano Concerto Cadenza." In *Wolfgang Amadè Mozart: Essays on His Life and His Music*, edited by Stanley Sadie, 161–77. Oxford: Clarendon Press, 1996.

Dreyfus, Laurence. "Mozart as Early Music: A Romantic Antidote." *Early Music* 20, no. 2 (1992): 297–309.

Edge, Dexter. "Mozart's Viennese Copyists." PhD diss., University of Southern California, 2001.

Einstein, Alfred. *Mozart, His Character, His Work*. Translated by Arthur Mendel and Nathan Broder. 1945. Reprint, New York: Oxford University Press, 1962.

Epstein, David. *Beyond Orpheus: Studies in Musical Structure*. Cambridge, MA: MIT Press, 1979.

Feldman, Martha. "Staging the Virtuoso: Ritornello Procedure in Mozart, from Aria to Concerto." In *Mozart's Piano Concertos: Text, Context, Interpretation*, edited by Neal Zaslaw, 149–86. Ann Arbor: University of Michigan Press, 1996.

Gjerdingen, Robert O. *Music in the Galant Style*. New York: Oxford University Press, 2007.

Goehring, Edmund J. *Coming to Terms with Our Musical Past: An Essay on Mozart and Modernist Aesthetics*. Rochester, NY: University of Rochester Press, 2018.

Gooley, Dana. *Fantasies of Improvisation: Free Playing in Nineteenth-Century Music*. New York: Oxford University Press, 2018.

Grayson, David. "Whose Authenticity? Ornaments by Hummel and Cramer for Mozart's Piano Concertos." In *Mozart's Piano Concertos: Text, Context, Interpretation*, edited by Neal Zaslaw, 373–91. Ann Arbor: University of Michigan Press, 1996.

Greenberg, Yoel. *How Sonata Forms: A Bottom-Up Approach to Musical Form*. New York: Oxford University Press, 2022.

———. "Precedents for the 'Secondary Development' from Bach to Mozart and Their Implications for Understanding Early Sonata Form." *Bach Perspectives* 14 (2022): 23–37.

Guymer, Sheila. "Eloquent Performance: The Pronuntiatio of Topics." In *The Oxford Handbook of Topic Theory*, edited by Danuta Mirka, 577–96. Oxford: Oxford University Press, 2014.

Hatten, Robert. *A Theory of Virtual Agency for Western Art Music*. Bloomington: Indiana University Press, 2018.

Heartz, Daniel. *Haydn, Mozart and the Viennese School: 1740–1780*. New York: W. W. Norton, 1995.

———. *Mozart's Operas*. Berkeley: University of California Press, 1992.

———. "Susanna's Hat." *Early Music* 19, no. 1 (1991): 585–89.

Hepokoski, James, and Warren Darcy. *Elements of Sonata Theory: Norms, Types, and Deformations in the Late-Eighteenth-Century Sonata*. New York: Oxford University Press, 2006.

Hoeprich, Eric. *The Clarinet*. New Haven, CT: Yale University Press, 2008.

Holtmeier, Ludwig. "Zur Komplexität Mozarts: Analytischer Versuch über eine Sequenz." *Musik & Ästhetik* 16, no. 4 (2000): 5–23.

Irving, John. *Mozart's Piano Sonatas: Contexts, Sources, Style*. Cambridge: Cambridge University Press, 1997.

Ivanovitch, Roman. "Mozart and the Environment of Variation." PhD diss., Yale University, 2004.

———. "Mozart's Art of Retransition." *Music Analysis* 30, no. 1 (2011): 1–36.

———. "Showing Off: Variation in the Display Episodes of Mozart's Piano Concertos." *Journal of Music Theory* 52, no. 2 (2008): 181–218.

Jan, Steven. "The Evolution of a 'Memeplex' in Late Mozart: Replicated Structures in Pamina's 'Ach ich fühl's.'" *Journal of the Royal Musical Association* 128, no. 1 (2003): 30–70.

———. *The Memetics of Music: A Neo-Darwinian View of Musical Structure and Culture*. Aldershot: Ashgate, 2007.

Jonas, Oswald. "Improvisation in Mozarts Klavierwerken." In *Mozart-Jahrbuch 1967*, 176–81. Salzburg: Internationalen Stiftung Mozarteum, 1968.

Keefe, Simon P. "Dramatic Dialogue in Mozart's Viennese Piano Concertos: A Study of Competition and Cooperation in Three First Movements." *Musical Quarterly* 83, no. 2 (1999): 169–204.

———. *Mozart in Vienna: The Final Decade*. Cambridge: Cambridge University Press, 2017.

———. *Mozart's Piano Concertos: Dramatic Dialogue in the Age of Enlightenment*. Woodbridge: Boydell Press, 2001.

———. *Mozart's Requiem: Reception, Work, Completion*. Cambridge: Cambridge University Press, 2012.

———. *Mozart's Viennese Instrumental Music: A Study of Stylistic Re-invention*. Woodbridge: Boydell Press, 2007.

———. "'We Hardly Knew What We Should Pay Attention to First': Mozart the Performer-Composer at Work on the Viennese Piano Concertos." *Journal of the Royal Musical Association* 134, no. 2 (2009): 185–242.

Kerman, Joseph. "Critics and the Classics." In *Write All These Down: Essays on Music*, 51–72. Berkeley: University of California Press, 1998.

Kinderman, William. *Beethoven*. 2nd ed. New York: Oxford University Press, 2009.

———. *The Creative Process in Music from Mozart to Kurtág*. Urbana: University of Illinois Press, 2012.

———. *Mozart's Piano Music*. Oxford: Oxford University Press, 2006.

Kivy, Peter. *Authenticities*. Ithaca, NY: Cornell University Press, 1997.

Klorman, Edward. *Mozart's Music of Friends: Social Interplay in the Chamber Works*. Cambridge: Cambridge University Press, 2016.

Kobb, Christina. "Viennese Piano Technique of the 1820s and Implications for Today's Pianists." *Music & Practice* 4 (2019). https://www.musicandpractice.org/volume-4/viennese-piano-technique-of-the-1820s-and-implications-for-todays-pianists/.

Komlós, Katalin. "'Ich praeludirte und spielte Variazionen': Mozart the Fortepianist." In

Perspectives on Mozart Performance, edited by R. Larry Todd and Peter Williams, 27–54. Cambridge: Cambridge University Press, 1991.

———. "Mozart the Performer." In *The Cambridge Companion to Mozart*, edited by Simon P. Keefe, 215–26. Cambridge: Cambridge University Press, 2003.

Konrad, Ulrich. "Mozart the Letter Writer and His Language." In *Mozart Studies 2*, edited by Simon P. Keefe, 1–22. Cambridge: Cambridge University Press, 2015.

Kramer, Richard. *Cherubino's Leap: In Search of the Enlightenment Moment*. Chicago: University of Chicago Press, 2016.

———. "Diderot's *Paradoxe* and C.P.E. Bach's *Empfindung*." In *C.P.E. Bach Studies*, edited by Annette Richards, 6–24. Cambridge: Cambridge University Press, 2006.

Kroll, Mark. *Johann Nepomuk Hummel: A Musician's Life and World*. Lanham, MD: Scarecrow Press, 2007.

Kunze, Stefan. *Mozarts Opern*. Stuttgart: Reclam, 1984.

Leeson, Daniel N. "A Revisit: Mozart's Serenade for Thirteen Instruments, K. 361 (370a), the 'Gran Partita.'" In *Mozart-Jahrbuch 1997*, 181–223. Kassel: Bärenreiter, 1997.

Le Guin, Elisabeth. *Boccherini's Body: An Essay in Carnal Musicology*. Berkeley: University of California Press, 2006.

Lester, Joel. *Compositional Theory in the Eighteenth Century*. Cambridge, MA: Harvard University Press, 1992.

Levin, Robert D. "Improvised Embellishments in Mozart's Keyboard Music." *Early Music* 20, no. 2 (1992): 221–33.

———. "Instrumental Ornamentation, Improvisation, and Cadenzas." In *Performance Practice: Music after 1600*, edited by Howard Mayer Brown and Stanley Sadie, 267–92. London: Macmillan, 1990.

———. *Introduction: Klavierkonzert C-Moll, KV 491*. Bärenreiter Facsimile. Kassel: Bärenreiter, 2014.

———. "Mozart's Non-Metrical Keyboard Preludes." In *The Keyboard in Baroque Europe*, edited by Christopher Hogwood, 198–216. Cambridge: Cambridge University Press, 2003.

———. "Mozart's Solo Keyboard Music." In *Eighteenth-Century Keyboard Music*, edited by Robert L. Marshall, 308–49. New York: Routledge, 2003.

———. "Mozart's Working Methods in the Keyboard Concertos." In *The Century of Bach and Mozart: Perspectives on Historiography, Composition, Theory, and Performance*, edited by Sean Gallagher and Thomas Forrest Kelly, 379–406. Cambridge, MA: Harvard Publications in Music, 2008.

———. Review of *Ornamentation and Improvisation in Mozart* by Frederick Neumann. *Journal of the American Musicological Society* 41, no. 2 (1988): 355–68.

Lorenz, Michael. "'Mademoiselle Jeunehomme.' Zur Lösung eines Mozart-Rätsels." In *Mozart: Experiment Aufklärung im Wien des Ausgehenden 18. Jahrhunderts*, edited by Herbert Lachmayer, 423–29. Vienna: Hatje Cantz, 2006.

Lowe, Melanie. *Pleasure and Meaning in the Classical Symphony*. Bloomington: Indiana University Press, 2007.

Lowinsky, Edward T. "On Mozart's Rhythm." In *The Creative World of Mozart*, edited by Paul Henry Lang. New York: W. W. Norton, 1991.

Maliniak, Omer, and Yoel Greenberg. "Follow the Solo." *Music Theory Spectrum* 44, no. 2 (2022): 231–59.

Marshall, Robert L. *Mozart Speaks: Views on Music, Musicians, and the World.* New York: Schirmer Books, 1991.

Maus, Fred Everett. "Music as Drama." *Music Theory Spectrum* 10 (1988): 56–73.

McKee, Eric. "Ballroom Dances of the Late Eighteenth Century." In *The Oxford Handbook of Topic Theory*, edited by Danuta Mirka, 164–93. Oxford: Oxford University Press, 2014.

Meyer, Leonard B. *Emotion and Meaning in Music.* Chicago: University of Chicago Press, 1956.

———. *Explaining Music.* Berkeley: University of California Press, 1973.

———. "Process and Morphology in the Music of Mozart." In *The Spheres of Music*, 126–56. Chicago: University of Chicago Press, 2000.

———. *Style and Music: Theory, History, and Ideology.* Chicago: University of Chicago Press, 1989.

Mirka, Danuta, ed. *The Oxford Handbook of Topic Theory.* New York: Oxford University Press, 2014.

Monahan, Seth. "Action and Agency Revisited." *Journal of Music Theory* 57, no. 2 (2013): 321–71.

Moseley, Roger. *Keys to Play: Music as a Ludic Medium from Apollo to Nintendo.* Oakland: University of California Press, 2016.

Mozart, Leopold. *A Treatise on the Fundamental Principles of Violin Playing.* Translated by Editha Knocker. 1951. Reprint, Oxford: Oxford University Press, 1986. First published 1756 as *Versuch einer gründlichen Violinschule* by Verlag des Verfassers (Augsburg).

Mozart, Wolfgang Amadeus. *Mozarts Briefe und Aufzeichnungen: Gesamtausgabe.* [*MBA*] Collected and annotated by Wilhelm A. Bauer and Otto Erich Deutsch, 3 vols. Kassel: Bärenreiter, 2005.

———. *Neue Ausgabe sämtlicher Werke* [*Neue Mozart-Ausgabe: NMA*]. Kassel: Bärenreiter, 1955–2007. Available at Digital Mozart Edition, http://dme.mozarteum.at.

Mueller, Adline. *Mozart and the Mediation of Childhood.* Chicago: University of Chicago Press, 2021.

Neumann, Frederick. *Ornamentation and Improvisation in Mozart.* Princeton, NJ: Princeton University Press, 1986.

———. "Some Problems of Mozart Ornamentation: A Response to Robert Levin." In *New Essays on Performance Practice*, 155–67. Rochester, NY: University of Rochester Press, 1989.

Nguyen, C. Thi. *Games: Agency as Art.* New York: Oxford University Press, 2020.

Niemetschek, Franz. *Lebensbeschreibung des K.K. Kapelmeisters Wolfgang Amadeus Mozart, aus Originalquellen.* Prague, 1808. First published 1798.

Nissen, Georg Nikolaus. *Biographie W.A. Mozarts.* Leipzig, 1828.

Notley, Margaret. "Late-Nineteenth-Century Chamber Music and the Cult of the Classical Adagio." *19th-Century Music* 23, no. 1 (1999): 33–61.

Novello, Vincent, and Mary Novello. *A Mozart Pilgrimage: Being the Travel Diaries of Vincent and Mary Novello in the Year 1829.* Edited by Rosemary Hughes. London: Eulenberg, 1975.

Pesic, Peter. "The Child and the Daemon: Mozart and Deep Play." *19th-Century Music* 25, no. 2/3 (2001/2002): 91–107.

Peters, Gary. *The Philosophy of Improvisation.* Chicago: University of Chicago Press, 2009.

Popper, Karl. *The Logic of Scientific Discovery*. Rev. ed. London: Routledge Classics, 2002.

———. *Objective Knowledge: An Evolutionary Approach*. Rev. ed. Oxford: Clarendon Press, 1979.

Rabinovitch, Gilad. "Reimagining Historical Improvisation: An Analysis of Robert Levin's Fantasy on Themes by W.A. Mozart, October 29, 2012." *Music Theory Online* 26, no. 2 (2020).

Ratner, Leonard. "Ars Combinatoria: Chance and Choice in Eighteenth-Century Music." In *Studies in Eighteenth-Century Music: A Tribute to Karl Geiringer on His Seventieth Birthday*, edited by H. C. Robbins Landon, 343–63. London: Allen and Unwin, 1970.

———. *Classic Music: Expression, Form, and Style*. New York: Schirmer Books, 1980.

Remeš, Derek. "Some (Dis)Assembly Required: Modularity in the Keyboard Improvisation Pedagogy of Jacob Adlung and Johann Vallade." *Music Theory Online* 26, no. 1 (2020).

Richards, Annette. *The Free Fantasia and the Musical Picturesque*. Cambridge: Cambridge University Press, 2001.

Rohringer, Stefan. "Don Ottavio and the History of the Tenor Voice." In *Dramma Giocoso: Four Contemporary Perspectives on the Mozart/Da Ponte Operas*. Leuven: Leuven University Press, 2012.

Rom, Uri B. "Tonartbezogenes Denken in Mozarts Werken unter besonderer Berücksichtigung des Instrumentalwerks." PhD diss., Technische Universität Berlin, 2011.

Rose, Stephen. *Musical Authorship from Schütz to Bach*. Cambridge: Cambridge University Press, 2019.

Rosen, Charles. *The Classical Style: Haydn, Mozart, Beethoven*. Enl. ed. New York: W. W. Norton, 1997.

———. *The Romantic Generation*. Cambridge, MA: Harvard University Press, 1998.

———. *Sonata Forms*. Rev. ed. New York: W. W. Norton, 1988.

———. "Tradition without Convention: The Impossible Nineteenth-Century Project." In *The Tanner Lectures on Human Values*, edited by Grethe B. Peterson, 351–88. Salt Lake City: University of Utah Press, 2002.

Rosen, David. "'Unexpectedness' and 'Inevitability' in Mozart's Piano Concertos." In *Mozart's Piano Concertos: Text, Context, Interpretation*, edited by Neal Zaslaw, 261–84. Ann Arbor: University of Michigan Press, 1996.

Rosenblum, Sandra P. *Performance Practices in Classic Piano Music: Their Principles and Applications*. Bloomington: Indiana University Press, 1991.

Rumph, Stephen. "Topical Figurae: The Double Articulation of Topics." In *The Oxford Handbook of Topic Theory*, edited by Danuta Mirka, 493–513. Oxford: Oxford University Press, 2014.

Rushton, Julian. "'By Their Arias Shall Ye Know Them': Characterization in Aria-Based Opera." In *Dramma Giocoso: Four Contemporary Perspectives on the Mozart/Da Ponte Operas*, 11–32. Leuven: Leuven University Press, 2012.

———. *Mozart*. New York: Oxford University Press, 2006.

Sadie, Stanley. *Mozart: The Early Years 1756–1781*. Oxford: Oxford University Press, 2006.

Sawyer, R. Keith. "Improvisation and the Creative Process: Dewey, Collingwood, and the Aesthetics of Spontaneity." *Journal of Aesthetics and Art Criticism* 58, no. 2 (2000): 149–61.

Schachter, Carl. "20th-Century Analysis and Mozart Performance." *Early Music* 19, no. 4 (1991): 620–28.

Scruton, Roger. *Art and Imagination: A Study in the Philosophy of Mind*. London: Methuan, 1974.

Sherman, Bernard D. "Restoring Ingredients: Malcolm Bilson on the Fortepiano." In *Inside Early Music: Conversations with Performers*, 297–314. London: Oxford University Press, 2003.

Sisman, Elaine. *Haydn and the Classical Variation*. Cambridge, MA: Harvard University Press, 1993.

———. *Mozart: The "Jupiter" Symphony*. Cambridge: Cambridge University Press, 1993.

———. "Six of One: The Opus Concept in the Eighteenth Century." In *The Century of Bach and Mozart: Perspectives on Historiography, Composition, Theory, and Performance*, edited by Sean Gallagher and Thomas Forrest Kelly, 79–107. Cambridge, MA: Harvard Publications in Music, 2008.

Somfai, László. "Mozart's First Thoughts: The Two Versions of the Sonata in D Major, K. 284." *Early Music* 19, no. 4 (1991): 601–13.

Spitzer, John, and Neal Zaslaw. *The Birth of the Orchestra: History of an Institution, 1650–1815*. New York: Oxford University Press, 2004.

Steblin, Rita. *A History of Key Characteristics in the Eighteenth and Early Nineteenth Centuries*. 3rd ed. Rochester, NY: University of Rochester Press, 1996.

Stowell, Robin. *Violin Technique and Performance Practice in the Late Eighteenth and Early Nineteenth Centuries*. Cambridge: Cambridge University Press, 1990.

Suits, Bernard. *The Grasshopper: Games, Life and Utopia*. Toronto: University of Toronto Press, 1978.

Sutcliffe, W. Dean. *Instrumental Music in an Age of Sociability: Haydn, Mozart and Friends*. Cambridge: Cambridge University Press, 2020.

Swinkin, Jeffrey. *Performative Analysis: Reimagining Music Theory for Performance*. Rochester, NY: University of Rochester Press, 2016.

———. "Variation as Thematic Actualisation: The Case of Brahms's Op. 9." *Music Analysis* 31, no. 1 (2012): 37–89.

Taruskin, Richard. *Text and Act: Essays on Music and Performance*. New York: Oxford University Press, 1995.

Tovey, Donald Francis. *A Companion to Beethoven's Pianoforte Sonatas*. London: Associated Board of the Royal Schools of Music, 1931.

Türk, Daniel Gottlob. *School of Clavier Playing*. Translated by Raymond H. Haggh. Lincoln: University of Nebraska Press, 1982. First published 1789 as *Clavierschule, oder Anweisung zum Clavierspielen* by Schwichert (Leipzig).

Tyson, Alan. *Mozart: Studies of the Autograph Scores*. Cambridge, MA: Harvard University Press, 1987.

———. "Proposed New Dates for Many Works and Fragments Written by Mozart from March 1781 to December 1791." In *Mozart Studies*, edited by Cliff Eisen, 213–26. Oxford: Clarendon Press, 1991.

Waldoff, Jessica. "Mozart and Finances." In *Mozart in Context*, edited by Simon P. Keefe, 170–80. Cambridge: Cambridge University Press, 2019.

———. *Recognition in Mozart's Operas*. New York: Oxford University Press, 2006.

Watkins, Holly. *Metaphors of Depth in German Musical Thought*. Cambridge: Cambridge University Press, 2011.

Webster, James. "The Analysis of Mozart's Arias." In *Mozart Studies*, edited by Cliff Eisen, 101–99. Oxford: Clarendon Press, 1991.

———. "Are Mozart's Concertos 'Dramatic'? Concerto Ritornellos versus Aria Introductions in the 1780s." In *Mozart's Piano Concertos: Text, Context, Interpretation*, edited by Neal Zaslaw, 107–37. Ann Arbor: University of Michigan Press, 1996.

———. *Haydn's "Farewell" Symphony and the Idea of Classical Style: Through-Composition and Cyclic Integration in His Instrumental Music*. Cambridge: Cambridge University Press, 1991.

———. "The Rhetoric of Improvisation in Haydn's Keyboard Music." In *Haydn and the Performance of Rhetoric*, edited by Tom Beghin and Sander M. Goldberg, 172–212. Chicago: University of Chicago Press, 2007.

Wheelock, Gretchen A. *Haydn's Ingenious Jesting with Art: Contexts of Musical Wit and Humor*. New York: Schirmer Books, 1992.

Wolf, Eugene K. "The Rediscovered Autograph of Mozart's Fantasy and Sonata in C Minor, K. 475/457." *Journal of Musicology* 10, no. 1 (1992): 3–47.

Wolff, Christoph. "The Challenge of Blank Paper: Mozart the Composer." In *On Mozart*, edited by James M. Morris, 113–29. Cambridge: Cambridge University Press; Washington, DC: Woodrow Wilson Center Press, 1994.

———. "The Many Faces of Authenticity: Problems of a Critical Edition of Mozart's Piano Concertos." In *Mozart's Piano Concertos: Text, Context, Interpretation*, edited by Neal Zaslaw, 19–28. Ann Arbor: University of Michigan Press, 1996.

———. *Mozart at the Gateway to His Fortune: Serving the Emperor, 1788–1791*. New York: W. W. Norton, 2012.

Woodfield, Ian. "Reactions to Mozart in His Lifetime." In *Mozart in Context*, edited by Simon P. Keefe, 239–45. Cambridge: Cambridge University Press, 2019.

Zaslaw, Neal. "The Adagio in F Major, K3 Anhang 206a = K6 Anhang A 65." In *Haydn, Mozart, and Beethoven: Studies in the Music of the Classical Period (Essays in Honour of Alan Tyson)*, edited by Sieghard Brandenburg, 101–13. Oxford: Clarendon Press, 1998.

———. "Mozart as a Working Stiff." In *On Mozart*, edited by James M. Morris, 102–12. Cambridge: Cambridge University Press; Washington, DC: Woodrow Wilson Center Press, 1994.

———. "Mozart's Modular Minuet Machine." In *Essays in Honor of László Somfai on His 70th Birthday: Studies in the Sources and the Interpretation of Music*, edited by László Vikárius and Vera Lampert, 219–35. Lanham, MD: Scarecrow Press, 2005.

———. *Mozart's Symphonies: Context, Performance Practice, Reception*. New York: Oxford University Press, 1989.

Zemach, Eddy, and Tamara Balter. "The Structure of Irony and How It Functions in Music." In *Philosophers on Music: Experience, Meaning, and Work*, edited by Kathleen Stock, 178–206. Oxford: Oxford University Press, 2007.

INDEX OF MOZART'S COMPOSITIONS

Page numbers in italics refer to examples.

SUBJECT INDEX

Page numbers in italics refer to examples.